POEMS

by

VICTOR HUGO

Copyright © 2016 Read Books Ltd.
This book is copyright and may not be
reproduced or copied in any way without
the express permission of the publisher in writing

British Library Cataloguing-in-Publication Data
A catalogue record for this book is available from
the British Library

CONTENTS

Victor Hugo...11
MEMOIR OF VICTOR MARIE HUGO..................17
EARLY POEMS..27
    MOSES ON THE NILE. 27
    ENVY AND AVARICE.............................31
ODES.—1818-28.....................................34
    KING LOUIS XVII................................34
    THE FEAST OF FREEDOM........................38
    TO YE KINGS....................................38
    GENIUS..40
    THE GIRL OF OTAHEITE.........................42
    NERO'S INCENDIARY SONG......................43
    REGRET..46
    THE MORNING OF LIFE..........................48
    BELOVED NAME..................................49
    THE PORTRAIT OF A CHILD......................50
BALLADES.—1823-28................................52
    THE GRANDMOTHER............................52
    THE GIANT IN GLEE.............................54
    THE CYMBALEER'S BRIDE. 57
    BATTLE OF THE NORSEMEN AND THE GAELS.......61
    MADELAINE.....................................63
    THE FAY AND THE PERI..........................65

- LES ORIENTALES.—1829. 70
  - THE SCOURGE OF HEAVEN. 70
  - PIRATES' SONG. 83
  - THE TURKISH CAPTIVE. 85
  - MOONLIGHT ON THE BOSPHORUS. 88
  - THE VEIL. 89
  - THE SISTER. 90
  - THE FAVORITE SULTANA. 92
  - THE PASHA AND THE DERVISH. 95
  - THE LOST BATTLE. 97
  - THE GREEK BOY. 101
  - ZARA, THE BATHER. 102
  - EXPECTATION.. 107
  - THE LOVER'S WISH. 108
  - THE SACKING OF THE CITY. 109
  - NOORMAHAL THE FAIR.{1} 111
  - THE DJINNS. 112
  - THE OBDURATE BEAUTY. 117
  - DON RODRIGO. 118
  - CORNFLOWERS. 120
  - MAZEPPA. 124
  - THE DANUBE IN WRATH. 124
  - OLD OCEAN. 125
  - MY NAPOLEON. 126
- LES FEUILLES D'AUTOMNE.—1831.. 129
  - THE PATIENCE OF THE PEOPLE. 129
  - DICTATED BEFORE THE RHONE GLACIER. 130
  - THE POET'S LOVE FOR LIVELINESS.. 132
  - INFANTILE INFLUENCE.. 133
  - THE WATCHING ANGEL. 136

SUNSET. 138
THE UNIVERSAL PRAYER. 139
II. 141

LES CHANTS DU CRÉPUSCULE.—1849. 145
    PRELUDE TO "THE SONGS OF TWILIGHT." 145
    THE LAND OF FABLE. 147
    THE THREE GLORIOUS DAYS. 148
    TRIBUTE TO THE VANQUISHED. 150
    ANGEL OR DEMON. 151
    THE ERUPTION OF VESUVIUS. 152
    MARRIAGE AND FEASTS. 154
    THE MORROW OF GRANDEUR. 158
    THE EAGLET MOURNED. 161
    INVOCATION. 163
    OUTSIDE THE BALL-ROOM. 164
    PRAYER FOR FRANCE. 166
    TO CANARIS, THE GREEK PATRIOT. 167
    POLAND. 169
    INSULT NOT THE FALLEN. 170
    MORNING. 171
    SONG OF LOVE. 172
    SWEET CHARMER.{1}. 174
    MORE STRONG THAN TIME. 175
    ROSES AND BUTTERFLIES. 176
    THE POET TO HIS WIFE. 177

LES VOIX INTÉRIEURES.—1840. 178
    THE BLINDED BOURBONS. 178
    TO ALBERT DÜRER. 180
    TO HIS MUSE. 182
    THE COW. 184

MOTHERS..186
　　TO SOME BIRDS FLOWN AWAY....................187
　　MY THOUGHTS OF YE..............................196
　　THE BEACON IN THE STORM........................198
　　LOVE'S TREACHEROUS POOL.......................199
　　THE ROSE AND THE GRAVE........................200

LES RAYONS ET LES OMBRES.—1840..................202
　　HOLYROOD PALACE.................................202
　　THE HUMBLE HOME.................................203
　　THE EIGHTEENTH CENTURY........................204
　　STILL BE A CHILD..................................205
　　THE POOL AND THE SOUL..........................207
　　YE MARINERS WHO SPREAD YOUR SAILS..........207
　　ON A FLEMISH WINDOW-PANE.....................209
　　THE PRECEPTOR....................................210
　　GASTIBELZA..211
　　GUITAR SONG......................................215
　　COME WHEN I SLEEP...............................216
　　EARLY LOVE REVISITED............................217
　　SWEET MEMORY OF LOVE..........................219
　　THE MARBLE FAUN..................................220
　　BABY'S SEASIDE GRAVE............................224

LES CHÂTIMENTS.—1853.............................226
　　INDIGNATION!......................................226
　　IMPERIAL REVELS..................................227
　　POOR LITTLE CHILDREN............................229
　　APOSTROPHE TO NATURE.........................230
　　NAPOLEON "THE LITTLE."..........................230
　　FACT OR FABLE?...................................231
　　NO ASSASSINATION................................233

THE DESPATCH OF THE DOOM............235
THE SEAMAN'S SONG..................235
THE RETREAT FROM MOSCOW............236
THE OCEAN'S SONG...................239
THE TRUMPETS OF THE MIND...........240
AFTER THE COUP D'ÉTAT..............242
PATRIA.{1}.........................243
THE UNIVERSAL REPUBLIC.............245

LES CONTEMPLATIONS.—1830-56...........248
  THE VALE TO YOU, TO ME THE HEIGHTS..........248
  CHILDHOOD......................250
  SATIRE ON THE EARTH............251
  HOW BUTTERFLIES ARE BORN.......252
  HAVE YOU NOTHING TO SAY FOR YOURSELF?......253
  INSCRIPTION FOR A CRUCIFIX.{1}.........254
  DEATH, IN LIFE.................254
  THE DYING CHILD TO ITS MOTHER..........255
  EPITAPH........................257
  ST. JOHN.......................258
  THE POET'S SIMPLE FAITH........259

LA LÉGENDE DES SIÈCLES................261
  CAIN...........................261
  BOAZ ASLEEP....................263
  SONG OF THE GERMAN LANZKNECHT..........266
  KING CANUTE....................269
  THE BOY-KING'S PRAYER..........273
  EVIRADNUS......................275
  THE SOUDAN, THE SPHINXES, THE CUP, THE LAMP.328
  SEA-ADVENTURERS' SONG..........345
  THE SWISS MERCENARIES..........349

  THE CUP ON THE BATTLE-FIELD... 353
  HOW GOOD ARE THE POOR. ... 355

LA VOIX DE GUERNESEY... 361
  MENTANA. {1}... 361

LES CHANSONS DES RUES ET DES BOIS. ... 370
  LOVE OF THE WOODLAND... 370
  SHOOTING STARS. ... 371

L'ANNÉE TERRIBLE. ... 372
  TO LITTLE JEANNE... 372
  TO A SICK CHILD DURING THE SIEGE OF PARIS... 375
  THE CARRIER PIGEON... 376
  TOYS AND TRAGEDY. ... 377
  MOURNING... 377
  THE LESSON OF THE PATRIOT DEAD... 379
  THE BOY ON THE BARRICADE. ... 380
  TO HIS ORPHAN GRANDCHILDREN... 383
  TO THE CANNON "VICTOR HUGO."... 386

L'ART D'ÊTRE GRANDPÊRE... 388
  THE CHILDREN OF THE POOR. ... 388
  THE EPIC OF THE LION. ... 389

LES QUATRE VENTS DE L'ESPRIT... 395
  ON HEARING THE PRINCESS ROYAL{1} SING... 395
  MY HAPPIEST DREAM... 397
  AN OLD-TIME LAY... 398
  JERSEY... 399
  THEN, MOST, I SMILE. ... 401
  THE EXILE'S DESIRE... 402
  THE REFUGEE'S HAVEN... 403

VARIOUS PIECES..............................404
    TO THE NAPOLEON COLUMN....................404
    CHARITY...................................406
    SWEET SISTER..............................409
    THE PITY OF THE ANGELS....................410
    THE SOWER.................................410
    OH, WHY NOT BE HAPPY?{1}..................411
    FREEDOM AND THE WORLD.....................412
    SERENADE..................................413
    AN AUTUMNAL SIMILE........................414
    TO CRUEL OCEAN............................415
    ESMERALDA IN PRISON.......................415
    LOVER'S SONG..............................416
    LORD ROCHESTER'S SONG.....................417
    THE BEGGAR'S QUATRAIN.....................418
    THE QUIET RURAL CHURCH....................419

DRAMATIC PIECES..............................420
    THE FATHER'S CURSE........................420
    PATERNAL LOVE.............................422
    THE DEGENERATE GALLANTS...................424
    THE OLD AND THE YOUNG BRIDEGROOM..........425
    THE SPANISH LADY'S LOVE...................427
    THE LOVER'S SACRIFICE.....................428
    THE OLD MAN'S LOVE........................430
    THE ROLL OF THE DE SILVA RACE.............432
    THE LOVERS' COLLOQUY......................434
    CROMWELL AND THE CROWN....................436
    MILTON'S APPEAL TO CROMWELL...............437
    FIRST LOVE................................441
    THE FIRST BLACK FLAG......................442

THE SON IN OLD AGE..............................444
THE EMPEROR'S RETURN.........................446

Victor Hugo

Victor Marie Hugo was born on 26th February 1802, in Besançon, Franche-Comté, France. He was a political campaigner, artist, poet, novelist and dramatist of the Romantic movement, considered one of the greatest French writers of all time.

Hugo's father was a freethinking republican who considered Napoléon a hero, and his mother was a Catholic Royalist, who was executed in 1812 for plotting against the legendary general. Hugo's childhood was a period of national political turmoil. Napoléon was proclaimed Emperor two years after Hugo's birth, and the Bourbon Monarchy was restored before his eighteenth birthday. The opposing political and religious views of Hugo's parents reflected the forces that would battle for supremacy in France throughout his life.

As a young man, his mother dominated his education and upbringing, and as a result Hugo's early work in poetry and fiction reflects her passionate devotion to both King and Faith. It was only later, during the events leading up to France's 1848 Revolution, that he would begin to rebel against his Catholic Royalist education and instead champion Republicanism and Freethought. Hugo was also a rebellious young man, and on falling in love with his childhood friend Adèle Foucher (1803–1868), became secretly engaged against his mothers wishes. Because of his close relationship with his mother, Hugo waited until after his mother's death (in 1821) to marry Adèle in 1822.

Hugo published his first novel the year following his marriage (*Han d'Islande*, 1823), and his second three years later (*Bug-Jargal*, 1826). Between 1829 and 1840 he would publish five more volumes of poetry, cementing his reputation as one of the greatest elegiac and lyric poets of his time. Victor Hugo's first mature work of fiction appeared in 1829, and reflected the acute social conscience that would infuse his later work. *The Last Day of a Condemned Man* would have a profound influence on later writers such as Albert Camus, Charles Dickens, and Fyodor Dostoevsky. It was soon followed by *The Hunchback of Notre-Dame* (in 1831), which was quickly translated into other language across Europe.

Adèle and Victor Hugo had their first child, Léopold, in 1823, but the boy died in infancy. The following year, on 28th August 1824, the couple's second child, Léopoldine was born, followed by Charles in 1826, François-Victor in 1828, and Adèle in 1830. Hugo's oldest and favourite daughter, Léopoldine, died at the age of nineteen in 1843, shortly after her marriage to Charles Vacquerie. On 4th September 1843, she drowned in the Seine at Villequier, pulled down by her heavy skirts, when a boat overturned. Her young husband also died trying to save her. The death left her father devastated; Hugo was travelling with his mistress at the time in the south of France, and first learned about Léopoldine's death from a newspaper he read in a cafe.

Hugo wrote many poems about his daughter's tragic life and death, and many biographers have claimed that he never completely recovered from this traumatic incident. His most famous poem is probably *Demain, Dès L'aube*, in which he describes visiting her grave. He began planning a major novel about social misery and injustice as early as the 1830s, but it would take a full seventeen years for *Les Misérables* to be realized and finally published in 1862. On its publication, the critical establishment was generally hostile to the novel, with Gustave Flaubert claiming he found within it 'neither truth nor greatness' and Baudelaire castigating it as 'tasteless and inept.' Despite this, *Les Misérables* was a massive hit with the public, and today remains Victor Hugo's most enduringly popular work.

After three unsuccessful attempts, Hugo was finally elected to the Académie Française in 1841, solidifying his position in the world of French arts and letters. He was also elevated to the peerage by King Louis-Philippe in the same year and entered the Higher Chamber as a *pair de France*, where he spoke against the death penalty and social injustice, and in favour of freedom of the press and self-government for Poland. In 1848, Hugo was elected to the Parliament as a conservative. In 1849 he broke with the conservatives when he gave a noted speech calling for the end of misery and poverty. When Louis Napoleon (Napoleon III) seized complete power in 1851, establishing an anti-parliamentary constitution, Hugo openly declared him a traitor to France.

Hugo decided to live in exile after Napoleon III's coup d'état at the end of 1851. After leaving France, he lived in Brussels briefly in 1851, before moving to the Channel Islands, first to Jersey (1852–1855) and then to the smaller island of Guernsey in 1855, where he stayed until 1870. Whilst in exile, Hugo published his famous political pamphlets against Napoleon III, *Napoléon le Petit* and *Histoire d'un Crime*, which whilst banned in France, had a strong impact. Although Napoleon III proclaimed a general amnesty in 1859, the author stayed in exile, only returning when Napoleon was forced from power in 1870. Hugo's next novel, *Troilers of the Sea* turned away from the social and political themes so prevalent in *Les Miserables*. It told the story of a man hoping to gain the approval of his beloved's father by rescuing his ship - thus battling the elements, mythical beasts and the sea itself. It was published in 1866, and was dedicated to the channel islands, in which Hugo found such a welcoming home.

Hugo returned to political and social issues in his next novel, *The Man Who Laughs*, which was published in 1869 and painted a critical picture of the aristocracy. The novel was not as successful as his previous efforts, and Hugo himself began to comment on the growing distance between himself and literary contemporaries such as Flaubert and Émile Zola, whose realist and naturalist novels were now exceeding the popularity of his own work. After the Siege of Paris, Hugo lived again in Guernsey from 1872 to 1873, before finally returning to France for the remainder of his life. His last novel, *Ninety-Three*, published in 1874, dealt with a subject that Hugo had previously avoided: the Reign of Terror during the French Revolution. Though Hugo's popularity was on the decline at the time of its publication, many now consider *Ninety-Three* to be a work on par with his earlier and better-known novels.

When Hugo returned to Paris in 1870, the country hailed him as a national hero. This was a sad time for the ageing writer however, as within a brief period he suffered a mild stoke, his daughter Adèle's internment in an insane asylum, and the death of his two sons. His wife Adèle had died in 1868. Hugo's mistress, Juliette Drouet, also died in 1883 – two years before Hugo's own death. Despite this, to honour the fact that he was entering his eightieth year, in 1882, one of the greatest tributes to a living writer was held. The celebrations began on 25th June when Hugo was presented with a Sèvres vase, the traditional gift for sovereigns, and on 27th June one of the largest parades in French history was held.

Victor Hugo's death from pneumonia on 22nd May 1885, at the age of eighty-three, generated intense national mourning. He was not only revered as a towering figure in literature, but he was also a statesman who shaped the Third Republic and democracy in France. More than two million people joined his funeral procession in Paris from the Arc de Triomphe to the Panthéon, where he was buried. He shares a crypt within the with Alexandre Dumas and Émile Zola.

MEMOIR OF VICTOR MARIE HUGO.

Towards the close of the First French Revolution, Joseph Leopold Sigisbert Hugo, son of a joiner at Nancy, and an officer risen from the ranks in the Republican army, married Sophie Trébuchet, daughter of a Nantes fitter-out of privateers, a Vendean royalist and devotee.

Victor Marie Hugo, their second son, was born on the 26th of February, 1802, at Besançon, France. Though a weakling, he was carried, with his boy-brothers, in the train of their father through the south of France, in pursuit of Fra Diavolo, the Italian brigand, and finally into Spain.

Colonel Hugo had become General, and there, besides being governor over three provinces, was Lord High Steward at King Joseph's court, where his eldest son Abel was installed as page. The other two were educated for similar posts among hostile young Spaniards under stern priestly tutors in the Nobles' College at Madrid, a palace become a monastery. Upon the English advance to free Spain of the invaders, the general and Abel remained at bay, whilst the mother and children hastened to Paris.

Again, in a house once a convent, Victor and his brother Eugène were taught by priests until, by the accident of their roof sheltering a comrade of their father's, a change of tutor was afforded them. This was General Lahorie, a man of superior education, main supporter of Malet in his daring plot to take the government into the Republicans' hands during the absence of Napoleon I. in Russia. Lahorie read old French and Latin with Victor till the police scented him out and led him to execution, October, 1812.

School claimed the young Hugos after this tragical episode, where they were oddities among the humdrum tradesmen's sons. Victor, thoughtful and taciturn, rhymed profusely in tragedies, "printing" in his books, "Châteaubriand or nothing!" and engaging his more animated brother to flourish the Cid's sword and roar the tyrant's speeches.

In 1814, both suffered a sympathetic anxiety as their father held out at Thionville against the Allies, finally repulsing them by a sortie. This was pure loyalty to the fallen Bonaparte, for Hugo had lost his all in Spain, his very savings having been sunk in real estate, through King Joseph's insistence on his adherents investing to prove they had "come to stay."

The Bourbons enthroned anew, General Hugo received, less for his neutrality than thanks to his wife's piety and loyalty, confirmation of his title and rank, and, moreover, a fieldmarshalship. Abel was accepted as a page, too, but there was no money awarded the ex-Bonapartist—money being what the Eaglet at Reichstadt most required for an attempt at his father's throne—and the poor officer was left in seclusion to write consolingly about his campaigns and "Defences of Fortified Towns."

Decidedly the pen had superseded the sword, for Victor and Eugène were scribbling away in ephemeral political sheets as apprenticeship to founding a periodical of their own.

Victor's poetry became remarkable in *La Muse Française* and *Le Conservateur Littéraire*, the odes being permeated with Legitimist and anti-revolutionary sentiments delightful to the taste of Madam Hugo, member as she was of the courtly Order of the Royal Lily.

Poems

In 1817, the French Academy honorably mentioned Victor's "Odes on the Advantages of Study," with a misgiving that some elder hand was masked under the line ascribing "scant fifteen years" to the author. At the Toulouse Floral Games he won prizes two years successively. His critical judgment was sound as well, for he had divined the powers of Lamartine.

His "Odes," collected in a volume, gave his ever-active mother her opportunity at Court. Louis XVIII. granted the boy-poet a pension of 1,500 francs.

It was the windfall for which the youth had been waiting to enable him to gratify his first love. In his childhood, his father and one M. Foucher, head of a War Office Department, had jokingly betrothed a son of the one to a daughter of the other. Abel had loftier views than alliance with a civil servant's child; Eugène was in love elsewhere; but Victor had fallen enamored with Adèle Foucher. It is true, when poverty beclouded the Hugos, the Fouchers had shrunk into their mantle of dignity, and the girl had been strictly forbidden to correspond with her child-sweetheart.

He, finding letters barred out, wrote a love story ("Hans of Iceland") in two weeks, where were recited his hopes, fears, and constancy, and this book she could read.

It pleased the public no less, and its sale, together with that of the "Odes" and a West Indian romance, "Buck Jargal," together with a royal pension, emboldened the poet to renew his love-suit. To refuse the recipient of court funds was not possible to a public functionary. M. Foucher consented to the betrothal in the summer of 1821.

So encloistered had Mdlle. Adèle been, her reading "Hans" the exceptional intrusion, that she only learnt on meeting her affianced that he was mourning his mother. In October, 1822, they were wed, the bride nineteen, the bridegroom but one year the elder. The dinner was marred by the sinister disaster of Eugène Hugo going mad. (He died in an asylum five years later.) The author terminated his wedding year with the "Ode to Louis XVIII.," read to a society after the President of the Academy had introduced him as "the most promising of our young lyrists."

In spite of new poems revealing a Napoleonic bias, Victor was invited to see Charles X. consecrated at Rheims, 29th of May, 1825, and was entered on the roll of the Legion of Honor repaying the favors with the verses expected. But though a son was born to him he was not restored to Conservatism; with his mother's death all that had vanished. His tragedy of "Cromwell" broke lances upon Royalists and upholders of the still reigning style of tragedy. The second collection of "Odes" preluding it, showed the spirit of the son of Napoleon's general, rather than of the Bourbonist field-marshal. On the occasion, too, of the Duke of Tarento being announced at the Austrian Ambassador's ball, February, 1827, as plain "Marshal Macdonald," Victor became the mouthpiece of indignant Bonapartists in his "Ode to the Napoleon Column" in the Place Vendôme.

His "Orientales," though written in a Parisian suburb by one who had not travelled, appealed for Grecian liberty, and depicted sultans and pashas as tyrants, many a line being deemed applicable to personages nearer the Seine than Stamboul.

"Cromwell" was not actable, and "Amy Robsart," in collaboration with his brother-in-law, Foucher, miserably failed, notwithstanding a finale "superior to Scott's 'Kenilworth.'" In one twelvemonth, there was this failure to record, the death of his father from apoplexy at his eldest son's marriage, and the birth of a second son to Victor towards the close.

Still imprudent, the young father again irritated the court with satire in "Marion Delorme" and "Hernani," two plays immediately suppressed by the Censure, all the more active as the Revolution of July, 1830, was surely seething up to the edge of the crater.

(At this juncture, the poet Châteaubriand, fading star to our rising sun, yielded up to him formally "his place at the poets' table.")

In the summer of 1831, a civil ceremony was performed over the insurgents killed in the previous year, and Hugo was constituted poet-laureate of the Revolution by having his hymn sung in the Pantheon over the biers.

Under Louis Philippe, "Marion Delorme" could be played, but livelier attention was turned to "Nôtre Dame de Paris," the historical romance in which Hugo vied with Sir Walter. It was to have been followed by others, but the publisher unfortunately secured a contract to monopolize all the new novelist's prose fictions for a term of years, and the author revenged himself by publishing poems and plays alone. Hence "Nôtre Dame" long stood unique: it was translated in all languages, and plays and operas were founded on it. Heine professed to see in the prominence of the hunchback a personal appeal of the author, who was slightly deformed by one shoulder being a trifle higher than the other; this malicious suggestion reposed also on the fact that the *quasi*-hero of "Le Roi s'Amuse" (1832, a tragedy suppressed after one representation, for its reflections on royalty), was also a contorted piece of humanity. This play was followed by "Lucrezia Borgia," "Marie Tudor," and "Angelo," written in a singular poetic prose. Spite of bald translations, their action was sufficiently dramatic to make them successes, and even still enduring on our stage. They have all been arranged as operas, whilst Hugo himself, to oblige the father of Louise Bertin, a magazine publisher of note, wrote "Esmeralda" for her music in 1835.

Thus, at 1837, when he was promoted to an officership in the Legion of Honor, it was acknowledged his due as a laborious worker in all fields of literature, however contestable the merits and tendencies of his essays.

In 1839, the Academy, having rejected him several times, elected him among the Forty Immortals. In the previous year had been successfully acted "Ruy Blas," for which play he had gone to Spanish sources; with and after the then imperative Rhine tour, came an unendurable "trilogy," the "Burgraves," played one long, long night in 1843. A real tragedy was to mark that year: his daughter Léopoldine being drowned in the Seine with her husband, who would not save himself when he found that her death-grasp on the sinking boat was not to be loosed.

For distraction, Hugo plunged into politics. A peer in 1845, he sat between Marshal Soult and Pontécoulant, the regicide-judge of Louis XVI. His maiden speech bore upon artistic copyright; but he rapidly became a power in much graver matters.

As fate would have it, his speech on the Bonapartes induced King Louis Philippe to allow Prince Louis Napoleon Bonaparte to return, and, there being no gratitude in politics, the emancipated outlaw rose as a rival candidate for the Presidency, for which Hugo had nominated himself in his newspaper the

Evènement. The story of the *Coup d'État* is well known; for the Republican's side, read Hugo's own "History of a Crime." Hugo, proscribed, betook himself to Brussels, London, and the Channel Islands, waiting to "return with right when the usurper should be expelled."

Meanwhile, he satirized the Third Napoleon and his congeners with ceaseless shafts, the principal being the famous "Napoleon the Little," based on the analogical reasoning that as the earth has moons, the lion the jackal, man himself his simian double, a minor Napoleon was inevitable as a standard of estimation, the grain by which a pyramid is measured. These flings were collected in "Les Châtiments," a volume preceded by "Les Contemplations" (mostly written in the '40's), and followed by "Les Chansons des Rues et des Bois."

The baffled publisher's close-time having expired, or, at least, his heirs being satisfied, three novels appeared, long heralded: in 1862, "Les Misérables" (Ye Wretched), wherein the author figures as Marius and his father as the Bonapartist officer: in 1866, "Les Travailleurs de la Mer" (Toilers of the Sea), its scene among the Channel Islands; and, in 1868, "L'Homme Qui Rit" (The Man who Grins), unfortunately laid in a fanciful England evolved from recondite reading through foreign spectacles. Whilst writing the final chapters, Hugo's wife died; and, as he had refused the Amnesty, he could only escort her remains to the Belgian frontier, August, 1868. All this while, in his Paris daily newspaper, *Le Rappel* (adorned with cuts of a Revolutionary drummer beating "to arms!"), he and his sons and son-in-law's family were reiterating blows at the throne. When it came down in 1870, and the Republic was proclaimed, Hugo hastened to Paris.

His poems, written during the War and Siege, collected under the title of "L'Année Terrible" (The Terrible Year, 1870-71), betray the long-tried exile, "almost alone in his gloom," after the death of his son Charles and his child. Fleeing to Brussels after the Commune, he nevertheless was so aggressive in sheltering and aiding its fugitives, that he was banished the kingdom, lest there should be a renewal of an assault on his house by the mob, supposed by his adherents to be, not "the honest Belgians," but the refugee Bonapartists and Royalists, who had not cared to fight for France in France endangered. Resting in Luxemburg, he prepared "L'Année Terrible" for the press, and thence returned to Paris, vainly to plead with President Thiers for the captured Communists' lives, and vainly, too, proposing himself for election to the new House.

In 1872, his novel of "'93" pleased the general public here, mainly by the adventures of three charming little children during the prevalence of an internecine war. These phases of a bounteously paternal mood reappeared in "L'Art d'être Grandpère," published in 1877, when he had become a life-senator.

"Hernani" was in the regular "stock" of the Théâtre Français, "Rigoletto" (Le Roi s'Amuse) always at the Italian opera-house, while the same subject, under the title of "The Fool's Revenge," held, as it still holds, a high position on the Anglo-American stage. Finally, the poetic romance of "Torquemada," for over thirty years promised, came forth in 1882, to prove that the wizard-wand had not lost its cunning.

After dolor, fêtes were come: on one birthday they crown his bust in the chief theatre; on another, all notable Paris parades under his window, where he sits with his grandchildren at his knee, in the shadow of the Triumphal Arch of Napoleon's Star. It is given to few men thus to see their own apotheosis.

Whilst he was dying, in May, 1885, Paris was but the first mourner for all France; and the magnificent funeral pageant which conducted the pauper's coffin, antithetically enshrining the remains considered worthy of the highest possible reverence and honors, from the Champs Elysées to the Pantheon, was the more memorable from all that was foremost in French art and letters having marched in the train, and laid a leaf or flower in the tomb of the protégé of Châteaubriand, the brother-in-arms of Dumas, the inspirer of Mars, Dorval, Le-maître, Rachel, and Bernhardt, and, above all, the Nemesis of the Third Empire.

EARLY POEMS.

MOSES ON THE NILE.

("Mes soeurs, l'onde est plus fraiche.")

{TO THE FLORAL GAMES, Toulouse, Feb. 10, 1820.}
"Sisters! the wave is freshest in the ray
Of the young morning; the reapers are asleep;
The river bank is lonely: come away!
The early murmurs of old Memphis creep
Faint on my ear; and here unseen we stray,—
Deep in the covert of the grove withdrawn,
Save by the dewy eye-glance of the dawn.

"Within my father's palace, fair to see,
Shine all the Arts, but oh! this river side,
Pranked with gay flowers, is dearer far to me
Than gold and porphyry vases bright and wide;
How glad in heaven the song-bird carols free!
Sweeter these zephyrs float than all the showers
Of costly odors in our royal bowers.

"The sky is pure, the sparkling stream is clear:
Unloose your zones, my maidens! and fling down
To float awhile upon these bushes near
Your blue transparent robes: take off my crown,

And take away my jealous veil; for here
To-day we shall be joyous while we lave
Our limbs amid the murmur of the wave.

"Hasten; but through the fleecy mists of morn,
What do I see? Look ye along the stream!
Nay, timid maidens—we must not return!
Coursing along the current, it would seem
An ancient palm-tree to the deep sea borne,
That from the distant wilderness proceeds,
Downwards, to view our wondrous Pyramids.

"But stay! if I may surely trust mine eye,—
It is the bark of Hermes, or the shell
Of Iris, wafted gently to the sighs
Of the light breeze along the rippling swell;
But no: it is a skiff where sweetly lies
An infant slumbering, and his peaceful rest
Looks as if pillowed on his mother's breast.

"He sleeps—oh, see! his little floating bed
Swims on the mighty river's fickle flow,
A white dove's nest; and there at hazard led
By the faint winds, and wandering to and fro,
The cot comes down; beneath his quiet head
The gulfs are moving, and each threatening wave
Appears to rock the child upon a grave.

"He wakes—ah, maids of Memphis! haste, oh, haste!
He cries! alas!—What mother could confide

Her offspring to the wild and watery waste?
He stretches out his arms, the rippling tide
Murmurs around him, where all rudely placed,
He rests but with a few frail reeds beneath,
Between such helpless innocence and death.

"Oh! take him up! Perchance he is of those
Dark sons of Israel whom my sire proscribes;
Ah! cruel was the mandate that arose
Against most guiltless of the stranger tribes!
Poor child! my heart is yearning for his woes,
I would I were his mother; but I'll give
If not his birth, at least the claim to live."

Thus Iphis spoke; the royal hope and pride
Of a great monarch; while her damsels nigh,
Wandered along the Nile's meandering side;
And these diminished beauties, standing by
The trembling mother; watching with eyes wide
Their graceful mistress, admired her as stood,
More lovely than the genius of the flood!

The waters broken by her delicate feet
Receive the eager wader, as alone
By gentlest pity led, she strives to meet
The wakened babe; and, see, the prize is won!
She holds the weeping burden with a sweet
And virgin glow of pride upon her brow,
That knew no flush save modesty's till now.

Opening with cautious hands the reedy couch,
She brought the rescued infant slowly out
Beyond the humid sands; at her approach
Her curious maidens hurried round about
To kiss the new-born brow with gentlest touch;
Greeting the child with smiles, and bending nigh
Their faces o'er his large, astonished eye!

Haste thou who, from afar, in doubt and fear,
Dost watch, with straining eyes, the fated boy—
The loved of heaven! come like a stranger near,
And clasp young Moses with maternal joy;
Nor fear the speechless transport and the tear
Will e'er betray thy fond and hidden claim,
For Iphis knows not yet a mother's name!

With a glad heart, and a triumphal face,
The princess to the haughty Pharaoh led
The humble infant of a hated race,
Bathed with the bitter tears a parent shed;
While loudly pealing round the holy place
Of Heaven's white Throne, the voice of angel choirs
Intoned the theme of their undying lyres!

"No longer mourn thy pilgrimage below—
O Jacob! let thy tears no longer swell
The torrent of the Egyptian river: Lo!
Soon on the Jordan's banks thy tents shall dwell;
And Goshen shall behold thy people go
Despite the power of Egypt's law and brand,

From their sad thrall to Canaan's promised land.

"The King of Plagues, the Chosen of Sinai,
Is he that, o'er the rushing waters driven,
A vigorous hand hath rescued for the sky;
Ye whose proud hearts disown the ways of heaven!
Attend, be humble! for its power is nigh
Israel! a cradle shall redeem thy worth—
A Cradle yet shall save the widespread earth!"

Dublin University Magazine, 1839

ENVY AND AVARICE.

("L'Avarice et l'Envie.")

{LE CONSERVATEUR LITÉRAIRE, 1820.}
Envy and Avarice, one summer day,
  Sauntering abroad
  In quest of the abode
Of some poor wretch or fool who lived that way—
You—or myself, perhaps—I cannot say—
Along the road, scarce heeding where it tended,
Their way in sullen, sulky silence wended;

For, though twin sisters, these two charming creatures,

Rivals in hideousness of form and features,
Wasted no love between them as they went.
 Pale Avarice,
  With gloating eyes,
And back and shoulders almost double bent,
Was hugging close that fatal box
 For which she's ever on the watch
 Some glance to catch
Suspiciously directed to its locks;
And Envy, too, no doubt with silent winking
 At her green, greedy orbs, no single minute
Withdrawn from it, was hard a-thinking
 Of all the shining dollars in it.

The only words that Avarice could utter,
Her constant doom, in a low, frightened mutter,
"There's not enough, enough, yet in my store!"
While Envy, as she scanned the glittering sight,
Groaned as she gnashed her yellow teeth with spite,
 "She's more than me, more, still forever more!"

Thus, each in her own fashion, as they wandered,
Upon the coffer's precious contents pondered,
 When suddenly, to their surprise,
 The God Desire stood before their eyes.
Desire, that courteous deity who grants
 All wishes, prayers, and wants;
Said he to the two sisters: "Beauteous ladies,
As I'm a gentleman, my task and trade is
 To be the slave of your behest—

Choose therefore at your own sweet will and pleasure,
Honors or treasure!
Or in one word, whatever you'd like best.
But, let us understand each other—she
Who speaks the first, her prayer shall certainly
Receive—the other, the same boon *redoubled!*"

Imagine how our amiable pair,
At this proposal, all so frank and fair,
 Were mutually troubled!
Misers and enviers, of our human race,
Say, what would you have done in such a case?
Each of the sisters murmured, sad and low
 "What boots it, oh, Desire, to me to have
 Crowns, treasures, all the goods that heart can crave,
Or power divine bestow,
Since still another must have always more?"

So each, lest she should speak before
The other, hesitating slow and long
Till the god lost all patience, held her tongue.
 He was enraged, in such a way,
 To be kept waiting there all day,
With two such beauties in the public road;
 Scarce able to be civil even,
 He wished them both—well, not in heaven.

Envy at last the silence broke,
 And smiling, with malignant sneer,
 Upon her sister dear,

Who stood in expectation by,
Ever implacable and cruel, spoke
"I would be blinded of *one* eye!"

American Keepsake

ODES.—1818-28.

KING LOUIS XVII.

("En ce temps-là du ciel les portes.")

{Bk. I. v., December, 1822.}
The golden gates were opened wide that day,
All through the unveiled heaven there seemed to play
Out of the Holiest of Holy, light;
And the elect beheld, crowd immortal,
A young soul, led up by young angels bright,
Stand in the starry portal.

A fair child fleeing from the world's fierce hate,
In his blue eye the shade of sorrow sate,
His golden hair hung all dishevelled down,
On wasted cheeks that told a mournful story,

And angels twined him with the innocent's crown,
The martyr's palm of glory.

The virgin souls that to the Lamb are near,
Called through the clouds with voices heavenly clear,
God hath prepared a glory for thy brow,
Rest in his arms, and all ye hosts that sing
His praises ever on untired string,
Chant, for a mortal comes among ye now;
Do homage—"'Tis a king."

And the pale shadow saith to God in heaven:
"I am an orphan and no king at all;
I was a weary prisoner yestereven,
My father's murderers fed my soul with gall.
Not me, O Lord, the regal name beseems.
Last night I fell asleep in dungeon drear,
But then I saw my mother in my dreams,
Say, shall I find her here?"

The angels said: "Thy Saviour bids thee come,
Out of an impure world He calls thee home,
From the mad earth, where horrid murder waves
 Over the broken cross her impure wings,
And regicides go down among the graves,
 Scenting the blood of kings."

He cries: "Then have I finished my long life?
Are all its evils over, all its strife,
And will no cruel jailer evermore

Wake me to pain, this blissful vision o'er?
Is it no dream that nothing else remains
Of all my torments but this answered cry,
And have I had, O God, amid my chains,
The happiness to die?

"For none can tell what cause I had to pine,
What pangs, what miseries, each day were mine;
And when I wept there was no mother near
To soothe my cries, and smile away my tear.
Poor victim of a punishment unending,
Torn like a sapling from its mother earth,
So young, I could not tell what crime impending
Had stained me from my birth.

"Yet far off in dim memory it seems,
With all its horror mingled happy dreams,
Strange cries of glory rocked my sleeping head,
And a glad people watched beside my bed.
One day into mysterious darkness thrown,
I saw the promise of my future close;
I was a little child, left all alone,
Alas! and I had foes.

"They cast me living in a dreary tomb,
Never mine eyes saw sunlight pierce the gloom,
Only ye, brother angels, used to sweep
Down from your heaven, and visit me in sleep.
'Neath blood-red hands my young life withered there.
Dear Lord, the bad are miserable all,

Be not Thou deaf, like them, unto my prayer,
It is for them I call."

The angels sang: "See heaven's high arch unfold,
Come, we will crown thee with the stars above,
Will give thee cherub-wings of blue and gold,
And thou shalt learn our ministry of love,
Shalt rock the cradle where some mother's tears
Are dropping o'er her restless little one,
Or, with thy luminous breath, in distant spheres,
Shalt kindle some cold sun."

Ceased the full choir, all heaven was hushed to hear,
Bowed the fair face, still wet with many a tear,
In depths of space, the rolling worlds were stayed,
Whilst the Eternal in the infinite said:

"O king, I kept thee far from human state,
Who hadst a dungeon only for thy throne,
O son, rejoice, and bless thy bitter fate,
The slavery of kings thou hast not known,
What if thy wasted arms are bleeding yet,
And wounded with the fetter's cruel trace,
No earthly diadem has ever set
A stain upon thy face.

"Child, life and hope were with thee at thy birth,
But life soon bowed thy tender form to earth,
And hope forsook thee in thy hour of need.
Come, for thy Saviour had His pains divine;

Come, for His brow was crowned with thorns like thine,
His sceptre was a reed."

Dublin University Magazine.

THE FEAST OF FREEDOM.

("Lorsqu'à l'antique Olympe immolant l'evangile.")

{Bk. II. v., 1823.}

{There was in Rome one antique usage as follows: On the eve of the
 execution day, the sufferers were given a public banquet—at the prison
 gate—known as the "Free Festival."—
CHATEAUBRIAND'S "Martyrs."}

TO YE KINGS.

When the Christians were doomed to the lions of old
By the priest and the praetor, combined to uphold

An idolatrous cause,
Forth they came while the vast Colosseum throughout
Gathered thousands looked on, and they fell 'mid the shout
   Of "the People's" applause.

On the eve of that day of their evenings the last!
At the gates of their dungeon a gorgeous repast,
   Rich, unstinted, unpriced,
That the doomed might (forsooth) gather strength ere they bled,
   With an ignorant pity the jailers would spread
   For the martyrs of Christ.

Oh, 'twas strange for a pupil of Paul to recline
On voluptuous couch, while Falernian wine
   Fill'd his cup to the brim!
Dulcet music of Greece, Asiatic repose,
Spicy fragrance of Araby, Italian rose,
   All united for him!

Every luxury known through the earth's wide expanse,
In profusion procured was put forth to enhance
   The repast that they gave;
And no Sybarite, nursed in the lap of delight,
Such a banquet ere tasted as welcomed that night
   The elect of the grave.

And the lion, meantime, shook his ponderous chain,
Loud and fierce howled the tiger, impatient to stain

The bloodthirsty arena;
Whilst the women of Rome, who applauded those deeds
And who hailed the forthcoming enjoyment, must needs
   Shame the restless hyena.

They who figured as guests on that ultimate eve,
In their turn on the morrow were destined to give
   To the lions their food;
For, behold, in the guise of a slave at that board,
Where his victims enjoyed all that life can afford,
   Death administering stood.

Such, O monarchs of earth! was your banquet of power,
But the tocsin has burst on your festival hour—
   'Tis your knell that it rings!
To the popular tiger a prey is decreed,
And the maw of Republican hunger will feed
   On *a banquet of Kings!*

"FATHER PROUT" (FRANK MAHONY)

GENIUS.

(DEDICATED TO CHATEAUBRIAND.)

{Bk. IV. vi., July, 1822.}

Woe unto him! the child of this sad earth,
Who, in a troubled world, unjust and blind,
Bears Genius—treasure of celestial birth,
Within his solitary soul enshrined.
Woe unto him! for Envy's pangs impure,
Like the undying vultures', will be driven
Into his noble heart, that must endure
Pangs for each triumph; and, still unforgiven,
Suffer Prometheus' doom, who ravished fire from Heaven.

Still though his destiny on earth may be
Grief and injustice; who would not endure
With joyful calm, each proffered agony;
Could he the prize of Genius thus ensure?
What mortal feeling kindled in his soul
That clear celestial flame, so pure and high,
O'er which nor time nor death can have control,
Would in inglorious pleasures basely fly
From sufferings whose reward is Immortality?
No! though the clamors of the envious crowd
Pursue the son of Genius, he will rise

From the dull clod, borne by an effort proud
Beyond the reach of vulgar enmities.
'Tis thus the eagle, with his pinions spread,
Reposing o'er the tempest, from that height
Sees the clouds reel and roll above our head,
While he, rejoicing in his tranquil flight,
More upward soars sublime in heaven's eternal light.

MRS. TORRE HULME

THE GIRL OF OTAHEITE.

("O! dis-moi, tu veux fuir?")

{Bk. IV, vii., Jan. 31, 1821.}
Forget? Can I forget the scented breath
Of breezes, sighing of thee, in mine ear;
The strange awaking from a dream of death,
The sudden thrill to find thee coming near?
Our huts were desolate, and far away
I heard thee calling me throughout the day,
  No one had seen thee pass,
  Trembling I came. Alas!
    Can I forget?

Once I was beautiful; my maiden charms
Died with the grief that from my bosom fell.
Ah! weary traveller! rest in my loving arms!
Let there be no regrets and no farewell!
  Here of thy mother sweet, where waters flow,
  Here of thy fatherland we whispered low;
  Here, music, praise, and prayer
  Filled the glad summer air.
    Can I forget?

Forget? My dear old home must I forget?
And wander forth and hear my people weep,
Far from the woods where, when the sun has set,
Fearless but weary to thy arms I creep;
Far from lush flow'rets and the palm-tree's moan
I could not live. Here let me rest alone!
Go! I must follow nigh,
With thee I'm doomed to die,
  Never forget!

CLEMENT SCOTT

NERO'S INCENDIARY SONG.

("Amis! ennui nous tue.")

{Bk. IV. xv., March, 1825.}

Aweary unto death, my friends, a mood by wise abhorred,
Come to the novel feast I spread, thrice-consul, Nero, lord,
The Caesar, master of the world, and eke of harmony,
Who plays the harp of many strings, a chief of minstrelsy.

My joyful call should instantly bring all who love me most,—
For ne'er were seen such arch delights from Greek or Roman host;

Nor at the free, control-less jousts, where, spite of cynic vaunts,
Austere but lenient Seneca no "Ercles" bumper daunts;

Nor where upon the Tiber floats Aglae in galley gay,
'Neath Asian tent of brilliant stripes, in gorgeous array;
Nor when to lutes and tambourines the wealthy prefect flings
A score of slaves, their fetters wreathed, to feed grim, greedy things.

I vow to show ye Rome aflame, the whole town in a mass;
Upon this tower we'll take our stand to watch the 'wildered pass;
How paltry fights of men and beasts! here be my combatants,—
The Seven Hills my circus form, and fiends shall lead the dance.

This is more meet for him who rules to drive away his stress—
He, being god, should lightnings hurl and make a wilderness—
But, haste! for night is darkling—soon, the festival it brings;
Already see the hydra show its tongues and sombre wings,

And mark upon a shrinking prey the rush of kindling breaths;
They tap and sap the threatened walls, and bear uncounted deaths;
And 'neath caresses scorching hot the palaces decay—
Oh, that I, too, could thus caress, and burn, and blight, and slay!

Hark to the hubbub! scent the fumes! Are those real men or ghosts?

The stillness spreads of Death abroad—down come the temple posts,
Their molten bronze is coursing fast and joins with silver waves
To leap with hiss of thousand snakes where Tiber writhes and raves.

All's lost! in jasper, marble, gold, the statues totter—crash!
Spite of the names divine engraved, they are but dust and ash.
The victor-scourge sweeps swollen on, whilst north winds sound the horn
To goad the flies of fire yet beyond the flight forlorn.

Proud capital! farewell for e'er! these flames nought can subdue—
The Aqueduct of Sylla gleams, a bridge o'er hellish brew.
'Tis Nero's whim! how good to see Rome brought the lowest down;
Yet, Queen of all the earth, give thanks for such a splendrous crown!

When I was young, the Sybils pledged eternal rule to thee;
That Time himself would lay his bones before thy unbent knee.
Ha! ha! how brief indeed the space ere this "immortal star"
Shall be consumed in its own glow, and vanished—oh, how far!

How lovely conflagrations look when night is utter dark!
The youth who fired Ephesus' fane falls low beneath my mark.
The pangs of people—when I sport, what matters?—See them whirl
About, as salamanders frisk and in the brazier curl.

Take from my brow this poor rose-crown—the flames have made it pine;

If blood rains on your festive gowns, wash off with Cretan wine!
I like not overmuch that red—good taste says "gild a crime?"
"To stifle shrieks by drinking-songs" is—thanks! a hint sublime!

I punish Rome, I am avenged; did she not offer prayers
Erst unto Jove, late unto Christ?—to e'en a Jew, she dares!
Now, in thy terror, own my right to rule above them all;
Alone I rest—except this pile, I leave no single hall.

Yet I destroy to build anew, and Rome shall fairer shine—
But out, my guards, and slay the dolts who thought me not divine.
The stiffnecks, haste! annihilate! make ruin all complete—
And, slaves, bring in fresh roses—what odor is more sweet?

H.L. WILLIAMS

REGRET.

("Oui, le bonheur bien vite a passé.")

{Bk. V. ii., February, 1821.}
Yes, Happiness hath left me soon behind!
Alas! we all pursue its steps! and when
We've sunk to rest within its arms entwined,
Like the Phoenician virgin, wake, and find
Ourselves alone again.

Then, through the distant future's boundless space,
We seek the lost companion of our days:
"Return, return!" we cry, and lo, apace
Pleasure appears! but not to fill the place
Of that we mourn always.

I, should unhallowed Pleasure woo me now,
Will to the wanton sorc'ress say, "Begone!
Respect the cypress on my mournful brow,
Lost Happiness hath left regret—but *thou*
Leavest remorse, alone."

Yet, haply lest I check the mounting fire,
O friends, that in your revelry appears!
With you I'll breathe the air which ye respire,
And, smiling, hide my melancholy lyre
When it is wet with tears.

Each in his secret heart perchance doth own
Some fond regret 'neath passing smiles concealed;—
Sufferers alike together and alone
Are we; with many a grief to others known,
How many unrevealed!

Alas! for natural tears and simple pains,
For tender recollections, cherished long,
For guileless griefs, which no compunction stains,
We blush; as if we wore these earthly chains
Only for sport and song!

Yes, my blest hours have fled without a trace:
In vain I strove their parting to delay;
Brightly they beamed, then left a cheerless space,
Like an o'erclouded smile, that in the face
Lightens, and fades away.

Fraser's Magazine

THE MORNING OF LIFE.

("Le voile du matin.")

{Bk. V. viii., April, 1822.}
The mist of the morning is torn by the peaks,
Old towers gleam white in the ray,
And already the glory so joyously seeks
The lark that's saluting the day.

Then smile away, man, at the heavens so fair,
Though, were you swept hence in the night,
From your dark, lonely tomb the owlets would stare
At the sun rising newly as bright.

But out of earth's trammels your soul would have flown
Where glitters Eternity's stream,

And you shall have waked 'midst pure glories unknown,
As sunshine disperses a dream.

BELOVED NAME.

("Le parfum d'un lis.")

{Bk. V. xiii.}
The lily's perfume pure, fame's crown of light,
The latest murmur of departing day,
Fond friendship's plaint, that melts at piteous sight,
The mystic farewell of each hour at flight,
The kiss which beauty grants with coy delay,—

The sevenfold scarf that parting storms bestow
As trophy to the proud, triumphant sun;
The thrilling accent of a voice we know,
The love-enthralled maiden's secret vow,
An infant's dream, ere life's first sands be run,—

The chant of distant choirs, the morning's sigh,
Which erst inspired the fabled Memnon's frame,—
The melodies that, hummed, so trembling die,—
The sweetest gems that 'mid thought's treasures lie,
Have naught of sweetness that can match HER NAME!

Low be its utterance, like a prayer divine,
Yet in each warbled song be heard the sound;
Be it the light in darksome fanes to shine,
The sacred word which at some hidden shrine,
The selfsame voice forever makes resound!

O friends! ere yet, in living strains of flame,
My muse, bewildered in her circlings wide,
With names the vaunting lips of pride proclaim,
Shall dare to blend the *one*, the purer name,
Which love a treasure in my breast doth hide,—

Must the wild lay my faithful harp can sing,
Be like the hymns which mortals, kneeling, hear;
To solemn harmonies attuned the string,
As, music show'ring from his viewless wing,
On heavenly airs some angel hovered near.

CAROLINE BOWLES (MRS. SOUTHEY)

THE PORTRAIT OF A CHILD.

("Oui, ce front, ce sourire.")

{Bk. V. xxii., November, 1825.}
That brow, that smile, that cheek so fair,

Beseem my child, who weeps and plays:
A heavenly spirit guards her ways,
From whom she stole that mixture rare.
Through all her features shining mild,
The poet sees an angel there,
The father sees a child.

And by their flame so pure and bright,
We see how lately those sweet eyes
Have wandered down from Paradise,
And still are lingering in its light.

All earthly things are but a shade
Through which she looks at things above,
And sees the holy Mother-maid,
Athwart her mother's glance of love.

She seems celestial songs to hear,
And virgin souls are whispering near.
Till by her radiant smile deceived,
  I say, "Young angel, lately given,
When was thy martyrdom achieved?
  And what name lost thou bear in heaven?"

Dublin University Magazine.

BALLADES.—1823-28.

THE GRANDMOTHER

("*Dors-tu? mère de notre mère.*")

{III., 1823.}

"To die—to sleep."—SHAKESPEARE.
Still asleep! We have been since the noon thus alone.
 Oh, the hours we have ceased to number!
Wake, grandmother!—speechless say why thou art grown.
Then, thy lips are so cold!—the Madonna of stone
 Is like thee in thy holy slumber.
We have watched thee in sleep, we have watched thee at prayer,
 But what can now betide thee?
Like thy hours of repose all thy orisons were,
And thy lips would still murmur a blessing whene'er
 Thy children stood beside thee.

Now thine eye is unclosed, and thy forehead is bent
 O'er the hearth, where ashes smoulder;
And behold, the watch-lamp will be speedily spent.
Art thou vexed? have we done aught amiss? Oh, relent!
 But—parent, thy hands grow colder!
Say, with ours wilt thou let us rekindle in thine

The glow that has departed?
Wilt thou sing us some song of the days of lang syne?
Wilt thou tell us some tale, from those volumes divine,
Of the brave and noble-hearted?

Of the dragon who, crouching in forest green glen,
  Lies in wait for the unwary—
Of the maid who was freed by her knight from the den
Of the ogre, whose club was uplifted, but then
  Turned aside by the wand of a fairy?
Wilt thou teach us spell-words that protect from all harm,
  And thoughts of evil banish?
What goblins the sign of the cross may disarm?
What saint it is good to invoke? and what charm
  Can make the demon vanish?

Or unfold to our gaze thy most wonderful book,
  So feared by hell and Satan;
At its hermits and martyrs in gold let us look,
At the virgins, and bishops with pastoral crook,
  And the hymns and the prayers in Latin.
Oft with legends of angels, who watch o'er the young,
  Thy voice was wont to gladden;
Have thy lips yet no language—no wisdom thy tongue?
Oh, see! the light wavers, and sinking, bath flung
  On the wall forms that sadden.

Wake! awake! evil spirits perhaps may presume
  To haunt thy holy dwelling;
Pale ghosts are, perhaps, stealing into the room—

Oh, would that the lamp were relit! with the gloom
 These fearful thoughts dispelling.
Thou hast told us our parents lie sleeping beneath
 The grass, in a churchyard lonely:
Now, thine eyes have no motion, thy mouth has no breath,
And thy limbs are all rigid! Oh, say, *Is this death*,
 Or thy prayer or thy slumber only?

ENVOY.

Sad vigil they kept by that grandmother's chair,
 Kind angels hovered o'er them—
And the dead-bell was tolled in the hamlet—and there,
On the following eve, knelt that innocent pair,
 With the missal-book before them.

"FATHER PROUT" (FRANK S. MAHONY).

THE GIANT IN GLEE.

("Ho, guerriers! je suis né dans le pays des Gaules.")

{V., March 11, 1825.}
Ho, warriors! I was reared in the land of the Gauls;
O'er the Rhine my ancestors came bounding like balls
Of the snow at the Pole, where, a babe, I was bathed

Ere in bear and in walrus-skin I was enswathed.

Then my father was strong, whom the years lowly bow,—
A bison could wallow in the grooves of his brow.
He is weak, very old—he can scarcely uptear
A young pine-tree for staff since his legs cease to bear;

But here's to replace him!—I can toy with his axe;
As I sit on the hill my feet swing in the flax,
And my knee caps the boulders and troubles the trees.
How they shiver, yea, quake if I happen to sneeze!

I was still but a springald when, cleaving the Alps,
I brushed snowy periwigs off granitic scalps,
And my head, o'er the pinnacles, stopped the fleet clouds,
Where I captured the eagles and caged them by crowds.

There were tempests! I blew them back into their source!
And put out their lightnings! More than once in a course,
Through the ocean I went wading after the whale,
And stirred up the bottom as did never a gale.

Fond of rambling, I hunted the shark 'long the beach,
And no osprey in ether soared out of my reach;
And the bear that I pinched 'twixt my finger and thumb,
Like the lynx and the wolf, perished harmless and dumb.

But these pleasures of childhood have lost all their zest;
It is warfare and carnage that now I love best:
The sounds that I wish to awaken and hear

Are the cheers raised by courage, the shrieks due to fear;

When the riot of flames, ruin, smoke, steel and blood,
Announces an army rolls along as a flood,
Which I follow, to harry the clamorous ranks,
Sharp-goading the laggards and pressing the flanks,
Till, a thresher 'mid ripest of corn, up I stand
With an oak for a flail in my unflagging hand.

Rise the groans! rise the screams! on my feet fall vain tears
As the roar of my laughter redoubles their fears.
I am naked. At armor of steel I should joke—
True, I'm helmed—a brass pot you could draw with ten yoke.

I look for no ladder to invade the king's hall—
I stride o'er the ramparts, and down the walls fall,
Till choked are the ditches with the stones, dead and quick,
Whilst the flagstaff I use 'midst my teeth as a pick.

Oh, when cometh my turn to succumb like my prey,
May brave men my body snatch away from th' array
Of the crows—may they heap on the rocks till they loom
Like a mountain, befitting a colossus' tomb!

Foreign Quarterly Review (adapted)

THE CYMBALEER'S BRIDE.

("Monseigneur le Duc de Bretagne.")

{VI., October, 1825.}
My lord the Duke of Brittany
  Has summoned his barons bold—
Their names make a fearful litany!
Among them you will not meet any
  But men of giant mould.

Proud earls, who dwell in donjon keep,
  And steel-clad knight and peer,
Whose forts are girt with a moat cut deep—
But none excel in soldiership
  My own loved cymbaleer.

Clashing his cymbals, forth he went,
  With a bold and gallant bearing;
Sure for a captain he was meant,
To judge his pride with courage blent,
  And the cloth of gold he's wearing.

But in my soul since then I feel
  A fear in secret creeping;
And to my patron saint I kneel,
That she may recommend his weal
  To his guardian-angel's keeping.

I've begged our abbot Bernardine
　His prayers not to relax;
And to procure him aid divine
I've burnt upon Saint Gilda's shrine
　Three pounds of virgin wax.

Our Lady of Loretto knows
　The pilgrimage I've vowed:
"To wear the scallop I propose,
If health and safety from the foes
　My lover be allowed."

No letter (fond affection's gage!)
　From him could I require,
The pain of absence to assuage—
A vassal-maid can have no page,
　A liegeman has no squire.

This day will witness, with the duke's,
　My cymbaleer's return:
Gladness and pride beam in my looks,
Delay my heart impatient brooks,
　All meaner thoughts I spurn.

Back from the battlefield elate
　His banner brings each peer;
Come, let us see, at the ancient gate,
The martial triumph pass in state—
　With the princes my cymbaleer.

We'll have from the rampart walls a glance
 Of the air his steed assumes;
His proud neck swells, his glad hoofs prance,
And on his head unceasing dance,
 In a gorgeous tuft, red plumes!

Be quick, my sisters! dress in haste!
 Come, see him bear the bell,
With laurels decked, with true love graced,
While in his bold hands, fitly placed,
 The bounding cymbals swell!

Mark well the mantle that he'll wear,
 Embroidered by his bride!
Admire his burnished helmet's glare,
O'ershadowed by the dark horsehair
 That waves in jet folds wide!

The gypsy (spiteful wench!) foretold,
 With a voice like a viper hissing.
(Though I had crossed her palm with gold),
That from the ranks a spirit bold
 Would be to-day found missing.

But I have prayed so much, I trust
 Her words may prove untrue;
Though in a tomb the hag accurst
Muttered: "Prepare thee for the worst!"
 Whilst the lamp burnt ghastly blue.

My joy her spells shall not prevent.
 Hark! I can hear the drums!
And ladies fair from silken tent
Peep forth, and every eye is bent
 On the cavalcade that comes!

Pikemen, dividing on both flanks,
 Open the pageantry;
Loud, as they tread, their armor clanks,
And silk-robed barons lead the ranks—
 The pink of gallantry!

In scarfs of gold the priests admire;
 The heralds on white steeds;
Armorial pride decks their attire,
Worn in remembrance of some sire
 Famed for heroic deeds.

Feared by the Paynim's dark divan,
 The Templars next advance;
Then the tall halberds of Lausanne,
Foremost to stand in battle van
 Against the foes of France.

Now hail the duke, with radiant brow,
 Girt with his cavaliers;
Round his triumphant banner bow
Those of his foe. Look, sisters, now!
 Here come the cymbaleers!

She spoke—with searching eye surveyed
 Their ranks—then, pale, aghast,
Sunk in the crowd! Death came in aid—
'Twas mercy to that loving maid—
 The cymbaleers had passed!

"FATHER PROUT" (FRANK S. MAHONY)

BATTLE OF THE NORSEMEN AND THE GAELS.

("Accourez tous, oiseaux de proie!")

{VII., September, 1825.}
Ho! hither flock, ye fowls of prey!
Ye wolves of war, make no delay!
For foemen 'neath our blades shall fall
Ere night may veil with purple pall.
The evening psalms are nearly o'er,
And priests who follow in our train
Have promised us the final gain,
 And filled with faith our valiant corps.

Let orphans weep, and widows brood!
To-morrow we shall wash the blood
Off saw-gapped sword and lances bent,

So, close the ranks and fire the tent!
And chill yon coward cavalcade
With brazen bugles blaring loud,
E'en though our chargers' neighing proud
Already has the host dismayed.

Spur, horsemen, spur! the charge resounds!
On Gaelic spear the Northman bounds!
Through helmet plumes the arrows flit,
And plated breasts the pikeheads split.
The double-axe fells human oaks,
And like the thistles in the field
See bristling up (where none must yield!)
The points hewn off by sweeping strokes!

We, heroes all, our wounds disdain;
Dismounted now, our horses slain,
Yet we advance—more courage show,
Though stricken, seek to overthrow
The victor-knights who tread in mud
The writhing slaves who bite the heel,
While on caparisons of steel
The maces thunder—cudgels thud!

Should daggers fail hide-coats to shred,
Seize each your man and hug him dead!
Who falls unslain will only make
A mouthful to the wolves who slake
Their month-whet thirst. No captives, none!
We die or win! but should we die,

The lopped-off hand will wave on high
The broken brand to hail the sun!

MADELAINE.

("Ecoute-moi, Madeline.")

{IX., September, 1825.}
List to me, O Madelaine!
Now the snows have left the plain,
  Which they warmly cloaked.
Come into the forest groves,
Where the notes that Echo loves
  Are from horns evoked.

Come! where Springtide, Madelaine,
Brings a sultry breath from Spain,
Giving buds their hue;
And, last night, to glad your eye,
Laid the floral marquetry,
Red and gold and blue.

Would I were, O Madelaine,
As the lamb whose wool you train
Through your tender hands.
Would I were the bird that whirls

Round, and comes to peck your curls,
Happy in such bands.

Were I e'en, O Madelaine,
Hermit whom the herd disdain
In his pious cell,
When your purest lips unfold
Sins which might to all be told,
As to him you tell.

Would I were, O Madelaine,
Moth that murmurs 'gainst your pane,
Peering at your rest,
As, so like its woolly wing,
Ceasing scarce its fluttering,
Heaves and sinks your breast.

If you seek it, Madelaine,
You may wish, and not in vain,
For a serving host,
And your splendid hall of state
Shall be envied by the great,
O'er the Jew-King's boast.

If you name it, Madelaine,
Round your head no more you'll train
Simple marguerites,
No! the coronet of peers,
Whom the queen herself oft fears,
And the monarch greets.

If you wish, O Madelaine!
Where you gaze you long shall reign—
For I'm ruler here!
I'm the lord who asks your hand
If you do not bid me stand
Loving shepherd here!

THE FAY AND THE PERI.

("Où vas-tu donc, jeune âme.")

{XV.}

THE PERI.

Beautiful spirit, come with me
Over the blue enchanted sea:
Morn and evening thou canst play
In my garden, where the breeze
Warbles through the fruity trees;
No shadow falls upon the day:
There thy mother's arms await
Her cherished infant at the gate.
Of Peris I the loveliest far—
My sisters, near the morning star,
In ever youthful bloom abide;

But pale their lustre by my side—
A silken turban wreathes my head,
Rubies on my arms are spread,
While sailing slowly through the sky,
By the uplooker's dazzled eye
Are seen my wings of purple hue,
Glittering with Elysian dew.
Whiter than a far-off sail
 My form of beauty glows,
Fair as on a summer night
Dawns the sleep star's gentle light;
 And fragrant as the early rose
That scents the green Arabian vale,
 Soothing the pilgrim as he goes.

THE FAY.

Beautiful infant (said the Fay),
In the region of the sun
I dwell, where in a rich array
The clouds encircle the king of day,
His radiant journey done.
My wings, pure golden, of radiant sheen
(Painted as amorous poet's strain),
Glimmer at night, when meadows green
Sparkle with the perfumed rain
While the sun's gone to come again.
And clear my hand, as stream that flows;
And sweet my breath as air of May;
And o'er my ivory shoulders stray

Locks of sunshine;—tunes still play
From my odorous lips of rose.

Follow, follow! I have caves
Of pearl beneath the azure waves,
And tents all woven pleasantly
In verdant glades of Faëry.
Come, belovèd child, with me,
And I will bear thee to the bowers
Where clouds are painted o'er like flowers,
And pour into thy charmed ear
Songs a mortal may not hear;
Harmonies so sweet and ripe
As no inspired shepherd's pipe
E'er breathed into Arcadian glen,
Far from the busy haunts of men.

THE PERI.

My home is afar in the bright Orient,
Where the sun, like a king, in his orange tent,
Reigneth for ever in gorgeous pride—
And wafting thee, princess of rich countree,
To the soft flute's lush melody,
My golden vessel will gently glide,
Kindling the water 'long the side.

Vast cities are mine of power and delight,
Lahore laid in lilies, Golconda, Cashmere;
And Ispahan, dear to the pilgrim's sight,

And Bagdad, whose towers to heaven uprear;
Alep, that pours on the startled ear,
From its restless masts the gathering roar,
As of ocean hamm'ring at night on the shore.

Mysore is a queen on her stately throne,
Thy white domes, Medina, gleam on the eye,—
 Thy radiant kiosques with their arrowy spires,
 Shooting afar their golden fires
 Into the flashing sky,—
Like a forest of spears that startle the gaze
Of the enemy with the vivid blaze.

Come there, beautiful child, with me,
Come to the arcades of Araby,
To the land of the date and the purple vine,
Where pleasure her rosy wreaths doth twine,
And gladness shall be alway thine;
Singing at sunset next thy bed,
Strewing flowers under thy head.
Beneath a verdant roof of leaves,
 Arching a flow'ry carpet o'er,
Thou mayst list to lutes on summer eves
 Their lays of rustic freshness pour,
 While upon the grassy floor
Light footsteps, in the hour of calm,
Ruffle the shadow of the palm.

THE FAY.

Come to the radiant homes of the blest,
Where meadows like fountain in light are drest,
And the grottoes of verdure never decay,
And the glow of the August dies not away.
Come where the autumn winds never can sweep,
And the streams of the woodland steep thee in sleep,
Like a fond sister charming the eyes of a brother,
Or a little lass lulled on the breast of her mother.
Beautiful! beautiful! hasten to me!
Colored with crimson thy wings shall be;
Flowers that fade not thy forehead shall twine,
Over thee sunlight that sets not shall shine.

The infant listened to the strain,
Now here, now there, its thoughts were driven—
But the Fay and the Peri waited in vain,
The soul soared above such a sensual gain—
The child rose to Heaven.

Asiatic Journal

LES ORIENTALES.—1829.

THE SCOURGE OF HEAVEN.

("*Là, voyez-vous passer, la nuée.*")

{I., November, 1828.}
I.

Hast seen it pass, that cloud of darkest rim?
Now red and glorious, and now gray and dim,
  Now sad as summer, barren in its heat?
One seems to see at once rush through the night
The smoke and turmoil from a burning site
  Of some great town in fiery grasp complete.

Whence comes it? From the sea, the hills, the sky?
Is it the flaming chariot from on high
  Which demons to some planet seem to bring?
Oh, horror! from its wondrous centre, lo!
A furious stream of lightning seems to flow
  Like a long snake uncoiling its fell ring.

II.

The sea! naught but the sea! waves on all sides!
Vainly the sea-bird would outstrip these tides!

Naught but an endless ebb and flow!
Wave upon wave advancing, then controlled
Beneath the depths a stream the eyes behold
Rolling in the involved abyss below!

Whilst here and there great fishes in the spray
Their silvery fins beneath the sun display,
  Or their blue tails lash up from out the surge,
Like to a flock the sea its fleece doth fling;
The horizon's edge bound by a brazen ring;
  Waters and sky in mutual azure merge.

"Am I to dry these seas?" exclaimed the cloud.
"No!" It went onward 'neath the breath of God.

III.

Green hills, which round a limpid bay
  Reflected, bask in the clear wave!
The javelin and its buffalo prey,
  The laughter and the joyous stave!
The tent, the manger! these describe
A hunting and a fishing tribe
Free as the air—their arrows fly
Swifter than lightning through the sky!
By them is breathed the purest air,
  Where'er their wanderings may chance!
Children and maidens young and fair,
  And warriors circling in the dance!
Upon the beach, around the fire,

Now quenched by wind, now burning higher,
Like spirits which our dreams inspire
 To hover o'er our trance.

Virgins, with skins of ebony,
 Beauteous as evening skies,
Laughed as their forms they dimly see
 In metal mirrors rise;
Others, as joyously as they,
Were drawing for their food by day,
With jet-black hands, white camels' whey,
 Camels with docile eyes.

Both men and women, bare,
 Plunged in the briny bay.
Who knows them? Whence they were?
 Where passed they yesterday?
Shrill sounds were hovering o'er,
Mixed with the ocean's roar,
Of cymbals from the shore,
 And whinnying courser's neigh.

"Is't there?" one moment asked the cloudy mass;
"Is't there?" An unknown utterance answered: "Pass!"

IV.

Whitened with grain see Egypt's lengthened plains,
Far as the eyesight farthest space contains,
 Like a rich carpet spread their varied hues.

The cold sea north, southwards the burying sand
Dispute o'er Egypt—while the smiling land
　Still mockingly their empire does refuse.

Three marble triangles seem to pierce the sky,
And hide their basements from the curious eye.
　Mountains—with waves of ashes covered o'er!
In graduated blocks of six feet square
From golden base to top, from earth to air
　Their ever heightening monstrous steps they bore.

No scorching blast could daunt the sleepless ken
Of roseate Sphinx, and god of marble green,
　Which stood as guardians o'er the sacred ground.
For a great port steered vessels huge and fleet,
A giant city bathed her marble feet
　In the bright waters round.

One heard the dread simoom in distance roar,
Whilst the crushed shell upon the pebbly shore
　Crackled beneath the crocodile's huge coil.
Westwards, like tiger's skin, each separate isle
Spotted the surface of the yellow Nile;
　Gray obelisks shot upwards from the soil.

The star-king set. The sea, it seemed to hold
In the calm mirror this live globe of gold,
　This world, the soul and torchbearer of our own.
In the red sky, and in the purple streak,
Like friendly kings who would each other seek,

Two meeting suns were shown.

"Shall I not stop?" exclaimed the impatient cloud.
"Seek!" trembling Tabor heard the voice of God.

V.

Sand, sand, and still more sand!
The desert! Fearful land!
Teeming with monsters dread
And plagues on every hand!
Here in an endless flow,
Sandhills of golden glow,
Where'er the tempests blow,
Like a great flood are spread.
Sometimes the sacred spot
Hears human sounds profane, when
As from Ophir or from Memphre
Stretches the caravan.
From far the eyes, its trail
Along the burning shale
Bending its wavering tail,
Like a mottled serpent scan.
These deserts are of God!
His are the bounds alone,
Here, where no feet have trod,
To Him its centre known!
And from this smoking sea
Veiled in obscurity,
The foam one seems to see

In fiery ashes thrown.

"Shall desert change to lake?" cried out the cloud.
"Still further!" from heaven's depths sounded that Voice aloud.

VI.

Like tumbled waves, which a huge rock surround;
Like heaps of ruined towers which strew the ground,
　See Babel now deserted and dismayed!
Huge witness to the folly of mankind;
Four distant mountains when the moonlight shined
　Seem covered with its shade.

O'er miles and miles the shattered ruins spread
Beneath its base, from captive tempests bred,
　The air seemed filled with harmony strange and dire;
While swarmed around the entire human race
A future Babel, on the world's whole space
　Fixed its eternal spire.

Up to the zenith rose its lengthening stair,
While each great granite mountain lent a share
　To form a stepping base;
Height upon height repeated seemed to rise,
For pyramid on pyramid the strainèd eyes
　Saw take their ceaseless place.

Through yawning walls huge elephants stalked by;

Under dark pillars rose a forestry,
 Pillars by madness multiplied;
As round some giant hive, all day and night,
Huge vultures, and red eagles' wheeling flight
 Was through each porch descried.

"Must I complete it?" said the angered cloud.
"On still!" "Lord, whither?" groaned it, deep not loud.

VII.

Two cities, strange, unknown in history's page,
Up to the clouds seemed scaling, stage by stage,
Noiseless their streets; their sleeping inmates lie,
Their gods, their chariots, in obscurity!
Like sisters sleeping 'neath the same moonlight,
O'er their twin towers crept the shades of night,
Whilst scarce distinguished in the black profound,
Stairs, aqueducts, great pillars, gleamed around,
And ruined capitals: then was seen a group
Of granite elephants 'neath a dome to stoop,
Shapeless, giant forms to view arise,
Monsters around, the spawn of hideous ties!
Then hanging gardens, with flowers and galleries:
O'er vast fountains bending grew ebon-trees;
Temples, where seated on their rich tiled thrones,
Bull-headed idols shone in jasper stones;
Vast halls, spanned by one block, where watch and stare
Each upon each, with straight and moveless glare,
Colossal heads in circles; the eye sees

Great gods of bronze, their hands upon their knees.
Sight seemed confounded, and to have lost its powers,
'Midst bridges, aqueducts, arches, and round towers,
Whilst unknown shapes fill up the devious views
Formed by these palaces and avenues.
Like capes, the lengthening shadows seem to rise
Of these dark buildings, pointed to the skies,
Immense entanglement in shroud of gloom!
The stars which gleamed in the empyrean dome,
Under the thousand arches in heaven's space
Shone as through meshes of the blackest lace.
Cities of hell, with foul desires demented,
And monstrous pleasures, hour by hour invented!
Each roof and home some monstrous mystery bore!
Which through the world spread like a twofold sore!
Yet all things slept, and scarce some pale late light
Flitted along the streets through the still night,
Lamps of debauch, forgotten and alone,
The feast's lost fires left there to flicker on;
The walls' large angles clove the light-lengthening shades
'Neath the white moon, or on some pool's face played.
Perchance one heard, faint in the plain beneath,
The kiss suppressed, the mingling of the breath;
And the two sister cities, tired of heat,
In love's embrace lay down in murmurs sweet!
Whilst sighing winds the scent of sycamore
From Sodom to Gomorrah softly bore!
Then over all spread out the blackened cloud,
"'Tis here!" the Voice on high exclaimed aloud.

VIII.

From a cavern wide
In the rent cloud's side,
In sulphurous showers
The red flame pours.
The palaces fall
In the lurid light,
Which casts a red pall
O'er their facades white!

Oh, Sodom! Gomorrah!
What a dome of horror
Rests now on your walls!
On you the cloud falls,
Nation perverse!
On your fated heads,
From its fell jaws, a curse
Its lightning fierce spreads!

The people awaken
Which godlessly slept;
Their palaces shaken,
Their offences unwept!
Their rolling cars all
Meet and crash in the street;
And the crowds, for a pall,
Find flames round their feet!

Numberless dead,

Round these high towers spread,
Still sleep in the shade
By their rugged heights made;
Colossi of rocks
In ill-steadied blocks!
So hang on a wall
Black ants, like a pall!

To escape is in vain
From this horrible rain!
Alas! all things die;
In the lightning's red flash
The bridges all crash;
'Neath the tiles the flame creeps;
From the fire-struck steeps
Falls on the pavements below,
All lurid in glow,
Rolling down from on high!

Beneath every spark,
The red, tyrannous fire
Mounts up in the dark
Ever redder and higher;
More swiftly than steed
Uncontrolled, see it pass!
 Horrid idols all twist,
  By the crumbling flame kissed
In their infamous dread,
Shrivelled members of brass!

It grows angry, flows on,
Silver towers fall down
Unforeseen, like a dream
In its green and red stream,
Which lights up the walls
Ere one crashes and falls,
Like the changeable scale
Of a lizard's bright mail.
Agate, porphyry, cracks
And is melted to wax!
Bend low to their doom
These stones of the tomb!
E'en the great marble giant
Called Nabo, sways pliant
Like a tree; whilst the flare
Seemed each column to scorch
As it blazed like a torch
Round and round in the air.

The magi, in vain,
From the heights to the plain
Their gods' images carry
In white tunic: they quake—
No idol can make
The blue sulphur tarry;
The temple e'en where they meet,
Swept under their feet
In the folds of its sheet!
Turns a palace to coal!
Whence the straitened cries roll

From its terrified flock;
With incendiary grips
It loosens a block,
Which smokes and then slips
From its place by the shock;
To the surface first sheers,
Then melts, disappears,
Like the glacier, the rock!
The high priest, full of years,
On the burnt site appears,
Whence the others have fled.
Lo! his tiara's caught fire
As the furnace burns higher,
And pale, full of dread,
See, the hand he would raise
To tear his crown from the blaze
Is flaming instead!

Men, women, in crowds
Hurry on—the fire shrouds
And blinds all their eyes
As, besieging each gate
Of these cities of fate
To the conscience-struck crowd,
In each fiery cloud,
Hell appears in the skies!

IX.

Men say that *then*, to see his foe's sad fall

As some old prisoner clings to his prison wall,
Babel, accomplice of their guilt, was seen
O'er the far hills to gaze with vision keen!
And as was worked this dispensation strange,
A wondrous noise filled the world's startled range;
Reached the dull hearing that deep, direful sound
Of their sad tribe who live below the ground.

X.

'Gainst this pitiless flame who condemned could prevail?
Who these walls, burnt and calcined, could venture to scale?
  Yet their vile hands they sought to uplift,
Yet they cared still to ask from what God, by what law?
In their last sad embrace, 'midst their honor and awe,
  Of this mighty volcano the drift.
'Neath great slabs of marble they hid them in vain,
'Gainst this everliving fire, God's own flaming rain!
  'Tis the rash whom God seeks out the first;
They call on their gods, who were deaf to their cries,
For the punishing flame caused their cold granite eyes
  In tears of hot lava to burst!
Thus away in the whirlwind did everything pass,
The man and the city, the soil and its grass!
  God burnt this sad, sterile champaign;
Naught living was left of this people destroyed,
And the unknown wind which blew over the void,
  Each mountain changed into a plain.

XI.

The palm-tree that grows on the rock to this day,
Feels its leaf growing yellow, its slight stem decay,
 In the blasting and ponderous air;
These towns are no more! but to mirror their past,
O'er their embers a cold lake spread far and spread fast,
 With smoke like a furnace, lies there!

J.N. FAZAKERLEY

PIRATES' SONG.

("Nous emmenions en esclavage.")

{VIII., March, 1828.}
We're bearing fivescore Christian dogs
To serve the cruel drivers:
Some are fair beauties gently born,
And some rough coral-divers.
We hardy skimmers of the sea
Are lucky in each sally,
And, eighty strong, we send along
The dreaded Pirate Galley.

A nunnery was spied ashore,

We lowered away the cutter,
And, landing, seized the youngest nun
Ere she a cry could utter;
Beside the creek, deaf to our oars,
She slumbered in green alley,
As, eighty strong, we sent along
The dreaded Pirate Galley.

"Be silent, darling, you must come—
The wind is off shore blowing;
You only change your prison dull
For one that's splendid, glowing!
His Highness doats on milky cheeks,
So do not make us dally"—
We, eighty strong, who send along
The dreaded Pirate Galley.

She sought to flee back to her cell,
And called us each a devil!
We dare do aught becomes Old Scratch,
But like a treatment civil,
So, spite of buffet, prayers, and calls—
Too late her friends to rally—
We, eighty strong, bore her along
Unto the Pirate Galley.

The fairer for her tears profuse,
As dews refresh the flower,
She is well worth three purses full,
And will adorn the bower—

For vain her vow to pine and die
Thus torn from her dear valley:
She reigns, and we still row along
The dreaded Pirate Galley.

THE TURKISH CAPTIVE.

("Si je n'était captive.")

{IX., July, 1828.}
Oh! were I not a captive,
I should love this fair countree;
Those fields with maize abounding,
This ever-plaintive sea:
I'd love those stars unnumbered,
If, passing in the shade,
Beneath our walls I saw not
The spahi's sparkling blade.

I am no Tartar maiden
That a blackamoor of price
Should tune my lute and hold to me
My glass of sherbet-ice.
Far from these haunts of vices,

In my dear countree, we
With sweethearts in the even
May chat and wander free.

But still I love this climate,
Where never wintry breeze
Invades, with chilly murmur,
These open lattices;
Where rain is warm in summer,
And the insect glossy green,
Most like a living emerald,
Shines 'mid the leafy screen.

With her chapelles fair Smyrna—
A gay princess is she!
Still, at her summons, round her
Unfading spring ye see.
And, as in beauteous vases,
Bright groups of flowers repose,
So, in her gulfs are lying
Her archipelagoes.

I love these tall red turrets;
These standards brave unrolled;
And, like an infant's playthings,
These houses decked with gold.
I love forsooth these reveries,
Though sandstorms make me pant,
Voluptuously swaying
Upon an elephant.

Here in this fairy palace,
Full of such melodies,
Methinks I hear deep murmurs
That in the deserts rise;
Soft mingling with the music
The Genii's voices pour,
Amid the air, unceasing,
Around us evermore.

I love the burning odors
This glowing region gives;
And, round each gilded lattice,
The trembling, wreathing leaves;
And, 'neath the bending palm-tree,
The gayly gushing spring;
And on the snow-white minaret,
The stork with snowier wing.

I love on mossy couch to sing
A Spanish roundelay,
And see my sweet companions
Around commingling gay,—
A roving band, light-hearted,
In frolicsome array,—
Who 'neath the screening parasols
Dance down the merry day.
But more than all enchanting
At night, it is to me,
To sit, where winds are sighing,

Lone, musing by the sea;
And, on its surface gazing,
To mark the moon so fair,
Her silver fan outspreading,
In trembling radiance there.

W.D., *Tait's Edin. Magazine*

MOONLIGHT ON THE BOSPHORUS.

("La lune était sereine.")

{X., September, 1828.}
Bright shone the merry moonbeams dancing o'er the wave;
  At the cool casement, to the evening breeze flung wide,
  Leans the Sultana, and delights to watch the tide,
With surge of silvery sheen, yon sleeping islets lave.

From her hand, as it falls, vibrates the light guitar.
  She listens—hark! that sound that echoes dull and low.
  Is it the beat upon the Archipelago
Of some long galley's oar, from Scio bound afar?

Is it the cormorants, whose black wings, one by one,
  Cut the blue wave that o'er them breaks in liquid pearls?

Is it some hovering sprite with whistling scream that hurls
Down to the deep from yon old tower a loosened stone?

Who thus disturbs the tide near the seraglio?
'Tis no dark cormorants that on the ripple float,
'Tis no dull plume of stone—no oars of Turkish boat,
With measured beat along the water creeping slow.

'Tis heavy sacks, borne each by voiceless dusky slaves;
And could you dare to sound the depths of yon dark tide,
Something like human form would stir within its side.
Bright shone the merry moonbeams dancing o'er the wave.

JOHN L. O'SULLIVAN.

THE VEIL.

("Qu'avez-vous, mes frères?")

{XI., September, 18288.}

"Have you prayed tonight, Desdemona?"

THE SISTER

What has happened, my brothers? Your spirit to-day
  Some secret sorrow damps
There's a cloud on your brow. What has happened? Oh, say,
  For your eyeballs glare out with a sinister ray
  Like the light of funeral lamps.
And the blades of your poniards are half unsheathed
  In your belt—and ye frown on me!
There's a woe untold, there's a pang unbreathed
  In your bosom, my brothers three!

ELDEST BROTHER.

Gulnara, make answer! Hast thou, since the dawn,
To the eye of a stranger thy veil withdrawn?

THE SISTER.

As I came, oh, my brother! at noon—from the bath—
  As I came—it was noon, my lords—
And your sister had then, as she constantly hath,
Drawn her veil close around her, aware that the path
  Is beset by these foreign hordes.
But the weight of the noonday's sultry hour
  Near the mosque was so oppressive
That—forgetting a moment the eye of the Giaour—
  I yielded to th' heat excessive.

SECOND BROTHER.

Gulnara, make answer! Whom, then, hast thou seen,
In a turban of white and a caftan of green?

THE SISTER.

Nay, *he* might have been there; but I muflled me so,
  He could scarcely have seen my figure.—
But why to your sister thus dark do you grow?
What words to yourselves do you mutter thus low,
  Of "blood" and "an intriguer"?
Oh! ye cannot of murder bring down the red guilt
  On your souls, my brothers, surely!
Though I fear—from the hands that are chafing the hilt,
  And the hints you give obscurely.

THIRD BROTHER.

Gulnara, this evening when sank the red sun,
Didst thou mark how like blood in descending it shone?

THE SISTER.

Mercy! Allah! have pity! oh, spare!
  See! I cling to your knees repenting!
Kind brothers, forgive me! for mercy, forbear!
Be appeased at the cry of a sister's despair,
  For our mother's sake relenting.

O God! must I die? They are deaf to my cries!
Their sister's life-blood shedding;
They have stabbed me each one—I faint—o'er my eyes
A *veil of Death* is spreading!

THE BROTHERS.

Gulnara, farewell! take *that* veil; 'tis the gift
Of thy brothers—a veil thou wilt never lift!

"FATHER PROUT" (FRANK S. MAHONY).

THE FAVORITE SULTANA.

("N'ai-je pas pour toi, belle juive.")

{XII., Oct. 27, 1828.}
To please you, Jewess, jewel!
I have thinned my harem out!
Must every flirting of your fan
Presage a dying shout?

Grace for the damsels tender
Who have fear to hear your laugh,
For seldom gladness gilds your lips
But blood you mean to quaff.

In jealousy so zealous,
Never was there woman worse;
You'd have no roses but those grown
Above some buried corse.

Am I not pinioned firmly?
Why be angered if the door
Repulses fifty suing maids
Who vainly there implore?

Let them live on—to envy
My own empress of the world,
To whom all Stamboul like a dog
Lies at the slippers curled.

To you my heroes lower
Those scarred ensigns none have cowed;
To you their turbans are depressed
That elsewhere march so proud.

To you Bassora offers
Her respect, and Trebizonde
Her carpets richly wrought, and spice
And gems, of which you're fond.

To you the Cyprus temples
Dare not bar or close the doors;
For you the mighty Danube sends
The choicest of its stores.

Fear you the Grecian maidens,
Pallid lilies of the isles?
Or the scorching-eyed sand-rover
From Baalbec's massy piles?

Compared with yours, oh, daughter
Of King Solomon the grand,
What are round ebon bosoms,
High brows from Hellas' strand?

You're neither blanched nor blackened,
For your tint of olive's clear;
Yours are lips of ripest cherry,
You are straight as Arab spear.

Hence, launch no longer lightning
On these paltry slaves of ours.
Why should your flow of tears be matched
By their mean life-blood showers?

Think only of our banquets
Brought and served by charming girls,
For beauties sultans must adorn
As dagger-hilts the pearls.

THE PASHA AND THE DERVISH.

("Un jour Ali passait.")

{XIII, Nov. 8, 1828.}
Ali came riding by—the highest head
Bent to the dust, o'ercharged with dread,
  Whilst "God be praised!" all cried;
But through the throng one dervish pressed,
Aged and bent, who dared arrest
  The pasha in his pride.

"Ali Tepelini, light of all light,
Who hold'st the Divan's upper seat by right,
  Whose fame Fame's trump hath burst—
Thou art the master of unnumbered hosts,
Shade of the Sultan—yet he only boasts
  In thee a dog accurst!

"An unseen tomb-torch flickers on thy path,
Whilst, as from vial full, thy spare-naught wrath
  Splashes this trembling race:
These are thy grass as thou their trenchant scythes
Cleaving their neck as 'twere a willow withe—
  Their blood none can efface.

"But ends thy tether! for Janina makes
A grave for thee where every turret quakes,
  And thou shalt drop below

To where the spirits, to a tree enchained,
Will clutch thee, there to be 'mid them retained
  For all to-come in woe!

"Or if, by happy chance, thy soul might flee
Thy victims, after, thou shouldst surely see
  And hear thy crimes relate;
Streaked with the guileless gore drained from their veins,
Greater in number than the reigns on reigns
  Thou hopedst for thy state.

"This so will be! and neither fleet nor fort
Can stay or aid thee as the deathly port
  Receives thy harried frame!
Though, like the cunning Hebrew knave of old,
To cheat the angel black, thou didst enfold
  In altered guise thy name."

Ali deemed anchorite or saint a pawn—
The crater of his blunderbuss did yawn,
  Sword, dagger hung at ease:
But he had let the holy man revile,
Though clouds o'erswept his brow; then, with a smile,
  He tossed him his pelisse.

THE LOST BATTLE.

("Allah! qui me rendra-")

{XVI., May, 1828.}
Oh, Allah! who will give me back my terrible array?
My emirs and my cavalry that shook the earth to-day;
My tent, my wide-extending camp, all dazzling to the sight,
Whose watchfires, kindled numberless beneath the brow of night,
Seemed oft unto the sentinel that watched the midnight hours,
As heaven along the sombre hill had rained its stars in showers?
Where are my beys so gorgeous, in their light pelisses gay,
And where my fierce Timariot bands, so fearless in the fray;
My dauntless khans, my spahis brave, swift thunderbolts of war;
My sunburnt Bedouins, trooping from the Pyramids afar,
Who laughed to see the laboring hind stand terrified at gaze,
And urged their desert horses on amid the ripening maize?
These horses with their fiery eyes, their slight untiring feet,
That flew along the fields of corn like grasshoppers so fleet—
What! to behold again no more, loud charging o'er the plain,
Their squadrons, in the hostile shot diminished all in vain,
Burst grandly on the heavy squares, like clouds that bear the storms,
Enveloping in lightning fires the dark resisting swarms!
Oh! they are dead! their housings bright are trailed amid their gore;

Dark blood is on their manes and sides, all deeply clotted o'er;
All vainly now the spur would strike these cold and rounded flanks,
To wake them to their wonted speed amid the rapid ranks:
Here the bold riders red and stark upon the sands lie down,
Who in their friendly shadows slept throughout the halt at noon.
Oh, Allah! who will give me back my terrible array?
See where it straggles 'long the fields for leagues on leagues away,
Like riches from a spendthrift's hand flung prodigal to earth.
Lo! steed and rider;—Tartar chiefs or of Arabian birth,
Their turbans and their cruel course, their banners and their cries,
Seem now as if a troubled dream had passed before mine eyes—
My valiant warriors and their steeds, thus doomed to fall and bleed!
Their voices rouse no echo now, their footsteps have no speed;
They sleep, and have forgot at last the sabre and the bit—
Yon vale, with all the corpses heaped, seems one wide charnel-pit.
Long shall the evil omen rest upon this plain of dread—
To-night, the taint of solemn blood; to-morrow, of the dead.
Alas! 'tis but a shadow now, that noble armament!
How terribly they strove, and struck from morn to eve unspent,
Amid the fatal fiery ring, enamoured of the fight!
Now o'er the dim horizon sinks the peaceful pall of night:
The brave have nobly done their work, and calmly sleep at last.

The crows begin, and o'er the dead are gathering dark and fast;
Already through their feathers black they pass their eager beaks.
Forth from the forest's distant depth, from bald and barren peaks,
They congregate in hungry flocks and rend their gory prey.
Woe to that flaunting army's pride, so vaunting yesterday!
That formidable host, alas! is coldly nerveless now
To drive the vulture from his gorge, or scare the carrion crow.
Were now that host again mine own, with banner broad unfurled,
With it I would advance and win the empire of the world.
Monarchs to it should yield their realms and veil their haughty brows;
My sister it should ever be, my lady and my spouse.
Oh! what will unrestoring Death, that jealous tyrant lord,
Do with the brave departed souls that cannot swing a sword?
Why turned the balls aside from me? Why struck no hostile hand
My head within its turban green upon the ruddy sand?
I stood all potent yesterday; my bravest captains three,
All stirless in their tigered selle, magnificent to see,
Hailed as before my gilded tent rose flowing to the gales,
Shorn from the tameless desert steeds, three dark and tossing tails.
But yesterday a hundred drums were heard when I went by;
Full forty agas turned their looks respectful on mine eye,
And trembled with contracted brows within their hall of state.
Instead of heavy catapults, of slow unwieldy weight,

I had bright cannons rolling on oak wheels in threatening tiers,
And calm and steady by their sides marched English cannoniers.
But yesterday, and I had towns, and castles strong and high,
And Greeks in thousands, for the base and merciless to buy.
But yesterday, and arsenals and harems were my own;
While now, defeated and proscribed, deserted and alone,
I flee away, a fugitive, and of my former power,
Allah! I have not now at least one battlemented tower.
And must he fly—the grand vizier! the pasha of three tails!
O'er the horizon's bounding hills, where distant vision fails,
All stealthily, with eyes on earth, and shrinking from the sight,
As a nocturnal robber holds his dark and breathless flight,
And thinks he sees the gibbet spread its arms in solemn wrath,
In every tree that dimly throws its shadow on his path!

> Thus, after his defeat, pale Reschid speaks.
> Among the dead we mourned a thousand Greeks.
> Lone from the field the Pasha fled afar,
> And, musing, wiped his reeking scimitar;
> His two dead steeds upon the sands were flung,
> And on their sides their empty stirrups hung.

W.D., *Bentley's Miscellany*, 1839.

THE GREEK BOY.

("Les Turcs ont passés là.")

{XVIII., June 10, 1828.}
All is a ruin where rage knew no bounds:
Chio is levelled, and loathed by the hounds,
 For shivered yest'reen was her lance;
Sulphurous vapors envenom the place
Where her true beauties of Beauty's true race
 Were lately linked close in the dance.

Dark is the desert, with one single soul;
Cerulean eyes! whence the burning tears roll
 In anguish of uttermost shame,
Under the shadow of one shrub of May,
Splashed still with ruddy drops, bent in decay
 Where fiercely the hand of Lust came.

"Soft and sweet urchin, still red with the lash
Of rein and of scabbard of wild Kuzzilbash,
 What lack you for changing your sob—
If not unto laughter beseeming a child—
To utterance milder, though they have defiled
 The graves which they shrank not to rob?

"Would'st thou a trinket, a flower, or scarf,
Would'st thou have silver? I'm ready with half
 These sequins a-shine in the sun!

Still more have I money—if you'll but speak!"
He spoke: and furious the cry of the Greek,
"Oh, give me your dagger and gun!"

ZARA, THE BATHER

("Sara, belle d'indolence.")

{XIX., August, 1828.}
In a swinging hammock lying,
 Lightly flying,
Zara, lovely indolent,
O'er a fountain's crystal wave
 There to lave
Her young beauty—see her bent.

As she leans, so sweet and soft,
 Flitting oft,
O'er the mirror to and fro,
Seems that airy floating bat,
 Like a feather
From some sea-gull's wing of snow.

Every time the frail boat laden
 With the maiden
Skims the water in its flight,

Starting from its trembling sheen,
 Swift are seen
A white foot and neck so white.

As that lithe foot's timid tips
 Quick she dips,
Passing, in the rippling pool,
(Blush, oh! snowiest ivory!)
 Frolic, she
Laughs to feel the pleasant cool.

Here displayed, but half concealed—
 Half revealed,
Each bright charm shall you behold,
In her innocence emerging,
 As a-verging
On the wave her hands grow cold.

For no star howe'er divine
 Has the shine
Of a maid's pure loveliness,
Frightened if a leaf but quivers
 As she shivers,
Veiled with naught but dripping trees.

By the happy breezes fanned
 See her stand,—
Blushing like a living rose,
On her bosom swelling high
 If a fly

Dare to seek a sweet repose.

In those eyes which maiden pride
 Fain would hide,
Mark how passion's lightnings sleep!
And their glance is brighter far
 Than the star
Brightest in heaven's bluest deep.

O'er her limbs the glittering current
 In soft torrent
Rains adown the gentle girl,
As if, drop by drop, should fall,
 One and all
From her necklace every pearl.

Lengthening still the reckless pleasure
 At her leisure,
Care-free Zara ever slow
As the hammock floats and swings
 Smiles and sings,
To herself, so sweet and low.

"Oh, were I a capitana,
 Or sultana,
Amber should be always mixt
In my bath of jewelled stone,
 Near my throne,
Griffins twain of gold betwixt.

"Then my hammock should be silk,
  White as milk;
And, more soft than down of dove,
Velvet cushions where I sit
  Should emit
Perfumes that inspire love.

"Then should I, no danger near,
  Free from fear,
Revel in my garden's stream;
Nor amid the shadows deep
  Dread the peep,
Of two dark eyes' kindling gleam.

"He who thus would play the spy,
  On the die
For such sight his head must throw;
In his blood the sabre naked
  Would be slakèd,
Of my slaves of ebon brow.

"Then my rich robes trailing show
  As I go,
None to chide should be so bold;
And upon my sandals fine
  How should shine
Rubies worked in cloth-of-gold!"

Fancying herself a queen,
  All unseen,

Thus vibrating in delight;
In her indolent coquetting
 Quite forgetting
How the hours wing their flight.

As she lists the showery tinkling
 Of the sprinkling
By her wanton curvets made;
Never pauses she to think
 Of the brink
Where her wrapper white is laid.

To the harvest-fields the while,
 In long file,
Speed her sisters' lively band,
Like a flock of birds in flight
 Streaming light,
Dancing onward hand in hand.

And they're singing, every one,
 As they run
This the burden of their lay:
"Fie upon such idleness!
 Not to dress
Earlier on harvest-day!"

JOHN L. O'SULLIVAN.

EXPECTATION.

("Moune, écureuil.")

{xx.}
Squirrel, mount yon oak so high,
To its twig that next the sky
  Bends and trembles as a flower!
Strain, O stork, thy pinion well,—
From thy nest 'neath old church-bell,
Mount to yon tall citadel,
  And its tallest donjon tower!
To your mountain, eagle old,
Mount, whose brow so white and cold,
  Kisses the last ray of even!
And, O thou that lov'st to mark
Morn's first sunbeam pierce the dark,
Mount, O mount, thou joyous lark—
  Joyous lark, O mount to heaven!
And now say, from topmost bough,
Towering shaft, and peak of snow,
  And heaven's arch—O, can you see
One white plume that like a star,
Streams along the plain afar,
And a steed that from the war
  Bears my lover back to me?

JOHN L. O'SULLIVAN.

THE LOVER'S WISH.

("Si j'étais la feuille.")

{XXII., September, 1828.}
Oh! were I the leaf that the wind of the West,
His course through the forest uncaring;
To sleep on the gale or the wave's placid breast
In a pendulous cradle is bearing.

All fresh with the morn's balmy kiss would I haste,
As the dewdrops upon me were glancing;
When Aurora sets out on the roseate waste,
And round her the breezes are dancing.

On the pinions of air I would fly, I would rush
Thro' the glens and the valleys to quiver;
Past the mountain ravine, past the grove's dreamy hush,
And the murmuring fall of the river.

By the darkening hollow and bramble-bush lane,
To catch the sweet breath of the roses;
Past the land would I speed, where the sand-driven plain
'Neath the heat of the noonday reposes.

Past the rocks that uprear their tall forms to the sky,
Whence the storm-fiend his anger is pouring;
Past lakes that lie dead, tho' the tempest roll nigh,
And the turbulent whirlwind be roaring.

On, on would I fly, till a charm stopped my way,
A charm that would lead to the bower;
Where the daughter of Araby sings to the day,
At the dawn and the vesper hour.

Then hovering down on her brow would I light,
'Midst her golden tresses entwining;
That gleam like the corn when the fields are bright,
And the sunbeams upon it shining.

A single frail gem on her beautiful head,
I should sit in the golden glory;
And prouder I'd be than the diadem spread
Round the brow of kings famous in story.

V., *Eton Observer.*

THE SACKING OF THE CITY.

("La flamme par ton ordre, O roi!")

{XXIII., November, 1825.}
Thy will, O King, is done! Lighting but to consume,
The roar of the fierce flames drowned even the shouts and shrieks;

Reddening each roof, like some day-dawn of bloody doom,
Seemed they in joyous flight to dance about their wrecks.

Slaughter his thousand giant arms hath tossed on high,
Fell fathers, husbands, wives, beneath his streaming steel;
Prostrate, the palaces, huge tombs of fire, lie,
While gathering overhead the vultures scream and wheel!

Died the pale mothers, and the virgins, from their arms,
O Caliph, fiercely torn, bewailed their young years' blight;
With stabs and kisses fouled, all their yet quivering charms,
At our fleet coursers' heels were dragged in mocking flight.

Lo! where the city lies mantled in pall of death;
Lo! where thy mighty hand hath passed, all things must bend!
Priests prayed, the sword estopped blaspheming breath,
Vainly their cheating book for shield did they extend.

Some infants yet survived, and the unsated steel
Still drinks the life-blood of each whelp of Christian-kind,
To kiss thy sandall'd foot, O King, thy people kneel,
And golden circlets to thy victor-ankle bind.

JOHN L. O'SULLIVAN.

Poems

NOORMAHAL THE FAIR.{1}

―――――――――――

("Entre deux rocs d'un noir d'ébène.")

{XXVII., November, 1828.}
Between two ebon rocks
Behold yon sombre den,
Where brambles bristle like the locks
Of wool between the horns of scapegoat banned by men!

Remote in ruddy fog
Still hear the tiger growl
At the lion and stripèd dog
That prowl with rusty throats to taunt and roar and howl;

Whilst other monsters fast
The hissing basilisk;
The hippopotamus so vast,
And the boa with waking appetite made brisk!

The orfrey showing tongue,
The fly in stinging mood,
The elephant that crushes strong
And elastic bamboos an the scorpion's brood;

And the men of the trees
With their families fierce,
Till there is not one scorching breeze
But brings here its venom—its horror to pierce—

Yet, rather there be lone,
'Mid all those horrors there,
Than hear the sickly honeyed tone
And see the swimming eyes of Noormahal the Fair!

{Footnote 1: Noormahal (Arabic) the light of the house; some of the
 Orientals deem fair hair and complexion a beauty.}

THE DJINNS.

("*Murs, ville et port.*")

{XXVIII., Aug. 28, 1828.}
Town, tower,
 Shore, deep,
Where lower
 Cliff's steep;
Waves gray,
Where play
Winds gay,
 All sleep.

Hark! a sound,
Far and slight,

Breathes around
On the night
High and higher,
Nigh and nigher,
Like a fire,
Roaring, bright.

Now, on 'tis sweeping
With rattling beat,
Like dwarf imp leaping
In gallop fleet
He flies, he prances,
In frolic fancies,
On wave-crest dances
With pattering feet.

Hark, the rising swell,
With each new burst!
Like the tolling bell
Of a convent curst;
Like the billowy roar
On a storm-lashed shore,—
Now hushed, but once more
Maddening to its worst.

O God! the deadly sound
Of the Djinn's fearful cry!
Quick, 'neath the spiral round
Of the deep staircase fly!
See, see our lamplight fade!

And of the balustrade
Mounts, mounts the circling shade
Up to the ceiling high!

'Tis the Djinns' wild streaming swarm
  Whistling in their tempest flight;
Snap the tall yews 'neath the storm,
  Like a pine flame crackling bright.
Swift though heavy, lo! their crowd
Through the heavens rushing loud
Like a livid thunder-cloud
  With its bolt of fiery might!

Ho! they are on us, close without!
Shut tight the shelter where we lie!
With hideous din the monster rout,
Dragon and vampire, fill the sky!
The loosened rafter overhead
Trembles and bends like quivering reed;
Shakes the old door with shuddering dread,
As from its rusty hinge 'twould fly!
Wild cries of hell! voices that howl and shriek!
The horrid troop before the tempest tossed—
O Heaven!—descends my lowly roof to seek:

Bends the strong wall beneath the furious host.
Totters the house as though, like dry leaf shorn
From autumn bough and on the mad blast borne,
Up from its deep foundations it were torn
To join the stormy whirl. Ah! all is lost!

O Prophet! if thy hand but now
Save from these hellish things,
A pilgrim at thy shrine I'll bow,
Laden with pious offerings.
Bid their hot breath its fiery rain
Stream on the faithful's door in vain;
Vainly upon my blackened pane
Grate the fierce claws of their dark wings!

They have passed!—and their wild legion
 Cease to thunder at my door;
Fleeting through night's rayless region,
 Hither they return no more.
Clanking chains and sounds of woe
Fill the forests as they go;
And the tall oaks cower low,
 Bent their flaming light before.

On! on! the storm of wings
 Bears far the fiery fear,
Till scarce the breeze now brings
 Dim murmurings to the ear;
Like locusts' humming hail,
Or thrash of tiny flail
Plied by the fitful gale
 On some old roof-tree sere.

 Fainter now are borne
  Feeble mutterings still;

As when Arab horn
  Swells its magic peal,
Shoreward o'er the deep
Fairy voices sweep,
And the infant's sleep
  Golden visions fill.

Each deadly Djinn,
  Dark child of fright,
Of death and sin,
  Speeds in wild flight.
Hark, the dull moan,
Like the deep tone
Of Ocean's groan,
  Afar, by night!

More and more
  Fades it slow,
As on shore
  Ripples flow,—
As the plaint
Far and faint
Of a saint
  Murmured low.

Hark! hist!
  Around,
I list!
  The bounds
Of space

All trace
Efface
Of sound.

JOHN L. O'SULLIVAN.

THE OBDURATE BEAUTY.

("A Juana la Grenadine!")

{XXIX., October, 1843.}
To Juana ever gay,
Sultan Achmet spoke one day
"Lo, the realms that kneel to own
Homage to my sword and crown
All I'd freely cast away,
Maiden dear, for thee alone."

"Be a Christian, noble king!
For it were a grievous thing:
Love to seek and find too well
In the arms of infidel.
Spain with cry of shame would ring,
If from honor faithful fell."

"By these pearls whose spotless chain,

Oh, my gentle sovereign,
Clasps thy neck of ivory,
Aught thou askest I will be,
If that necklace pure of stain
Thou wilt give for rosary."

JOHN L. O'SULLIVAN.

DON RODRIGO.

A MOORISH BALLAD.

("Don Roderique est à la chasse.")

{XXX., May, 1828.}
Unto the chase Rodrigo's gone,
With neither lance nor buckler;
A baleful light his eyes outshone—
To pity he's no truckler.

He follows not the royal stag,
But, full of fiery hating,
Beside the way one sees him lag,
Impatient at the waiting.

He longs his nephew's blood to spill,

Who 'scaped (the young Mudarra)
That trap he made and laid to kill
The seven sons of Lara.

Along the road—at last, no balk—
A youth looms on a jennet;
He rises like a sparrow-hawk
About to seize a linnet.

"What ho!" "Who calls?" "Art Christian knight,
Or basely born and boorish,
Or yet that thing I still more slight—
The spawn of some dog Moorish?

"I seek the by-born spawn of one
I e'er renounce as brother—
Who chose to make his latest son
Caress a Moor as mother.

"I've sought that cub in every hole,
'Midland, and coast, and islet,
For he's the thief who came and stole
Our sheathless jewelled stilet."

"If you well know the poniard worn
Without edge-dulling cover—
Look on it now—here, plain, upborne!
And further be no rover.

"Tis I—as sure as you're abhorred

Rodrigo—cruel slayer,
'Tis I am Vengeance, and your lord,
Who bids you crouch in prayer!

"I shall not grant the least delay—
Use what you have, defending,
I'll send you on that darksome way
Your victims late were wending.

"And if I wore this, with its crest—
Our seal with gems enwreathing—
In open air—'twas in your breast
To seek its fated sheathing!"

CORNFLOWERS.

("*Tandis que l'étoile inodore.*")

{XXXII.}
While bright but scentless azure stars
Be-gem the golden corn,
And spangle with their skyey tint
The furrows not yet shorn;
While still the pure white tufts of May
Ape each a snowy ball,—
Away, ye merry maids, and haste

To gather ere they fall!

Nowhere the sun of Spain outshines
Upon a fairer town
Than Peñafiel, or endows
More richly farming clown;
Nowhere a broader square reflects
Such brilliant mansions, tall,—
Away, ye merry maids, etc.

Nowhere a statelier abbey rears
Dome huger o'er a shrine,
Though seek ye from old Rome itself
To even Seville fine.
Here countless pilgrims come to pray
And promenade the Mall,—
Away, ye merry maids, etc.

Where glide the girls more joyfully
Than ours who dance at dusk,
With roses white upon their brows,
With waists that scorn the busk?
Mantillas elsewhere hide dull eyes—
Compared with these, how small!
Away, ye merry maids, etc.

A blossom in a city lane,
Alizia was our pride,
And oft the blundering bee, deceived,
Came buzzing to her side—

But, oh! for one that felt the sting,
And found, 'neath honey, gall—
Away, ye merry maids, etc.

Young, haughty, from still hotter lands,
A stranger hither came—
Was he a Moor or African,
Or Murcian known to fame?
None knew—least, she—or false or true,
The name by which to call.
Away, ye merry maids, etc.

Alizia asked not his degree,
She saw him but as Love,
And through Xarama's vale they strayed,
And tarried in the grove,—
Oh! curses on that fatal eve,
And on that leafy hall!
Away, ye merry maids, etc.

The darkened city breathed no more;
The moon was mantled long,
Till towers thrust the cloudy cloak
Upon the steeples' throng;
The crossway Christ, in ivy draped,
Shrank, grieving, 'neath the pall,—
Away, ye merry maids, etc.

But while, alone, they kept the shade,
The other dark-eyed dears

Were murmuring on the stifling air
Their jealous threats and fears;
Alizia was so blamed, that time,
Unheeded rang the call:
Away, ye merry maids, etc.

Although, above, the hawk describes
The circle round the lark,
It sleeps, unconscious, and our lass
Had eyes but for her spark—
A spark?—a sun! 'Twas Juan, King!
Who wears our coronal,—
Away, ye merry maids, etc.

A love so far above one's state
Ends sadly. Came a black
And guarded palanquin to bear
The girl that ne'er comes back;
By royal writ, some nunnery
Still shields her from us all
Away, ye merry maids, and haste
To gather ere they fall!

H. L. WILLIAMS

MAZEPPA.

("Ainsi, lorsqu'un mortel!")

{XXXIV., May, 1828.}

As when a mortal—Genius' prize, alack!
Is, living, bound upon thy fatal back,
 Thou reinless racing steed!
In vain he writhes, mere cloud upon a star,
Thou bearest him as went Mazeppa, far
 Out of the flow'ry mead,—
So—though thou speed'st implacable, (like him,
Spent, pallid, torn, bruised, weary, sore and dim,
 As if each stride the nearer bring
Him to the grave)—when comes *the time*,
After the fall, he rises—KING!

H.L. WILLIAMS

THE DANUBE IN WRATH.

("Quoi! ne pouvez-vous vivre ensemble?")

{XXXV., June, 1828.}

The River Deity upbraids his Daughters, the contributary Streams:—

Ye daughters mine! will naught abate
Your fierce interminable hate?
Still am I doomed to rue the fate
That such unfriendly neighbors made?
The while ye might, in peaceful cheer,
Mirror upon your waters clear,
Semlin! thy Gothic steeples dear,
And thy bright minarets, Belgrade!

Fraser's Magazine

OLD OCEAN.

("J'étais seul près des flots.")

{XXXVII., September 5, 1828.}
I stood by the waves, while the stars soared in sight,
Not a cloud specked the sky, not a sail shimmered bright;
Scenes beyond this dim world were revealed to mine eye;
And the woods, and the hills, and all nature around,
Seem'd to question with moody, mysterious sound,
The waves, and the pure stars on high.
And the clear constellations, that infinite throng,

While thousand rich harmonies swelled in their song,
Replying, bowed meekly their diamond-blaze—
And the blue waves, which nothing may bind or arrest,
Chorus'd forth, as they stooped the white foam of their crest
"Creator! we bless thee and praise!"

R.C. ELLWOOD

MY NAPOLEON.

("Toujours lui! lui partout!")

{XL., December, 1828.}
Above all others, everywhere I see
His image cold or burning!
My brain it thrills, and oftentime sets free
The thoughts within me yearning.
My quivering lips pour forth the words
That cluster in his name of glory—
The star gigantic with its rays of swords
Whose gleams irradiate all modern story.

I see his finger pointing where the shell
Should fall to slay most rabble,
And save foul regicides; or strike the knell

Of weaklings 'mid the tribunes' babble.
A Consul then, o'er young but proud,
With midnight poring thinned, and sallow,
But dreams of Empire pierce the transient cloud,
And round pale face and lank locks form the halo.

And soon the Caesar, with an eye a-flame
Whole nations' contact urging
To gain his soldiers gold and fame
Oh, Sun on high emerging,
Whose dazzling lustre fired the hells
Embosomed in grim bronze, which, free, arose
To change five hundred thousand base-born Tells,
Into his host of half-a-million heroes!

What! next a captive? Yea, and caged apart.
No weight of arms enfolded
Can crush the turmoil in that seething heart
Which Nature—not her journeymen—self-moulded.
Let sordid jailers vex their prize;
But only bends that brow to lightning,
As gazing from the seaward rock, his sighs
Cleave through the storm and haste where France looms bright'ning.

Alone, but greater! Broke the sceptre, true!
Yet lingers still some power—
In tears of woe man's metal may renew
The temper of high hour;
For, bating breath, e'er list the kings

The pinions clipped may grow! the Eagle
May burst, in frantic thirst for home, the rings
And rend the Bulldog, Fox, and Bear, and Beagle!

And, lastly, grandest! 'tween dark sea and here
Eternal brightness coming!
The eye so weary's freshened with a tear
As rises distant drumming,
And wailing cheer—they pass the pale
His army mourns though still's the end hid;
And from his war-stained cloak, he answers "Hail!"
And spurns the bed of gloom for throne aye-splendid!

H.L. WILLIAMS.

LES FEUILLES D'AUTOMNE.—1831.

THE PATIENCE OF THE PEOPLE.

("Il s'est dit tant de fois.")

{III., May, 1830.}
How often have the people said: "What's power?"
Who reigns soon is dethroned? each fleeting hour
Has onward borne, as in a fevered dream,
Such quick reverses, like a judge supreme—
Austere but just, they contemplate the end
To which the current of events must tend.
Self-confidence has taught them to forbear,
And in the vastness of their strength, they spare.
Armed with impunity, for *one in vain*
Resists a *nation*, they let others reign.

G.W.M. REYNOLDS.

DICTATED BEFORE THE RHONE GLACIER.

("Souvent quand mon esprit riche.")

{VII., May 18, 1828.}
When my mind, on the ocean of poesy hurled,
Floats on in repose round this wonderful world,
  Oft the sacred fire from heaven—
Mysterious sun, that gives light to the soul—
Strikes mine with its ray, and above the pole
  Its upward course is driven,

  Like a wandering cloud, then, my eager thought
  Capriciously flies, to no guidance brought,
    With every quarter's wind;
  It regards from those radiant vaults on high,
  Earth's cities below, and again doth fly,
    And leaves but its shadow behind.

In the glistening gold of the morning bright,
It shines, detaching some lance of light,
  Or, as warrior's armor rings;
It forages forests that ferment around,
Or bathed in the sun-red gleams is found,
  Where the west its radiance flings.

Or, on mountain peak, that rears its head
Where snow-clad Alps around are spread,
  By furious gale 'tis thrown.

From the yawning abyss see the cloud scud away,
And the glacier appears, with its multiform ray,
 The giant mountain's crown!

Like Parnassian pinnacle yet to be scaled,
In its form from afar, by the aspirant hailed;
 On its side the rainbow plays,
And at eve, when the shadow sinks sleeping below,
The last slanting ray on its crest of snow
 Makes its cap like a crater to blaze.

In the darkness, its front seems some pale orb of light,
The chamois with fear flashes on in its flight,
 The eagle afar is driven;
The deluge but roars in despair to its feet,
And scarce dare the eye its aspect to meet,
 So near doth it rise to heaven.

Alone on these altitudes, feeling no fear,
Forgetful of earth, my spirit draws near;
 On the starry vault to gaze,
And nearer, to gaze on those glories of night,
On th' horizon high heaving, like arches of light,
 Till again the sun shall blaze.

For then will the glacier with glory be graced,
On its prisms will light streaked with darkness be placed,
 The morn its echoes greet;
Like a torrent it falls on the ocean of life,
Like Chaos unformed, with the sea-stormy strife,

When waters on waters meet.

As the spirit of poesy touches my thought,
It is thus my ideas in a circle are brought,
  From earth, with the waters of pain.
As under a sunbeam a cloud ascends,
These fly to the heavens—their course never ends,
  But descend to the ocean again.

Author of "Critical Essays."

THE POET'S LOVE FOR LIVELINESS.

("Moi, quelque soit le monde.")

{XV., May 11, 1830.}
For me, whate'er my life and lot may show,
Years blank with gloom or cheered by mem'ry's glow,
Turmoil or peace; never be it mine, I pray,
To be a dweller of the peopled earth,
Save 'neath a roof alive with children's mirth
Loud through the livelong day.

So, if my hap it be to see once more
Those scenes my footsteps tottered in before,
An infant follower in Napoleon's train:

Rodrigo's holds, Valencia and Leon,
And both Castiles, and mated Aragon;
Ne'er be it mine, O Spain!

To pass thy plains with cities scant between,
Thy stately arches flung o'er deep ravine,
Thy palaces, of Moor's or Roman's time;
Or the swift makings of thy Guadalquiver,
Save in those gilded cars, where bells forever
Ring their melodious chime.

Fraser's Magazine

INFANTILE INFLUENCE.

("Lorsque l'enfant parait.")

{XIX., May 11, 1830.}
The child comes toddling in, and young and old
With smiling eyes its smiling eyes behold,
 And artless, babyish joy;
A playful welcome greets it through the room,
The saddest brow unfolds its wrinkled gloom,
 To greet the happy boy.

If June with flowers has spangled all the ground,

Or winter bleak the flickering hearth around
  Draws close the circling seat;
The child still sheds a never-failing light;
We call; Mamma with mingled joy and fright
  Watches its tottering feet.

Perhaps at eve as round the fire we draw,
We speak of heaven, or poetry, or law,
  Or politics, or prayer;
The child comes in, 'tis now all smiles and play,
Farewell to grave discourse and poet's lay,
  Philosophy and care.

When fancy wakes, but sense in heaviest sleep
Lies steeped, and like the sobs of them that weep
  The dark stream sinks and swells,
The dawn, like Pharos gleaming o'er the sea,
Bursts forth, and sudden wakes the minstrelsy
  Of birds and chiming bells;

Thou art my dawn; my soul is as the field,
Where sweetest flowers their balmy perfumes yield
  When breathed upon by thee,
Of forest, where thy voice like zephyr plays,
And morn pours out its flood of golden rays,
  When thy sweet smile I see.

Oh, sweetest eyes, like founts of liquid blue;
And little hands that evil never knew,
  Pure as the new-formed snow;

Thy feet are still unstained by this world's mire,
Thy golden locks like aureole of fire
  Circle thy cherub brow!

Dove of our ark, thine angel spirit flies
On azure wings forth from thy beaming eyes.
  Though weak thine infant feet,
What strange amaze this new and strange world gives
To thy sweet virgin soul, that spotless lives
  In virgin body sweet.

Oh, gentle face, radiant with happy smile,
And eager prattling tongue that knows no guile,
  Quick changing tears and bliss;
Thy soul expands to catch this new world's light,
Thy mazed eyes to drink each wondrous sight,
  Thy lips to taste the kiss.

Oh, God! bless me and mine, and these I love,
And e'en my foes that still triumphant prove
  Victors by force or guile;
A flowerless summer may we never see,
Or nest of bird bereft, or hive of bee,
  Or home of infant's smile.

HENRY HIGHTON, M.A.

THE WATCHING ANGEL.

("Dans l'alcôve sombre.")

{XX., November, 1831.}
In the dusky nook,
Near the altar laid,
Sleeps the child in shadow
Of his mother's bed:
Softly he reposes,
And his lid of roses,
Closed to earth, uncloses
On the heaven o'erhead.

Many a dream is with him,
Fresh from fairyland,
Spangled o'er with diamonds
Seems the ocean sand;
Suns are flaming there,
Troops of ladies fair
Souls of infants bear
In each charming hand.

Oh, enchanting vision!
Lo, a rill upsprings,
And from out its bosom
Comes a voice that sings
Lovelier there appear
Sire and sisters dear,

While his mother near
Plumes her new-born wings.

But a brighter vision
Yet his eyes behold;
Roses pied and lilies
Every path enfold;
Lakes delicious sleeping,
Silver fishes leaping,
Through the wavelets creeping
Up to reeds of gold.

Slumber on, sweet infant,
Slumber peacefully
Thy young soul yet knows not
What thy lot may be.
Like dead weeds that sweep
O'er the dol'rous deep,
Thou art borne in sleep.
What is all to thee?

Thou canst slumber by the way;
Thou hast learnt to borrow
Naught from study, naught from care;
The cold hand of sorrow
On thy brow unwrinkled yet,
Where young truth and candor sit,
Ne'er with rugged nail hath writ
That sad word, "To-morrow!"

Innocent! thou sleepest—
See the angelic band,
Who foreknow the trials
That for man are planned;
Seeing him unarmed,
Unfearing, unalarmed,
With their tears have warmed
This unconscious hand.

Still they, hovering o'er him,
Kiss him where he lies,
Hark, he sees them weeping,
"Gabriel!" he cries;
"Hush!" the angel says,
On his lip he lays
One finger, one displays
His native skies.

Foreign Quarterly Review

SUNSET.

("Le soleil s'est couché")

{XXXV. vi., April, 1829.}
The sun set this evening in masses of cloud,

The storm comes to-morrow, then calm be the night,
Then the Dawn in her chariot refulgent and proud,
Then more nights, and still days, steps of Time in his flight.
The days shall pass rapid as swifts on the wing.
O'er the face of the hills, o'er the face of the seas,
O'er streamlets of silver, and forests that ring
With a dirge for the dead, chanted low by the breeze;
The face of the waters, the brow of the mounts
Deep scarred but not shrivelled, and woods tufted green,
Their youth shall renew; and the rocks to the founts
Shall yield what these yielded to ocean their queen.
But day by day bending still lower my head,
Still chilled in the sunlight, soon I shall have cast,
At height of the banquet, my lot with the dead,
Unmissed by creation aye joyous and vast.

TORU DUTT.

THE UNIVERSAL PRAYER.

("Ma fille, va prier!")

{XXXVII., June, 1830.}
I.

Come, child, to prayer; the busy day is done,
A golden star gleams through the dusk of night;
The hills are trembling in the rising mist,
The rumbling wain looms dim upon the sight;
All things wend home to rest; the roadside trees
Shake off their dust, stirred by the evening breeze.

The sparkling stars gush forth in sudden blaze,
As twilight open flings the doors of night;
The fringe of carmine narrows in the west,
The rippling waves are tipped with silver light;
The bush, the path—all blend in one dull gray;
The doubtful traveller gropes his anxious way.

Oh, day! with toil, with wrong, with hatred rife;
Oh, blessed night! with sober calmness sweet,
The sad winds moaning through the ruined tower,
The age-worn hind, the sheep's sad broken bleat—
All nature groans opprest with toil and care,
And wearied craves for rest, and love, and prayer.

At eve the babes with angels converse hold,
While we to our strange pleasures wend our way,
Each with its little face upraised to heaven,
With folded hands, barefoot kneels down to pray,
At selfsame hour with selfsame words they call
On God, the common Father of them all.

And then they sleep, and golden dreams anon,
Born as the busy day's last murmurs die,

In swarms tumultuous flitting through the gloom
Their breathing lips and golden locks descry.
And as the bees o'er bright flowers joyous roam,
Around their curtained cradles clustering come.

Oh, prayer of childhood! simple, innocent;
Oh, infant slumbers! peaceful, pure, and light;
Oh, happy worship! ever gay with smiles,
Meet prelude to the harmonies of night;
As birds beneath the wing enfold their head,
Nestled in prayer the infant seeks its bed.

HENRY HIGHTON, M.A.

II.

To prayer, my child! and O, be thy first prayer
For her who, many nights, with anxious care,
Rocked thy first cradle; who took thy infant soul
From heaven and gave it to the world; then rife
With love, still drank herself the gall of life,
And left for thy young lips the honeyed bowl.

And then—I need it more—then pray for me!
For she is gentle, artless, true like thee;—
She has a guileless heart, brow placid still;

Pity she has for all, envy for none;
Gentle and wise, she patiently lives on;
And she endures, nor knows who does the ill.

In culling flowers, her novice hand has ne'er
Touched e'en the outer rind of vice; no snare
With smiling show has lured her steps aside:
On her the past has left no staining mark;
Nor knows she aught of those bad thoughts which, dark
Like shade on waters, o'er the spirit glide.

She knows not—nor mayest thou—the miseries
In which our spirits mingle: vanities,
Remorse, soul-gnawing cares, Pleasure's false show:
Passions which float upon the heart like foam,
Bitter remembrances which o'er us come,
And Shame's red spot spread sudden o'er the brow.

I know life better! when thou'rt older grown
I'll tell thee—it is needful to be known—
Of the pursuit of wealth—art, power; the cost.
That it is folly, nothingness: that shame
For glory is oft thrown us in the game
Of Fortune; chances where the soul is lost.

The soul will change. Although of everything
The cause and end be clear, yet wildering
We roam through life (of vice and error full).
We wander as we go; we feel the load
Of doubt; and to the briars upon the road

Man leaves his virtue, as the sheep its wool.

Then go, go pray for me! And as the prayer
Gushes in words, be this the form they bear:—
"Lord, Lord, our Father! God, my prayer attend;
Pardon! Thou art good! Pardon—Thou art great!"
Let them go freely forth, fear not their fate!
Where thy soul sends them, thitherward they tend.

There's nothing here below which does not find
Its tendency. O'er plains the rivers wind,
And reach the sea; the bee, by instinct driven,
Finds out the honeyed flowers; the eagle flies
To seek the sun; the vulture where death lies;
The swallow to the spring; the prayer to Heaven!

And when thy voice is raised to God for me,
I'm like the slave whom in the vale we see
Seated to rest, his heavy load laid by;
I feel refreshed—the load of faults and woe
Which, groaning, I drag with me as I go,
Thy wingèd prayer bears off rejoicingly!

Pray for thy father! that his dreams be bright
With visitings of angel forms of light,
And his soul burn as incense flaming wide,
Let thy pure breath all his dark sins efface,
So that his heart be like that holy place,
An altar pavement each eve purified!

Poems

C., *Tait's Magazine*

Poems

LES CHANTS DU CRÉPUSCULE.—1849.

PRELUDE TO "THE SONGS OF TWILIGHT."

("De quel non te nommer?")

{PRELUDE, a, Oct. 20, 1835.}
How shall I note thee, line of troubled years,
Which mark existence in our little span?
One constant twilight in the heaven appears—
One constant twilight in the mind of man!

Creed, hope, anticipation and despair,
Are but a mingling, as of day and night;
The globe, surrounded by deceptive air,
Is all enveloped in the same half-light.

And voice is deadened by the evening breeze,
The shepherd's song, or maiden's in her bower,
Mix with the rustling of the neighboring trees,
Within whose foliage is lulled the power.

Yet all unites! The winding path that leads
Thro' fields where verdure meets the trav'ller's eye.
The river's margin, blurred with wavy reeds,
The muffled anthem, echoing to the sky!

The ivy smothering the armèd tower;
The dying wind that mocks the pilot's ear;
The lordly equipage at midnight hour,
Draws into danger in a fog the peer;

The votaries of Satan or of Jove;
The wretched mendicant absorbed in woe;
The din of multitudes that onward move;
The voice of conscience in the heart below;

The waves, which Thou, O Lord, alone canst still;
Th' elastic air; the streamlet on its way;
And all that man projects, or sovereigns will;
Or things inanimate might seem to say;

The strain of gondolier slow streaming by;
The lively barks that o'er the waters bound;
The trees that shake their foliage to the sky;
The wailing voice that fills the cots around;

And man, who studies with an aching heart—
For now, when smiles are rarely deemed sincere,
In vain the sceptic bids his doubts depart—
Those doubts at length will arguments appear!

Hence, reader, know the subject of my song—
A mystic age, resembling twilight gloom,
Wherein we smile at birth, or bear along,
With noiseless steps, a victim to the tomb!

G.W.M. REYNOLDS

THE LAND OF FABLE.

("L'Orient! qu'y voyez-vous, poëtes?")

{PRELUDE, b.}
Now, vot'ries of the Muses, turn your eyes,
Unto the East, and say what there appears!
"Alas!" the voice of Poesy replies,
"Mystic's that light between the hemispheres!"

"Yes, dread's the mystic light in yonder heaven—
Dull is the gleam behind the distant hill;
Like feeble flashes in the welkin driven,
When the far thunder seems as it were still!

"But who can tell if that uncertain glare
Be Phoebus' self, adorned with glowing vest;
Or, if illusions, pregnant in the air,
Have drawn our glances to the radiant west?

"Haply the sunset has deceived the sight—
Perchance 'tis evening, while we look for morning;
Bewildered in the mazes of twilight,
That lucid sunset may *appear* a dawning!"

G.W.M. REYNOLDS

THE THREE GLORIOUS DAYS.

("Frères, vous avez vos journées.")

{I., July, 1830.}
Youth of France, sons of the bold,
Your oak-leaf victor-wreaths behold!
Our civic-laurels—honored dead!
So bright your triumphs in life's morn,
Your maiden-standards hacked and torn,
On Austerlitz might lustre shed.

All that your fathers did re-done—
A people's rights all nobly won—
Ye tore them living from the shroud!
Three glorious days bright July's gift,
The Bastiles off our hearts ye lift!
Oh! of such deeds be ever proud!

Of patriot sires ye lineage claim,
Their souls shone in your eye of flame;
Commencing the great work was theirs;
On you the task to finish laid

Your fruitful mother, France, who bade
Flow in one day a hundred years.

E'en chilly Albion admires,
The grand example Europe fires;
America shall clap her hands,
When swiftly o'er the Atlantic wave,
Fame sounds the news of how the brave,
In three bright days, have burst their bands!

With tyrant dead your fathers traced
A circle wide, with battles graced;
Victorious garland, red and vast!
Which blooming out from home did go
To Cadiz, Cairo, Rome, Moscow,
From Jemappes to Montmirail passed!

Of warlike Lyceums{1} ye are
The favored sons; there, deeds of war
Formed e'en your plays, while o'er you shook
The battle-flags in air aloft!
Passing your lines, Napoleon oft
Electrified you with a look!

Eagle of France! whose vivid wing
Did in a hundred places fling
A bloody feather, till one night
The arrow whelmed thee 'neath the wave!
Look up—rejoice—for now thy brave
And worthy eaglets dare the light.

ELIZABETH COLLINS.

{Footnote 1: The pupils of the Polytechnic Military School distinguished
  themselves by their patriotic zeal and military skill, through all the
    troubles.}

TRIBUTE TO THE VANQUISHED.

("Laissez-moi pleurer sur cette race.")

{I. v.}
Oh! let me weep that race whose day is past,
 By exile given, by exile claimed once more,
Thrice swept away upon that fatal blast.
 Whate'er its blame, escort we to our shore
 These relics of the monarchy of yore;
 And to th' outmarching oriflamme be paid
War's honors by the flag on Fleurus' field displayed!

Fraser's Magazine

ANGEL OR DEMON.

("Tu domines notre âge; ange ou démon, qu'importe!")

{I. vii.}
Angel or demon! thou,—whether of light
The minister, or darkness—still dost sway
This age of ours; thine eagle's soaring flight
Bears us, all breathless, after it away.
The eye that from thy presence fain would stray,
Shuns thee in vain; thy mighty shadow thrown
Rests on all pictures of the living day,
And on the threshold of our time alone,
Dazzling, yet sombre, stands thy form, Napoleon!

Thus, when the admiring stranger's steps explore
The subject-lands that 'neath Vesuvius be,
Whether he wind along the enchanting shore
To Portici from fair Parthenope,
Or, lingering long in dreamy reverie,
O'er loveliest Ischia's od'rous isle he stray,
Wooed by whose breath the soft and am'rous sea
Seems like some languishing sultana's lay,
A voice for very sweets that scarce can win its way.

Him, whether Paestum's solemn fane detain,
Shrouding his soul with meditation's power;
Or at Pozzuoli, to the sprightly strain
Of tarantella danced 'neath Tuscan tower,

Listening, he while away the evening hour;
Or wake the echoes, mournful, lone and deep,
Of that sad city, in its dreaming bower
By the volcano seized, where mansions keep
The likeness which they wore at that last fatal sleep;

Or be his bark at Posillippo laid,
While as the swarthy boatman at his side
Chants Tasso's lays to Virgil's pleased shade,
Ever he sees, throughout that circuit wide,
From shaded nook or sunny lawn espied,
From rocky headland viewed, or flow'ry shore,
From sea, and spreading mead alike descried,
The Giant Mount, tow'ring all objects o'er,
And black'ning with its breath th' horizon evermore!

Fraser's Magazine

THE ERUPTION OF VESUVIUS.

("Quand longtemps a grondé la bouche du Vésuve.")

{I. vii.}
When huge Vesuvius in its torment long,
Threatening has growled its cavernous jaws among,
When its hot lava, like the bubbling wine,

Foaming doth all its monstrous edge incarnadine,
Then is alarm in Naples.

   With dismay,
Wanton and wild her weeping thousands pour,
Convulsive grasp the ground, its rage to stay,
Implore the angry Mount—in vain implore!
For lo! a column tow'ring more and more,
Of smoke and ashes from the burning crest
Shoots like a vulture's neck reared from its airy nest.

Sudden a flash, and from th' enormous den
Th' eruption's lurid mass bursts forth amain,
Bounding in frantic ecstasy. Ah! then
Farewell to Grecian fount and Tuscan fane!
Sails in the bay imbibe the purpling stain,
The while the lava in profusion wide
Flings o'er the mountain's neck its showery locks untied.

It comes—it comes! that lava deep and rich,
That dower which fertilizes fields and fills
New moles upon the waters, bay and beach.
Broad sea and clustered isles, one terror thrills
As roll the red inexorable rills;
While Naples trembles in her palaces,
More helpless than the leaves when tempests shake the trees.

Prodigious chaos, streets in ashes lost,
   Dwellings devoured and vomited again.

Roof against neighbor-roof, bewildered, tossed.
The waters boiling and the burning plain;
While clang the giant steeples as they reel,
Unprompted, their own tocsin peal.

Yet 'mid the wreck of cities, and the pride
Of the green valleys and the isles laid low,
The crash of walls, the tumult waste and wide,
O'er sea and land; 'mid all this work of woe,
Vesuvius still, though close its crater-glow,
Forgetful spares—Heaven wills that it should spare,
The lonely cell where kneels an aged priest in prayer.

Fraser's Magazine.

MARRIAGE AND FEASTS.

("La salle est magnifique.")

{IV. Aug. 23, 1839.}
The hall is gay with limpid lustre bright—
The feast to pampered palate gives delight—
The sated guests pick at the spicy food,
And drink profusely, for the cheer is good;
And at that table—where the wise are few—
Both sexes and all ages meet the view;

The sturdy warrior with a thoughtful face—
The am'rous youth, the maid replete with grace,
The prattling infant, and the hoary hair
Of second childhood's proselytes—are there;—
And the most gaudy in that spacious hall,
Are e'er the young, or oldest of them all
Helmet and banner, ornament and crest,
The lion rampant, and the jewelled vest,
The silver star that glitters fair and white,
The arms that tell of many a nation's might—
Heraldic blazonry, ancestral pride,
And all mankind invents for pomp beside,
The wingèd leopard, and the eagle wild—
All these encircle woman, chief and child;
Shine on the carpet burying their feet,
Adorn the dishes that contain their meat;
And hang upon the drapery, which around
Falls from the lofty ceiling to the ground,
Till on the floor its waving fringe is spread,
As the bird's wing may sweep the roses' bed.—

Thus is the banquet ruled by Noise and Light,
Since Light and Noise are foremost on the site.

The chamber echoes to the joy of them
Who throng around, each with his diadem—
Each seated on proud throne—but, lesson vain!
Each sceptre holds its master with a chain!
Thus hope of flight were futile from that hall,
Where chiefest guest was most enslaved of all!

The godlike-making draught that fires the soul
The Love—sweet poison-honey—past control,
(Formed of the sexual breath—an idle name,
Offspring of Fancy and a nervous frame)—
Pleasure, mad daughter of the darksome Night,
Whose languid eye flames when is fading light—
The gallant chases where a man is borne
By stalwart charger, to the sounding horn—
The sheeny silk, the bed of leaves of rose,
Made more to soothe the sight than court repose;
The mighty palaces that raise the sneer
Of jealous mendicants and wretches near—
The spacious parks, from which horizon blue
Arches o'er alabaster statues new;
Where Superstition still her walk will take,
Unto soft music stealing o'er the lake—
The innocent modesty by gems undone—
The qualms of judges by small brib'ry won—
The dread of children, trembling while they play—
The bliss of monarchs, potent in their sway—
The note of war struck by the culverin,
That snakes its brazen neck through battle din—
The military millipede
That tramples out the guilty seed—
The capital all pleasure and delight—
And all that like a town or army chokes
The gazer with foul dust or sulphur smokes.
The budget, prize for which ten thousand bait
A subtle hook, that ever, as they wait
Catches a weed, and drags them to their fate,

While gleamingly its golden scales still spread—
Such were the meats by which these guests were fed.

A hundred slaves for lazy master cared,
And served each one with what was e'er prepared
By him, who in a sombre vault below,
Peppered the royal pig with peoples' woe,
And grimly glad went laboring till late—
The morose alchemist we know as Fate!
That ev'ry guest might learn to suit his taste,
Behind had Conscience, real or mock'ry, placed;
Conscience a guide who every evil spies,
But royal nurses early pluck out both his eyes!

Oh! at the table there be all the great,
Whose lives are bubbles that best joys inflate!
Superb, magnificent of revels—doubt
That sagest lose their heads in such a rout!
In the long laughter, ceaseless roaming round,
Joy, mirth and glee give out a maelström's sound;
And the astonished gazer casts his care,
Where ev'ry eyeball glistens in the flare.

But oh! while yet the singing Hebes pour
Forgetfulness of those without the door—
At very hour when all are most in joy,
And the hid orchestra annuls annoy,
Woe—woe! with jollity a-top the heights,
With further tapers adding to the lights,
And gleaming 'tween the curtains on the street,

Where poor folks stare—hark to the heavy feet!
Some one smites roundly on the gilded grate,
Some one below will be admitted straight,
Some one, though not invited, who'll not wait!
Close not the door! Your orders are vain breath—
That stranger enters to be known as Death—
Or merely Exile—clothed in alien guise—
Death drags away—with *his* prey Exile flies!

Death is that sight. He promenades the hall,
And casts a gloomy shadow on them all,
'Neath which they bend like willows soft,
Ere seizing one—the dumbest monarch oft,
And bears him to eternal heat and drouth,
While still the toothsome morsel's in his mouth.

G.W.M. REYNOLDS.

THE MORROW OF GRANDEUR.

("Non, l'avenir n'est à personne!")

{V. ii., August, 1832.}
Sire, beware, the future's range
Is of God alone the power,
Naught below but augurs change,
E'en with ev'ry passing hour.

Future! mighty mystery!
All the earthly goods that be,
Fortune, glory, war's renown,
King or kaiser's sparkling crown,
Victory! with her burning wings,
Proud ambition's covetings,—
These may our grasp no more detain
Than the free bird who doth alight
Upon our roof, and takes its flight
High into air again.

Nor smile, nor tear, nor haughtiest lord's command,
Avails t' unclasp the cold and closèd hand.
Thy voice to disenthrall,
Dumb phantom, shadow ever at our side!
Veiled spectre, journeying with us stride for stride,
Whom men "To-morrow" call.

Oh, to-morrow! who may dare
Its realities to scan?
God to-morrow brings to bear
What to-day is sown by man.
'Tis the lightning in its shroud,
'Tis the star-concealing cloud,
Traitor, 'tis his purpose showing,
Engine, lofty tow'rs o'erthrowing,
Wand'ring star, its region changing,
"Lady of kingdoms," ever ranging.
To-morrow! 'Tis the rude display
Of the throne's framework, blank and cold,

That, rich with velvet, bright with gold,
Dazzles the eye to-day.

To-morrow! 'tis the foaming war-horse falling;
To-morrow! thy victorious march appalling,
'Tis the red fires from Moscow's tow'rs that wave;
'Tis thine Old Guard strewing the Belgian plain;
'Tis the lone island in th' Atlantic main:
To-morrow! 'tis the grave!

Into capitals subdued
Thou mayst ride with gallant rein,
Cut the knots of civil feud
With the trenchant steel in twain;
With thine edicts barricade
Haughty Thames' o'er-freighted trade;
Fickle Victory's self enthrall,
Captive to thy trumpet call;
Burst the stoutest gates asunder;
Leave the names of brightest wonder,
Pale and dim, behind thee far;
And to exhaustless armies yield
Thy glancing spur,—o'er Europe's field
A glory-guiding star.

God guards duration, if lends space to thee,
Thou mayst o'er-range mundane immensity,
Rise high as human head can rise sublime,
Snatch Europe from the stamp of Charlemagne,
Asia from Mahomet; but never gain

Power o'er the Morrow from the Lord of Time!

Fraser's Magazine.

THE EAGLET MOURNED.

("Encore si ce banni n'eût rien aimé sur terre.")

{V, iv., August, 1832.}
Too hard Napoleon's fate! if, lone,
No being he had loved, no single one,
  Less dark that doom had been.
But with the heart of might doth ever dwell
The heart of love! and in his island cell
  Two things there were—I ween.

Two things—a portrait and a map there were—
Here hung the pictured world, an infant there:
That framed his genius, this enshrined his love.
And as at eve he glanced round th' alcove,
Where jailers watched his very thoughts to spy,
What mused he *then*—what dream of years gone by
Stirred 'neath that discrowned brow, and fired that glistening eye?

'Twas not the steps of that heroic tale

That from Arcola marched to Montmirail
 On Glory's red degrees;
Nor Cairo-pashas' steel-devouring steeds,
Nor the tall shadows of the Pyramids—
 Ah! Twas not always these;

'Twas not the bursting shell, the iron sleet,
The whirlwind rush of battle 'neath his feet,
 Through twice ten years ago,
When at his beck, upon that sea of steel
Were launched the rustling banners—there to reel
 Like masts when tempests blow.

'Twas not Madrid, nor Kremlin of the Czar,
Nor Pharos on Old Egypt's coast afar,
Nor shrill *réveillé's* camp-awakening sound,
Nor bivouac couch'd its starry fires around,
Crested dragoons, grim, veteran grenadiers,
Nor the red lancers 'mid their wood of spears
Blazing like baleful poppies 'mong the golden ears.

No—'twas an infant's image, fresh and fair,
With rosy mouth half oped, as slumbering there.
 It lay beneath the smile,
Of her whose breast, soft-bending o'er its sleep,
Lingering upon that little lip doth keep
 One pendent drop the while.

Then, his sad head upon his hands inclined,
He wept; that father-heart all unconfined,

Outpoured in love alone.
My blessing on thy clay-cold head, poor child.
Sole being for whose sake his thoughts, beguiled,
Forgot the world's lost throne.

Fraser's Magazine

INVOCATION.

{V, vi., August, 1832.}
Say, Lord! for Thou alone canst tell
Where lurks the good invisible
Amid the depths of discord's sea—
That seem, alas! so dark to me!
Oppressive to a mighty state,
Contentions, feuds, the people's hate—
But who dare question that which fate
 Has ordered to have been?
Haply the earthquake may unfold
The resting-place of purest gold,
And haply surges up have rolled
 The pearls that were unseen!

G.W.M. REYNOLDS.

OUTSIDE THE BALL-ROOM.

("*Ainsi l'Hôtel de Ville illumine.*")

{VI., May, 1833.}
Behold the ball-room flashing on the sight,
From step to cornice one grand glare of light;
The noise of mirth and revelry resounds,
Like fairy melody on haunted grounds.
But who demands this profuse, wanton glee,
These shouts prolonged and wild festivity—
Not sure our city—web, more woe than bliss,
In any hour, requiring aught but this!

Deaf is the ear of all that jewelled crowd
To sorrow's sob, although its call be loud.
Better than waste long nights in idle show,
To help the indigent and raise the low—
To train the wicked to forsake his way,
And find th' industrious work from day to day!
Better to charity those hours afford,
Which now are wasted at the festal board!

And ye, O high-born beauties! in whose soul
Virtue resides, and Vice has no control;
Ye whom prosperity forbids to sin,
So fair without—so chaste, so pure within—
Whose honor Want ne'er threatened to betray,
Whose eyes are joyous, and whose heart is gay;

Around whose modesty a hundred arms,
Aided by pride, protect a thousand charms;
For you this ball is pregnant with delight;
As glitt'ring planets cheer the gloomy night:—
But, O, ye wist not, while your souls are glad,
How millions wander, homeless, sick and sad!
Hazard has placed you in a happy sphere,
And like your own to you all lots appear;
For blinded by the sun of bliss your eyes
Can see no dark horizon to the skies.

Such is the chance of life! Each gallant thane,
Prince, peer, and noble, follow in your train;—
They praise your loveliness, and in your ear
They whisper pleasing things, but insincere;
Thus, as the moths enamoured of the light,
Ye seek these realms of revelry each night.
But as ye travel thither, did ye know
What wretches walk the streets through which you go.
Sisters, whose gewgaws glitter in the glare
Of your great lustre, all expectant there,
Watching the passing crowd with avid eye,
Till one their love, or lust, or shame may buy;
Or, with commingling jealousy and rage,
They mark the progress of your equipage;
And their deceitful life essays the while
To mask their woe beneath a sickly smile!

G.W.M. REYNOLDS.

PRAYER FOR FRANCE.

("O Dieu, si vous avez la France.")

{VII., August, 1832.}
O God! if France be still thy guardian care,
Oh! spare these mercenary combats, spare!
The thrones that now are reared but to be broke;
The rights we render, and anon revoke;
The muddy stream of laws, ideas, needs,
Flooding our social life as it proceeds;
Opposing tribunes, even when seeming one—
Soft, yielding plaster put in place of stone;
Wave chasing wave in endless ebb and flow;
War, darker still and deeper in its woe;
One party fall'n, successor scarce preludes,
Than, straight, new views their furious feuds;
The great man's pressure on the poor for gold,
Rumors uncertain, conflicts, crimes untold;
Dark systems hatched in secret and in fear,
Telling of hate and strife to every ear,
That even to midnight sleep no peace is given,
For murd'rous cannon through our streets are driven.

J.S. MACRAE.

TO CANARIS, THE GREEK PATRIOT.

("Canaris! nous t'avons oublié.")

{VIII., October, 1832.}
O Canaris! O Canaris! the poet's song
Has blameful left untold thy deeds too long!
But when the tragic actor's part is done,
When clamor ceases, and the fights are won,
When heroes realize what Fate decreed,
When chieftains mark no more which thousands bleed;
When they have shone, as clouded or as bright,
As fitful meteor in the heaven at night,
And when the sycophant no more proclaims
To gaping crowds the glory of their names,—
'Tis then the mem'ries of warriors die,
And fall—alas!—into obscurity,
Until the poet, in whose verse alone
Exists a world—can make their actions known,
And in eternal epic measures, show
They are not yet forgotten here below.
And yet by us neglected! glory gloomed,
Thy name seems sealed apart, entombed,
Although our shouts to pigmies rise—no cries
To mark thy presence echo to the skies;
Farewell to Grecian heroes—silent is the lute,
And sets your sun without one Memnon bruit?

There was a time men gave no peace

To cheers for Athens, Bozzaris, Leonidas, and Greece!
And Canaris' more-worshipped name was found
On ev'ry lip, in ev'ry heart around.
But now is changed the scene! On hist'ry's page
Are writ o'er thine deeds of another age,
And thine are not remembered.—Greece, farewell!
The world no more thine heroes' deeds will tell.

Not that this matters to a man like thee!
To whom is left the dark blue open sea,
Thy gallant bark, that o'er the water flies,
And the bright planet guiding in clear skies;
All these remain, with accident and strife,
Hope, and the pleasures of a roving life,
Boon Nature's fairest prospects—land and main—
The noisy starting, glad return again;
The pride of freeman on a bounding deck
Which mocks at dangers and despises wreck,
And e'en if lightning-pinions cleave the sea,
'Tis all replete with joyousness to thee!

Yes, these remain! blue sky and ocean blue,
Thine eagles with one sweep beyond the view—
The sun in golden beauty ever pure,
The distance where rich warmth doth aye endure—
Thy language so mellifluously bland,
Mixed with sweet idioms from Italia's strand,
As Baya's streams to Samos' waters glide
And with them mingle in one placid tide.

Yes, these remain, and, Canaris! thy arms—
The sculptured sabre, faithful in alarms—
The broidered garb, the yataghan, the vest
Expressive of thy rank, to thee still rest!
And when thy vessel o'er the foaming sound
Is proud past storied coasts to blithely bound,
At once the point of beauty may restore
Smiles to thy lip, and smoothe thy brow once more.

G.W.M. REYNOLDS.

POLAND.

("Seule au pied de la tour.")

{IX., September, 1833.}
Alone, beneath the tower whence thunder forth
The mandates of the Tyrant of the North,
Poland's sad genius kneels, absorbed in tears,
Bound, vanquished, pallid with her fears—
Alas! the crucifix is all that's left
To her, of freedom and her sons bereft;
And on her royal robe foul marks are seen
Where Russian hectors' scornful feet have been.
Anon she hears the clank of murd'rous arms,—
The swordsmen come once more to spread alarms!

And while she weeps against the prison walls,
And waves her bleeding arm until it falls,
To France she hopeless turns her glazing eyes,
And sues her sister's succor ere she dies.

G.W.M. REYNOLDS.

INSULT NOT THE FALLEN.

("Oh! n'insultez jamais une femme qui tombe.")

{XIV., Sept. 6, 1835.}
I tell you, hush! no word of sneering scorn—
True, fallen; but God knows how deep her sorrow.
Poor girl! too many like her only born
To love one day—to sin—and die the morrow.
What know you of her struggles or her grief?
Or what wild storms of want and woe and pain
Tore down her soul from honor? As a leaf
From autumn branches, or a drop of rain
That hung in frailest splendor from a bough—
Bright, glistening in the sunlight of God's day—
So had she clung to virtue once. But now—
See Heaven's clear pearl polluted with earth's clay!
The sin is yours—with your accursed gold—
Man's wealth is master—woman's soul the slave!

Some purest water still the mire may hold.
Is there no hope for her—no power to save?
Yea, once again to draw up from the clay
The fallen raindrop, till it shine above,
Or save a fallen soul, needs but one ray
Of Heaven's sunshine, or of human love.

W.C.K. WILDE.

MORNING.

("L'aurore s'allume.")

{XX. a, December, 1834.}
Morning glances hither,
Now the shade is past;
Dream and fog fly thither
Where Night goes at last;
Open eyes and roses
As the darkness closes;
And the sound that grows is
Nature walking fast.

Murmuring all and singing,
Hark! the news is stirred,
Roof and creepers clinging,

Smoke and nest of bird;
Winds to oak-trees bear it,
Streams and fountains hear it,
Every breath and spirit
As a voice is heard.

All takes up its story,
Child resumes his play,
Hearth its ruddy glory,
Lute its lifted lay.
Wild or out of senses,
Through the world immense is
Sound as each commences
Schemes of yesterday.

W.M. HARDINGE.

SONG OF LOVE.

("S'il est un charmant gazon.")

{XXII, Feb. 18, 1834.}
If there be a velvet sward
By dewdrops pearly drest,
Where through all seasons fairies guard
Flowers by bees carest,

Where one may gather, day and night,
Roses, honeysuckle, lily white,
I fain would make of it a site
For thy foot to rest.

If there be a loving heart
Where Honor rules the breast,
Loyal and true in every part,
That changes ne'er molest,
Eager to run its noble race,
Intent to do some work of grace,
I fain would make of it a place
For thy brow to rest.

And if there be of love a dream
Rose-scented as the west,
Which shows, each time it comes, a gleam,—
A something sweet and blest,—
A dream of which heaven is the pole,
A dream that mingles soul and soul,
I fain of it would make the goal
Where thy mind should rest.

TORU DUTT.

SWEET CHARMER.{1}

("L'aube naît et ta porte est close.")

{XXIII., February, 18—.}
Though heaven's gate of light uncloses,
Thou stirr'st not—thou'rt laid to rest,
Waking are thy sister roses,
One only dreamest on thy breast.
  Hear me, sweet dreamer!
  Tell me all thy fears,
  Trembling in song,
  But to break in tears.

Lo! to greet thee, spirits pressing,
Soft music brings the gentle dove,
And fair light falleth like a blessing,
While my poor heart can bring thee only love.
Worship thee, angels love thee, sweet woman?
Yes; for that love perfects my soul.
None the less of heaven that my heart is human,
Blent in one exquisite, harmonious whole.

H.B. FARNIE.

{Footnote 1: Set to music by Sir Arthur Sullivan.}

Poems

MORE STRONG THAN TIME.

("Puisque j'ai mis ma lèvre à ta coupe.")

{XXV., Jan. 1, 1835.}
Since I have set my lips to your full cup, my sweet,
Since I my pallid face between your hands have laid,
Since I have known your soul, and all the bloom of it,
And all the perfume rare, now buried in the shade;

Since it was given to me to hear one happy while,
The words wherein your heart spoke all its mysteries,
Since I have seen you weep, and since I have seen you smile,
Your lips upon my lips, and your gaze upon my eyes;

Since I have known upon my forehead glance and gleam,
A ray, a single ray, of your star, veiled always,
Since I have felt the fall upon my lifetime's stream,
Of one rose-petal plucked from the roses of your days;

I now am bold to say to the swift-changing hours,
Pass—pass upon your way, for I grow never old.
Flee to the dark abysm with all your fading flowers,
One rose that none may pluck, within my heart I hold.

Your flying wings may smite, but they can never spill
The cup fulfilled of love, from which my lips are wet.
My heart has far more fire than you have frost to chill,

My soul more love than you can make my love forget.

A. LANG.

ROSES AND BUTTERFLIES.

("Roses et Papillons.")

{XXVII., Dec. 7, 1834.}
The grave receives us all:
Ye butterflies and roses gay and sweet
Why do ye linger, say?
Will ye not dwell together as is meet?
Somewhere high in the air
Would thy wing seek a home 'mid sunny skies,
In mead or mossy dell—
If there thy odors longest, sweetest rise.

Have where ye will your dwelling,
Or breath or tint whose praise we sing;
Butterfly shining bright,
Full-blown or bursting rosebud, flow'r or wing.
Dwell together ye fair,
'Tis a boon to the loveliest given;
Perchance ye then may choose your home
On the earth or in heaven.

W.C. WESTBROOK
A SIMILE.

("Soyez comme l'oiseau.")

{XXXIII. vi.}
Thou art like the bird
That alights and sings
Though the frail spray bends—
For he knows he has wings.

FANNY KEMBLE (BUTLER)

THE POET TO HIS WIFE.

("À toi, toujours à toi.")

{XXXIX., 1823}
To thee, all time to thee,
My lyre a voice shall be!
Above all earthly fashion,
Above mere mundane rage,
Your mind made it my passion
To write for noblest stage.

Whoe'er you be, send blessings to her—she
Was sister of my soul immortal, free!
My pride, my hope, my shelter, my resource,
When green hoped not to gray to run its course;
She was enthronèd Virtue under heaven's dome,
My idol in the shrine of curtained home.

LES VOIX INTÉRIEURES.—1840.

THE BLINDED BOURBONS.

("*Qui leur eût dit l'austère destineé?*")

{II. v., November, 1836.}
Who *then*, to them{1} had told the Future's story?
Or said that France, low bowed before their glory,
 One day would mindful be
Of them and of their mournful fate no more,
Than of the wrecks its waters have swept o'er
 The unremembering sea?

That their old Tuileries should see the fall
Of blazons from its high heraldic hall,
 Dismantled, crumbling, prone;{2}

Or that, o'er yon dark Louvre's architrave{3}
A Corsican, as yet unborn, should grave
  An eagle, then unknown?

That gay St. Cloud another lord awaited,
Or that in scenes Le Nôtre's art created
  For princely sport and ease,
Crimean steeds, trampling the velvet glade,
Should browse the bark beneath the stately shade
  Of the great Louis' trees?

Fraser's Magazine.

{Footnote 1: The young princes, afterwards Louis XVIII. and Charles X.}

{Footnote 2: The Tuileries, several times stormed by mobs, was so irreparably injured by the Communists that, in 1882, the Paris Town Council decided that the ruins should be cleared away.}

{Footnote 3: After the Eagle and the Bee superseded the Lily-flowers, the Third Napoleon's initial "N" flourished for two decades, but has been excised or plastered over, the words "National Property" or "Liberty, Equality, Fraternity" being cut in the stone profusely.}

TO ALBERT DÜRER.

("Dans les vieilles forêts.")

{X., April 20, 1837.}
Through ancient forests—where like flowing tide
The rising sap shoots vigor far and wide,
Mounting the column of the alder dark
And silv'ring o'er the birch's shining bark—
Hast thou not often, Albert Dürer, strayed
Pond'ring, awe-stricken—through the half-lit glade,
Pallid and trembling—glancing not behind
From mystic fear that did thy senses bind,
Yet made thee hasten with unsteady pace?
Oh, Master grave! whose musings lone we trace
Throughout thy works we look on reverently.
Amidst the gloomy umbrage thy mind's eye
Saw clearly, 'mong the shadows soft yet deep,
The web-toed faun, and Pan the green-eyed peep,
Who deck'd with flowers the cave where thou might'st rest,
Leaf-laden dryads, too, in verdure drest.
A strange weird world such forest was to thee,
Where mingled truth and dreams in mystery;
There leaned old ruminating pines, and there
The giant elms, whose boughs deformed and bare
A hundred rough and crooked elbows made;
And in this sombre group the wind had swayed,
Nor life—nor death—but life in death seemed found.
The cresses drink—the water flows—and round

Upon the slopes the mountain rowans meet,
And 'neath the brushwood plant their gnarled feet,
Intwining slowly where the creepers twine.
There, too, the lakes as mirrors brightly shine,
And show the swan-necked flowers, each line by line.
Chimeras roused take stranger shapes for thee,
The glittering scales of mailèd throat we see,
And claws tight pressed on huge old knotted tree;
While from a cavern dim the bright eyes glare.
Oh, vegetation! Spirit! Do we dare
Question of matter, and of forces found
'Neath a rude skin-in living verdure bound.
Oh, Master—I, like thee, have wandered oft
Where mighty trees made arches high aloft,
But ever with a consciousness of strife,
A surging struggle of the inner life.
Ever the trembling of the grass I say,
And the boughs rocking as the breezes play,
Have stirred deep thoughts in a bewild'ring way.
Oh, God! alone Great Witness of all deeds,
Of thoughts and acts, and all our human needs,
God only knows how often in such scenes
Of savage beauty under leafy screens,
I've felt the mighty oaks had spirit dower—
Like me knew mirth and sorrow—sentient power,
And whisp'ring each to each in twilight dim,
Had hearts that beat—and owned a soul from Him!

MRS. NEWTON CROSLAND

TO HIS MUSE.

("Puisqu'ici-bas tout âme.")

{XL, May 19, 1836.}

Since everything below,
Doth, in this mortal state,
Its tone, its fragrance, or its glow
Communicate;

Since all that lives and moves
Upon the earth, bestows
On what it seeks and what it loves
Its thorn or rose;

Since April to the trees
Gives a bewitching sound,
And sombre night to grief gives ease,
And peace profound;

Since day-spring on the flower
A fresh'ning drop confers,
And the fresh air on branch and bower
Its choristers;

Since the dark wave bestows
A soft caress, imprest
On the green bank to which it goes

Seeking its rest;

I give thee at this hour,
Thus fondly bent o'er thee,
The best of all the things in dow'r
That in me be.

Receive,-poor gift, 'tis true,
Which grief, not joy, endears,—
My thoughts, that like a shower of dew,
Reach thee in tears.

My vows untold receive,
All pure before thee laid;
Receive of all the days I live
The light or shade!

My hours with rapture fill'd,
Which no suspicion wrongs;
And all the blandishments distill'd
From all my songs.

My spirit, whose essay
Flies fearless, wild, and free,
And hath, and seeks, to guide its way
No star but thee.

No pensive, dreamy Muse,
Who, though all else should smile,
Oft as thou weep'st, with thee would choose,

To weep the while.

Oh, sweetest mine! this gift
Receive;—'tis throe alone;—
My heart, of which there's nothing left
When Love is gone!

Fraser's Magazine.

THE COW.

("Devant la blanche ferme.")

{XV., May, 1837.}
Before the farm where, o'er the porch, festoon
Wild creepers red, and gaffer sits at noon,
Whilst strutting fowl display their varied crests,
And the old watchdog slumberously rests,
They half-attentive to the clarion of their king,
Resplendent in the sunshine op'ning wing—
There stood a cow, with neck-bell jingling light,
Superb, enormous, dappled red and white—
Soft, gentle, patient as a hind unto its young,
Letting the children swarm until they hung
Around her, under—rustics with their teeth
Whiter than marble their ripe lips beneath,

And bushy hair fresh and more brown
Than mossy walls at old gates of a town,
Calling to one another with loud cries
For younger imps to be in at the prize;
Stealing without concern but tremulous with fear
They glance around lest Doll the maid appear;—
Their jolly lips—that haply cause some pain,
And all those busy fingers, pressing now and 'gain,
The teeming udders whose small, thousand pores
Gush out the nectar 'mid their laughing roars,
While she, good mother, gives and gives in heaps,
And never moves. Anon there creeps
A vague soft shiver o'er the hide unmarred,
As sharp they pull, she seems of stone most hard.
Dreamy of large eye, seeks she no release,
And shrinks not while there's one still to appease.
Thus Nature—refuge 'gainst the slings of fate!
Mother of all, indulgent as she's great!
Lets us, the hungered of each age and rank,
Shadow and milk seek in the eternal flank;
Mystic and carnal, foolish, wise, repair,
The souls retiring and those that dare,
Sages with halos, poets laurel-crowned,
All creep beneath or cluster close around,
And with unending greed and joyous cries,
From sources full, draw need's supplies,
Quench hearty thirst, obtain what must eftsoon
Form blood and mind, in freest boon,
Respire at length thy sacred flaming light,
From all that greets our ears, touch, scent or sight—

Brown leaves, blue mountains, yellow gleams, green sod—
Thou undistracted still dost dream of God.

TORU DUTT.

MOTHERS.

("Regardez: les enfants.")

{XX., June, 1884.}
See all the children gathered there,
Their mother near; so young, so fair,
An elder sister she might be,
And yet she hears, amid their games,
The shaking of their unknown names
In the dark urn of destiny.

She wakes their smiles, she soothes their cares,
On that pure heart so like to theirs,
Her spirit with such life is rife
That in its golden rays we see,
Touched into graceful poesy,
The dull cold commonplace of life.

Still following, watching, whether burn
The Christmas log in winter stern,

While merry plays go round;
Or streamlets laugh to breeze of May
That shakes the leaf to break away—
A shadow falling to the ground.

If some poor man with hungry eyes
Her baby's coral bauble spies,
She marks his look with famine wild,
For Christ's dear sake she makes with joy
An alms-gift of the silver toy—
A smiling angel of the child.

Dublin University Magazine

TO SOME BIRDS FLOWN AWAY.

("Enfants! Oh! revenez!")

{XXII, April, 1837}
Children, come back—come back, I say—
You whom my folly chased away
A moment since, from this my room,
With bristling wrath and words of doom!
What had you done, you bandits small,
With lips as red as roses all?
What crime?—what wild and hapless deed?

What porcelain vase by you was split
To thousand pieces? Did you need
For pastime, as you handled it,
Some Gothic missal to enrich
With your designs fantastical?
Or did your tearing fingers fall
On some old picture? Which, oh, which
Your dreadful fault? Not one of these;
Only when left yourselves to please
This morning but a moment here
'Mid papers tinted by my mind
You took some embryo verses near—
Half formed, but fully well designed
To open out. Your hearts desire
Was but to throw them on the fire,
Then watch the tinder, for the sight
Of shining sparks that twinkle bright
As little boats that sail at night,
Or like the window lights that spring
From out the dark at evening.

'Twas all, and you were well content.
Fine loss was this for anger's vent—
A strophe ill made midst your play,
Sweet sound that chased the words away
In stormy flight. An ode quite new,
With rhymes inflated—stanzas, too,
That panted, moving lazily,
And heavy Alexandrine lines
That seemed to jostle bodily,

Like children full of play designs
That spring at once from schoolroom's form.
Instead of all this angry storm,
Another might have thanked you well
For saving prey from that grim cell,
That hollowed den 'neath journals great,
Where editors who poets flout
With their demoniac laughter shout.
And I have scolded you! What fate
For charming dwarfs who never meant
To anger Hercules! And I
Have frightened you!—My chair I sent
Back to the wall, and then let fly
A shower of words the envious use—
"Get out," I said, with hard abuse,
"Leave me alone—alone I say."
Poor man alone! Ah, well-a-day,
What fine result—what triumph rare!
As one turns from the coffin'd dead
So left you me:—I could but stare
Upon the door through which you fled—
I proud and grave—but punished quite.
And what care you for this my plight!—
You have recovered liberty,
Fresh air and lovely scenery,
The spacious park and wished-for grass;
The running stream, where you can throw
A blade to watch what comes to pass;
Blue sky, and all the spring can show;
Nature, serenely fair to see;

The book of birds and spirits free,
God's poem, worth much more than mine,
Where flowers for perfect stanzas shine—
Flowers that a child may pluck in play,
No harsh voice frightening it away.
And I'm alone—all pleasure o'er—
Alone with pedant called "Ennui,"
For since the morning at my door
Ennui has waited patiently.
That docto-r-London born, you mark,
One Sunday in December dark,
Poor little ones—he loved you not,
And waited till the chance he got
To enter as you passed away,
And in the very corner where
You played with frolic laughter gay,
He sighs and yawns with weary air.

What can I do? Shall I read books,
Or write more verse—or turn fond looks
Upon enamels blue, sea-green,
And white—on insects rare as seen
Upon my Dresden china ware?
Or shall I touch the globe, and care
To make the heavens turn upon
Its axis? No, not one—not one
Of all these things care I to do;
All wearies me—I think of you.
In truth with you my sunshine fled,
And gayety with your light tread—

Glad noise that set me dreaming still.
'Twas my delight to watch your will,
And mark you point with finger-tips
To help your spelling out a word;
To see the pearls between your lips
When I your joyous laughter heard;
Your honest brows that looked so true,
And said "Oh, yes!" to each intent;
Your great bright eyes, that loved to view
With admiration innocent
My fine old Sèvres; the eager thought
That every kind of knowledge sought;
The elbow push with "Come and see!"

Oh, certes! spirits, sylphs, there be,
And fays the wind blows often here;
The gnomes that squat the ceiling near,
In corners made by old books dim;
The long-backed dwarfs, those goblins grim
That seem at home 'mong vases rare,
And chat to them with friendly air—
Oh, how the joyous demon throng
Must all have laughed with laughter long
To see you on my rough drafts fall,
My bald hexameters, and all
The mournful, miserable band,
And drag them with relentless hand
From out their box, with true delight
To set them each and all a-light,
And then with clapping hands to lean

Above the stove and watch the scene,
How to the mass deformed there came
A soul that showed itself in flame!

Bright tricksy children—oh, I pray
Come back and sing and dance away,
And chatter too—sometimes you may,
A giddy group, a big book seize—
Or sometimes, if it so you please,
With nimble step you'll run to me
And push the arm that holds the pen,
Till on my finished verse will be
A stroke that's like a steeple when
Seen suddenly upon a plain.
My soul longs for your breath again
To warm it. Oh, return—come here
With laugh and babble—and no fear
When with your shadow you obscure
The book I read, for I am sure,
Oh, madcaps terrible and dear,
That you were right and I was wrong.
But who has ne'er with scolding tongue
Blamed out of season. Pardon me!
You must forgive—for sad are we.

The young should not be hard and cold
And unforgiving to the old.
Children each morn your souls ope out
Like windows to the shining day,
Oh, miracle that comes about,

The miracle that children gay
Have happiness and goodness too,
Caressed by destiny are you,
Charming you are, if you but play.
But we with living overwrought,
And full of grave and sombre thought,
Are snappish oft: dear little men,
We have ill-tempered days, and then,
Are quite unjust and full of care;
It rained this morning and the air
Was chill; but clouds that dimm'd the sky
Have passed. Things spited me, and why?
But now my heart repents. Behold
What 'twas that made me cross, and scold!
All by-and-by you'll understand,
When brows are mark'd by Time's stern hand;
Then you will comprehend, be sure,
When older—that's to say, less pure.

The fault I freely own was mine.
But oh, for pardon now I pine!
Enough my punishment to meet,
You must forgive, I do entreat
With clasped hands praying—oh, come back,
Make peace, and you shall nothing lack.
See now my pencils—paper—here,
And pointless compasses, and dear
Old lacquer-work; and stoneware clear
Through glass protecting; all man's toys
So coveted by girls and boys.

Great China monsters—bodies much
Like cucumbers—you all shall touch.
I yield up all! my picture rare
Found beneath antique rubbish heap,
My great and tapestried oak chair
I will from you no longer keep.
You shall about my table climb,
And dance, or drag, without a cry
From me as if it were a crime.
Even I'll look on patiently
If you your jagged toys all throw
Upon my carved bench, till it show
The wood is torn; and freely too,
I'll leave in your own hands to view,
My pictured Bible—oft desired—
But which to touch your fear inspired—
With God in emperor's robes attired.

Then if to see my verses burn,
Should seem to you a pleasant turn,
Take them to freely tear away
Or burn. But, oh! not so I'd say,
If this were Méry's room to-day.
That noble poet! Happy town,
Marseilles the Greek, that him doth own!
Daughter of Homer, fair to see,
Of Virgil's son the mother she.
To you I'd say, Hold, children all,
Let but your eyes on his work fall;
These papers are the sacred nest

In which his crooning fancies rest;
To-morrow winged to Heaven they'll soar,
For new-born verse imprisoned still
In manuscript may suffer sore
At your small hands and childish will,
Without a thought of bad intent,
Of cruelty quite innocent.
You wound their feet, and bruise their wings,
And make them suffer those ill things
That children's play to young birds brings.

But mine! no matter what you do,
My poetry is all in you;
You are my inspiration bright
That gives my verse its purest light.
Children whose life is made of hope,
Whose joy, within its mystic scope,
Owes all to ignorance of ill,
You have not suffered, and you still
Know not what gloomy thoughts weigh down
The poet-writer weary grown.
What warmth is shed by your sweet smile!
How much he needs to gaze awhile
Upon your shining placid brow,
When his own brow its ache doth know;
With what delight he loves to hear
Your frolic play 'neath tree that's near,
Your joyous voices mixing well
With his own song's all-mournful swell!
Come back then, children! come to me,

If you wish not that I should be
As lonely now that you're afar
As fisherman of Etrétat,
Who listless on his elbow leans
Through all the weary winter scenes,
As tired of thought—as on Time flies—
And watching only rainy skies!

MRS. NEWTON CROSLAND.

MY THOUGHTS OF YE.

("À quoi je songe?")

{XXIII., July, 1836.}
What do I dream of? Far from the low roof,
Where now ye are, children, I dream of you;
Of your young heads that are the hope and crown
Of my full summer, ripening to its fall.
Branches whose shadow grows along my wall,
Sweet souls scarce open to the breath of day,
Still dazzled with the brightness of your dawn.
I dream of those two little ones at play,
Making the threshold vocal with their cries,
Half tears, half laughter, mingled sport and strife,
Like two flowers knocked together by the wind.

Or of the elder two—more anxious thought—
Breasting already broader waves of life,
A conscious innocence on either face,
My pensive daughter and my curious boy.
Thus do I dream, while the light sailors sing,
At even moored beneath some steepy shore,
While the waves opening all their nostrils breathe
A thousand sea-scents to the wandering wind,
And the whole air is full of wondrous sounds,
From sea to strand, from land to sea, given back
Alone and sad, thus do I dream of you.
Children, and house and home, the table set,
The glowing hearth, and all the pious care
Of tender mother, and of grandsire kind;
And while before me, spotted with white sails,
The limpid ocean mirrors all the stars,
And while the pilot, from the infinite main,
Looks with calm eye into the infinite heaven,
I dreaming of you only, seek to scan
And fathom all my soul's deep love for you—
Love sweet, and powerful, and everlasting—
And find that the great sea is small beside it.

Dublin University Magazine.

THE BEACON IN THE STORM.

("Quels sont ces bruits sourds?")

{XXIV., July 17, 1836.}
Hark to that solemn sound!
It steals towards the strand.—
Whose is that voice profound
Which mourns the swallowed land,
  With moans,
  Or groans,
New threats of ruin close at hand?
It is Triton—the storm to scorn
Who doth wind his sonorous horn.

How thick the rain to-night!
And all along the coast
The sky shows naught of light
Is it a storm, my host?
  Too soon
  The boon
Of pleasant weather will be lost
Yes, 'tis Triton, etc.

Are seamen on that speck
Afar in deepening dark?
Is that a splitting deck
Of some ill-fated bark?
  Fend harm!

Send calm!
O Venus! show thy starry spark!
Though 'tis Triton, etc.

The thousand-toothèd gale,—
Adventurers too bold!—
Rips up your toughest sail
And tears your anchor-hold.
  You forge
  Through surge,
To be in rending breakers rolled.
While old Triton, etc.

Do sailors stare this way,
Cramped on the Needle's sheaf,
To hail the sudden ray
Which promises relief?
  Then, bright;
  Shine, light!
Of hope upon the beacon reef!
Though 'tis Triton, etc.

LOVE'S TREACHEROUS POOL

("Jeune fille, l'amour c'est un miroir.")

{XXVI., February, 1835.}
Young maiden, true love is a pool all mirroring clear,
Where coquettish girls come to linger in long delight,
For it banishes afar from the face all the clouds that besmear
The soul truly bright;
But tempts you to ruffle its surface; drawing your foot
To subtilest sinking! and farther and farther the brink
That vainly you snatch—for repentance, 'tis weed without root,—
And struggling, you sink!

THE ROSE AND THE GRAVE.

("La tombe dit à la rose.")

{XXXI., June 3, 1837}
The Grave said to the rose
"What of the dews of dawn,
Love's flower, what end is theirs?"
"And what of spirits flown,
The souls whereon doth close
The tomb's mouth unawares?"
The Rose said to the Grave.

The Rose said: "In the shade

From the dawn's tears is made
A perfume faint and strange,
Amber and honey sweet."
"And all the spirits fleet
Do suffer a sky-change,
More strangely than the dew,
To God's own angels new,"
The Grave said to the Rose.

A. LANG.

LES RAYONS ET LES OMBRES.—1840.

HOLYROOD PALACE.

("O palais, sois bénié.")

{II., June, 1839.}
Palace and ruin, bless thee evermore!
Grateful we bow thy gloomy tow'rs before;
For the old King of France{1} hath found in thee
That melancholy hospitality
Which in their royal fortune's evil day,
Stuarts and Bourbons to each other pay.

Fraser's Magazine.

{Footnote 1: King Charles X.}

THE HUMBLE HOME.

("L'église est vaste et haute.")

{IV., June 29, 1839.}

The Church{1} is vast; its towering pride, its steeples loom on high;
The bristling stones with leaf and flower are sculptured wondrously;
 The portal glows resplendent with its "rose,"
 And 'neath the vault immense at evening swarm
 Figures of angel, saint, or demon's form,
  As oft a fearful world our dreams disclose.
But not the huge Cathedral's height, nor yet its vault sublime,
Nor porch, nor glass, nor streaks of light, nor shadows deep with time;
 Nor massy towers, that fascinate mine eyes;
 No, 'tis that spot—the mind's tranquillity—
 Chamber wherefrom the song mounts cheerily,
  Placed like a joyful nest well nigh the skies.

Yea! glorious is the Church, I ween, but Meekness dwelleth here;
Less do I love the lofty oak than mossy nest it bear;
 More dear is meadow breath than stormy wind:
 And when my mind for meditation's meant,
 The seaweed is preferred to the shore's extent,—
  The swallow to the main it leaves behind.

Author of "Critical Essays."
{Footnote 1: The Cathedral Nôtre Dame of Paris, which is the scene of the author's romance, "Nôtre Dame."}

THE EIGHTEENTH CENTURY.

("O dix-huitième siècle!")

{IV. vi}
O Eighteenth Century! by Heaven chastised!
Godless thou livedst, by God thy doom was fixed.
Thou in one ruin sword and sceptre mixed,
Then outraged love, and pity's claim despised.
Thy life a banquet—but its board a scaffold at the close,
Where far from Christ's beatic reign, Satanic deeds arose!
Thy writers, like thyself, by good men scorned—
Yet, from thy crimes, renown has decked thy name,
As the smoke emplumes the furnace flame,
A revolution's deeds have thine adorned!

Author of "Critical Essays."

STILL BE A CHILD.

("O vous que votre âge défende")

{IX., February, 1840.}
In youthful spirits wild,
Smile, for all beams on thee;
Sport, sing, be still the child,
The flower, the honey-bee.

Bring not the future near,
For Joy too soon declines—
What is man's mission here?
Toil, where no sunlight shines!

Our lot is hard, we know;
From eyes so gayly beaming,
Whence rays of beauty flow,
Salt tears most oft are streaming.

Free from emotions past,
All joy and hope possessing,
With mind in pureness cast,
Sweet ignorance confessing.

Plant, safe from winds and showers,
Heart with soft visions glowing,
In childhood's happy hours
A mother's rapture showing.

Loved by each anxious friend,
No carking care within—
When summer gambols end,
My winter sports begin.

Sweet poesy from heaven
Around thy form is placed,
A mother's beauty given,
By father's thought is graced!

Seize, then, each blissful second,
Live, for joy *sinks in night*,
And those whose tale is reckoned,
Have had their days of light.

Then, oh! before we part,
The poet's blessing take,
Ere bleeds that aged heart,
Or child the woman make.

Dublin University Magazine.

THE POOL AND THE SOUL.

("Comme dans les étangs.")

{X., May, 1839.}
As in some stagnant pool by forest-side,
In human souls two things are oft descried;
The sky,—which tints the surface of the pool
With all its rays, and all its shadows cool;
The basin next,—where gloomy, dark and deep,
Through slime and mud black reptiles vaguely creep.

R.F. HODGSON

YE MARINERS WHO SPREAD YOUR SAILS.

("Matelôts, vous déploirez les voiles.")

{XVI., May 5, 1839.}
Ye mariners! ye mariners! each sail to the breeze unfurled,
In joy or sorrow still pursue your course around the world;
And when the stars next sunset shine, ye anxiously will gaze
Upon the shore, a friend or foe, as the windy quarter lays.

Ye envious souls, with spiteful tooth, the statue's base will bite;
Ye birds will sing, ye bending boughs with verdure glad the sight;
The ivy root in the stone entwined, will cause old gates to fall;
The church-bell sound to work or rest the villagers will call.

Ye glorious oaks will still increase in solitude profound,
Where the far west in distance lies as evening veils around;
Ye willows, to the earth your arms in mournful trail will bend,
And back again your mirror'd forms the water's surface send.

Ye nests will oscillate beneath the youthful progeny;
Embraced in furrows of the earth the germing grain will lie;
Ye lightning-torches still your streams will cast into the air,
Which like a troubled spirit's course float wildly here and there.

Ye thunder-peals will God proclaim, as doth the ocean wave;
Ye violets will nourish still the flower that April gave;
Upon your ambient tides will be man's sternest shadow cast;
Your waters ever will roll on when man himself is past.

All things that are, or being have, or those that mutely lie,
Have each its course to follow out, or object to descry;
Contributing its little share to that stupendous whole,
Where with man's teeming race combined creation's wonders roll.

The poet, too, will contemplate th' Almighty Father's love,
Who to our restless minds, with light and darkness from above,
Hath given the heavens that glorious urn of tranquil majesty,
Whence in unceasing stores we draw calm and serenity.

Author of "Critical Essays."

ON A FLEMISH WINDOW-PANE.

("J'aime le carillon dans tes cités antiques.")

{XVIII., August, 1837.}
Within thy cities of the olden time
Dearly I love to list the ringing chime,
Thou faithful guardian of domestic worth,
Noble old Flanders! where the rigid North
A flush of rich meridian glow doth feel,
Caught from reflected suns of bright Castile.
The chime, the clinking chime! To Fancy's eye—
Prompt her affections to personify—
It is the fresh and frolic hour, arrayed
In guise of Andalusian dancing maid,
Appealing by a crevice fine and rare,
As of a door oped in "th' incorporal air."
She comes! o'er drowsy roofs, inert and dull,

Shaking her lap, of silv'ry music full,
Rousing without remorse the drones abed,
Tripping like joyous bird with tiniest tread,
Quiv'ring like dart that trembles in the targe,
By a frail crystal stair, whose viewless marge
Bears her slight footfall, tim'rous half, yet free,
In innocent extravagance of glee
The graceful elf alights from out the spheres,
While the quick spirit—thing of eyes and ears—
As now she goes, now comes, mounts, and anon
Descends, those delicate degrees upon,
Hears her melodious spirit from step to step run on.

Fraser's Magazine

THE PRECEPTOR.

("Homme chauve et noir.")

{XIX., May, 1839.}
A gruesome man, bald, clad in black,
Who kept us youthful drudges in the track,
Thinking it good for them to leave home care,
And for a while a harsher yoke to bear;
Surrender all the careless ease of home,
And be forbid from schoolyard bounds to roam;

For this with blandest smiles he softly asks
That they with him will prosecute their tasks;
Receives them in his solemn chilly lair,
The rigid lot of discipline to share.
At dingy desks they toil by day; at night
To gloomy chambers go uncheered by light,
Where pillars rudely grayed by rusty nail
Of heavy hours reveal the weary tale;
Where spiteful ushers grin, all pleased to make
Long scribbled lines the price of each mistake.
By four unpitying walls environed there
The homesick students pace the pavements bare.

E.E. FREWER

GASTIBELZA.

("Gastibelza, l'homme à la carabine.")

{XXII., March, 1837.}
Gastibelza, with gun the measure beating,
   Would often sing:
"Has one o' ye with sweet Sabine been meeting,
   As, gay, ye bring
Your songs and steps which, by the music,
   Are reconciled—

Oh! this chill wind across the mountain rushing
  Will drive me wild!

"You stare as though you hardly knew my lady—
  Sabine's her name!
Her dam inhabits yonder cavern shady,
  A witch of shame,
Who shrieks o' nights upon the Haunted Tower,
  With horrors piled—
Oh! this chill wind, etc.

"Sing on and leap—enjoying all the favors
  Good heaven sends;
She, too, was young—her lips had peachy savors
  With honey blends;
Give to that hag—not always old—a penny,
  Though crime-defiled—
Oh! this chill wind, etc.

"The queen beside her looked a wench uncomely,
  When, near to-night,
She proudly stalked a-past the maids so homely,
  In bodice tight
And collar old as reign of wicked Julian,
  By fiend beguiled—
Oh! this chill wind, etc.

"The king himself proclaimed her peerless beauty
  Before the court,
And held it were to win a kiss his duty

To give a fort,
Or, more, to sign away all bright Dorado,
   Tho' gold-plate tiled—
Oh! this chill wind, etc.

"Love her? at least, I know I am most lonely
   Without her nigh;
I'm but a hound to follow her, and only
   At her feet die.
I'd gayly spend of toilsome years a dozen—
   A felon styled—
Oh! this chill wind, etc.

"One summer day when long—so long? I'd missed her,
   She came anew,
To play i' the fount alone but for her sister,
   And bared to view
The finest, rosiest, most tempting ankle,
   Like that of child—
Oh! this chill wind, etc.

"When I beheld her, I—a lowly shepherd—
   Grew in my mind
Till I was Caesar—she that crownèd leopard
   He crouched behind,
No Roman stern, but in her silken leashes
   A captive mild—
Oh! this chill wind, etc.

"Yet dance and sing, tho' night be thickly falling;—

In selfsame time
Poor Sabine heard in ecstasy the calling,
  In winning rhyme,
Of Saldane's earl so noble, ay, and wealthy,
  Name e'er reviled—
Oh! this chill wind, etc.

"(Let me upon this bench be shortly resting,
  So weary, I!)
That noble bore her smiling, unresisting,
  By yonder high
And ragged road that snakes towards the summit
  Where crags are piled—
Oh! this chill wind, etc.

"I saw her pass beside my lofty station—
  A glance—'twas all!
And yet I loathe my daily honest ration,
  The air's turned gall!
My soul's in chase, my body chafes to wander—
  My dagger's filed—
Oh! this chill wind may change, and o'er the mountain
  May drive me wild!"

HENRY L. WILLIAMS.

GUITAR SONG.

("Comment, disaient-ils.")

{XXIII., July 18, 1838.}
How shall we flee sorrow—flee sorrow? said he.
How, how! How shall we flee sorrow—flee sorrow? said he.
How—how—how? answered she.

How shall we see pleasure—see pleasure? said he.
How, how! How shall we see pleasure—see pleasure? said he.
Dream—dream—dream! answered she.

How shall we be happy—be happy? said he.
How, how! How shall we be happy—be happy? said he.
Love—love—love! whispered she.

EVELYN JERROLD

COME WHEN I SLEEP.

("Oh, quand je dors.")

{XXVII.}
Oh! when I sleep, come near my resting-place,
As Laura came to bless her poet's heart,
And let thy breath in passing touch my face—
  At once a space
  My lips will part.

And on my brow where too long weighed supreme
A vision—haply spent now—black as night,
Let thy look as a star arise and beam—
  At once my dream
  Will seem of light.

Then press my lips, where plays a flame of bliss—
A pure and holy love-light—and forsake
The angel for the woman in a kiss—
  At once, I wis,
  My soul will wake!

WM. W. TOMLINSON.

EARLY LOVE REVISITED.

("O douleur! j'ai voulu savoir.")

{XXXIV. i., October, 183-.}
I have wished in the grief of my heart to know
If the vase yet treasured that nectar so clear,
And to see what this beautiful valley could show
Of all that was once to my soul most dear.
In how short a span doth all Nature change,
How quickly she smoothes with her hand serene—
And how rarely she snaps, in her ceaseless range,
The links that bound our hearts to the scene.

Our beautiful bowers are all laid waste;
The fir is felled that our names once bore;
Our rows of roses, by urchins' haste,
Are destroyed where they leap the barrier o'er.
The fount is walled in where, at noonday pride,
She so gayly drank, from the wood descending;
In her fairy hand was transformed the tide,
And it turned to pearls through her fingers wending

The wild, rugged path is paved with spars,
Where erst in the sand her footsteps were traced,
When so small were the prints that the surface mars,
That they seemed *to smile* ere by mine effaced.
The bank on the side of the road, day by day,
Where of old she awaited my loved approach,

Is now become the traveller's way
To avoid the track of the thundering coach.

Here the forest contracts, there the mead extends,
Of all that was ours, there is little left—
Like the ashes that wildly are whisked by winds,
Of all souvenirs is the place bereft.
Do we live no more—is our hour then gone?
Will it give back naught to our hungry cry?
The breeze answers my call with a mocking tone,
The house that was mine makes no reply.

True! others shall pass, as we have passed,
As we have come, so others shall meet,
And the dream that our mind had sketched in haste,
Shall others continue, but never complete.
For none upon earth can achieve his scheme,
The best as the worst are futile here:
We awake at the selfsame point cf the dream—
All is here begun, and finished elsewhere.

Yes! others shall come in the bloom of the heart,
To enjoy in this pure and happy retreat,
All that nature to timid love can impart
Of solemn repose and communion sweet.
In *our* fields, in *our* paths, shall strangers stray,
In *thy* wood, my dearest, new lovers go lost,
And other fair forms in the stream shall play
Which of old thy delicate feet have crossed.

Author of "Critical Essays."

SWEET MEMORY OF LOVE.
———————————

("Toutes les passions s'éloignent avec l'âge.")

{XXXIV. ii., October, 183-.}
As life wanes on, the passions slow depart,
One with his grinning mask, one with his steel;
Like to a strolling troupe of Thespian art,
Whose pace decreases, winding past the hill.
But naught can Love's all charming power efface,
That light, our misty tracks suspended o'er,
In joy thou'rt ours, more dear thy tearful grace,
The young may curse thee, but the old adore.

But when the weight of years bow down the head,
And man feels all his energies decline,
His projects gone, himself tomb'd with the dead,
Where virtues lie, nor more illusions shine,
When all our lofty thoughts dispersed and o'er,
We count within our hearts so near congealed,
Each grief that's past, each dream, exhausted ore!
As counting dead upon the battle-field.

As one who walks by the lamp's flickering blaze,

Far from the hum of men, the joys of earth—
Our mind arrives at last by tortuous ways,
At that drear gulf where but despair has birth.
E'en there, amid the darkness of that night,
When all seems closing round in empty air,
Is seen through thickening gloom one trembling light!
'Tis Love's sweet memory that lingers there!

Author of "Critical Essays."

THE MARBLE FAUN.

("Il semblait grelotter.")

{XXXVI., December, 1837.}
He seemed to shiver, for the wind was keen.
'Twas a poor statue underneath a mass
Of leafless branches, with a blackened back
And a green foot—an isolated Faun
In old deserted park, who, bending forward,
Half-merged himself in the entangled boughs,
Half in his marble settings. He was there,
Pensive, and bound to earth; and, as all things
Devoid of movement, he was there—forgotten.

Trees were around him, whipped by icy blasts—

Gigantic chestnuts, without leaf or bird,
And, like himself, grown old in that same place.
Through the dark network of their undergrowth,
Pallid his aspect; and the earth was brown.
Starless and moonless, a rough winter's night
Was letting down her lappets o'er the mist.
This—nothing more: old Faun, dull sky, dark wood.

Poor, helpless marble, how I've pitied it!
Less often man—the harder of the two.

So, then, without a word that might offend
His ear deformed—for well the marble hears
The voice of thought—I said to him: "You hail
From the gay amorous age. O Faun, what saw you
When you were happy? Were you of the Court?

"Speak to me, comely Faun, as you would speak
To tree, or zephyr, or untrodden grass.
Have you, O Greek, O mocker of old days,
Have you not sometimes with that oblique eye
Winked at the Farnese Hercules?—Alone,
Have you, O Faun, considerately turned
From side to side when counsel-seekers came,
And now advised as shepherd, now as satyr?—
Have you sometimes, upon this very bench,
Seen, at mid-day, Vincent de Paul instilling
Grace into Gondi?—Have you ever thrown
That searching glance on Louis with Fontange,
On Anne with Buckingham; and did they not

Start, with flushed cheeks, to hear your laugh ring forth
From corner of the wood?—Was your advice
As to the thyrsis or the ivy asked,
When, in grand ballet of fantastic form,
God Phoebus, or God Pan, and all his court,
Turned the fair head of the proud Montespan,
Calling her Amaryllis?—La Fontaine,
Flying the courtiers' ears of stone, came he,
Tears on his eyelids, to reveal to you
The sorrows of his nymphs of Vaux?—What said
Boileau to you—to you—O lettered Faun,
Who once with Virgil, in the Eclogue, held
That charming dialogue?—Say, have you seen
Young beauties sporting on the sward?—Have you
Been honored with a sight of Molière
In dreamy mood?—Has he perchance, at eve,
When here the thinker homeward went, has he,
Who—seeing souls all naked—could not fear
Your nudity, in his inquiring mind,
Confronted you with Man?"

Under the thickly-tangled branches, thus
Did I speak to him; he no answer gave.

I shook my head, and moved myself away;
Then, from the copses, and from secret caves
Hid in the wood, methought a ghostly voice
Came forth and woke an echo in my souls
As in the hollow of an amphora.

"Imprudent poet," thus it seemed to say,
"What dost thou here? Leave the forsaken Fauns
In peace beneath their trees! Dost thou not know,
Poet, that ever it is impious deemed,
In desert spots where drowsy shades repose—
Though love itself might prompt thee—to shake down
The moss that hangs from ruined centuries,
And, with the vain noise of throe ill-timed words,
To mar the recollections of the dead?"

Then to the gardens all enwrapped in mist
I hurried, dreaming of the vanished days,
And still behind me—hieroglyph obscure
Of antique alphabet—the lonely Faun
Held to his laughter, through the falling night.

I went my way; but yet—in saddened spirit
Pondering on all that had my vision crossed,
Leaves of old summers, fair ones of old time—
Through all, at distance, would my fancy see,
In the woods, statues; shadows in the past!

WILLIAM YOUNG
A LOVE FOR WINGED THINGS.

{XXXVII., April 12, 1840.}
My love flowed e'er for things with wings.
When boy I sought for forest fowl,
And caged them in rude rushes' mesh,
And fed them with my breakfast roll;

So that, though fragile were the door,
They rarely fled, and even then
Would flutter back at faintest call!

Man-grown, I charm for men.

BABY'S SEASIDE GRAVE.

("Vieux lierre, frais gazon.")

{XXXVIII., 1840.}
Brown ivy old, green herbage new;
Soft seaweed stealing up the shingle;
An ancient chapel where a crew,
Ere sailing, in the prayer commingle.
A far-off forest's darkling frown,
Which makes the prudent start and tremble,
Whilst rotten nuts are rattling down,
And clouds in demon hordes assemble.

Land birds which twit the mews that scream
Round walls where lolls the languid lizard;
Brine-bubbling brooks where fishes stream
Past caves fit for an ocean wizard.
Alow, aloft, no lull—all life,
But far aside its whirls are keeping,

As wishfully to let its strife
Spare still the mother vainly weeping
O'er baby, lost not long, a-sleeping.

LES CHÂTIMENTS.—1853.

INDIGNATION!

("Toi qu'aimais Juvénal.")

{Nox (PRELUDE) ix., Jersey, November, 1852.}
Thou who loved Juvenal, and filed
His style so sharp to scar imperial brows,
And lent the lustre lightening
The gloom in Dante's murky verse that flows—
Muse Indignation! haste, and help
My building up before this roseate realm,
And its so fruitless victories,
Whence transient shame Right's prophets overwhelm,
So many pillories, deserved!
That eyes to come will pry without avail,
Upon the wood impenetrant,
And spy no glimmer of its tarnished tale.

IMPERIAL REVELS.

("Courtisans! attablés dans le splendide orgie.")

{Bk. I. x., Jersey, December, 1852.}
Cheer, courtiers! round the banquet spread—
The board that groans with shame and plate,
Still fawning to the sham-crowned head
That hopes front brazen turneth fate!
Drink till the comer last is full,
And never hear in revels' lull,
Grim Vengeance forging arrows fleet,
  Whilst I gnaw at the crust
  Of Exile in the dust—
But *Honor* makes it sweet!

Ye cheaters in the tricksters' fane,
Who dupe yourself and trickster-chief,
In blazing *cafés* spend the gain,
But draw the blind, lest at *his* thief
Some fresh-made beggar gives a glance
And interrupts with steel the dance!
But let him toilsomely tramp by,
  As I myself afar
  Follow no gilded car
In ways of *Honesty*.

Ye troopers who shot mothers down,
And marshals whose brave cannonade

Broke infant arms and split the stone
Where slumbered age and guileless maid—
Though blood is in the cup you fill,
Pretend it "rosy" wine, and still
Hail Cannon "King!" and Steel the "Queen!"
 But I prefer to sup
 From Philip Sidney's cup—
True soldier's draught serene.

Oh, workmen, seen by me sublime,
When from the tyrant wrenched ye peace,
Can you be dazed by tinselled crime,
And spy no wolf beneath the fleece?
Build palaces where Fortunes feast,
And bear your loads like well-trained beast,
Though once such masters you made flee!
 But then, like me, you ate
 Food of a blessed *fête*—
The bread of *Liberty*!

H.L.W.

POOR LITTLE CHILDREN.

("La femelle! elle est morte.")

{Bk. I. xiii., Jersey, February, 1853.}
Mother birdie stiff and cold,
Puss has hushed the other's singing;
Winds go whistling o'er the wold,—
Empty nest in sport a-flinging.
 Poor little birdies!

Faithless shepherd strayed afar,
Playful dog the gadflies catching;
Wolves bound boldly o'er the bar,
Not a friend the fold is watching—
 Poor little lambkins!

Father into prison fell,
Mother begging through the parish;
Baby's cot they, too, will sell,—
Who will now feed, clothe and cherish?
 Poor little children!

APOSTROPHE TO NATURE.

("O Soleil!")

{Bk. II. iv., Anniversary of the Coup d'État, 1852.}
O Sun! thou countenance divine!
Wild flowers of the glen,
Caves swoll'n with shadow, where sunshine
Has pierced not, far from men;
Ye sacred hills and antique rocks,
Ye oaks that worsted time,
Ye limpid lakes which snow-slide shocks
Hurl up in storms sublime;
And sky above, unruflfed blue,
Chaste rills that alway ran
From stainless source a course still true,
What think ye of this man?

NAPOLEON "THE LITTLE."

("Ah! tu finiras bien par hurler!")

{Bk. III. ii., Jersey, August, 1852.}
How well I knew this stealthy wolf would howl,
When in the eagle talons ta'en in air!

Aglow, I snatched thee from thy prey—thou fowl—
I held thee, abject conqueror, just where
All see the stigma of a fitting name
As deeply red as deeply black thy shame!
And though thy matchless impudence may frame
Some mask of seeming courage—spite thy sneer,
And thou assurest sloth and skunk: "It does not smart!"
Thou feel'st it burning, in and in,—and fear
None will forget it till shall fall the deadly dart!

FACT OR FABLE?

(BISMARCK AND NAPOLEON III.)

("Un jour, sentant un royal appétit.")

{Bk. III. iii., Jersey, September, 1852.}
One fasting day, itched by his appetite,
A monkey took a fallen tiger's hide,
And, where the wearer had been savage, tried
To overpass his model. Scratch and bite
Gave place, however, to mere gnash of teeth and screams,
But, as he prowled, he made his hearers fly
With crying often: "See the Terror of your dreams!"
Till, for too long, none ventured thither nigh.
Left undisturbed to snatch, and clog his brambled den,

With sleepers' bones and plumes of daunted doves,
And other spoil of beasts as timid as the men,
Who shrank when he mock-roared, from glens and groves—
He begged his fellows view the crannies crammed with pelf
Sordid and tawdry, stained and tinselled things,
As ample proof he was the Royal Tiger's self!
Year in, year out, thus still he purrs and sings
Till tramps a butcher by—he risks his head—
In darts the hand and crushes out the yell,
And plucks the hide—as from a nut the shell—
He holds him nude, and sneers: "An ape you dread!"

H.L.W.
A LAMENT.

("Sentiers où l'herbe se balance.")

{Bk. III. xi., July, 1853.}
O paths whereon wild grasses wave!
O valleys! hillsides! forests hoar!
Why are ye silent as the grave?
For One, who came, and comes no more!

Why is thy window closed of late?
And why thy garden in its sear?
O house! where doth thy master wait?
I only know he is not here.

Good dog! thou watchest; yet no hand
Will feed thee. In the house is none.

Whom weepest thou? child! My father. And
O wife! whom weepest thou? The Gone.

Where is he gone? Into the dark.—
O sad, and ever-plaining surge!
Whence art thou? From the convict-bark.
And why thy mournful voice? A dirge.

EDWIN ARNOLD, C.S.I.

NO ASSASSINATION.

("Laissons le glaive à Rome.")

{Bk. III. xvi., October, 1852.}
Pray Rome put up her poniard!
And Sparta sheathe the sword;
Be none too prompt to punish,
And cast indignant word!
Bear back your spectral Brutus
From robber Bonaparte;
Time rarely will refute us
Who doom the hateful heart.

Ye shall be o'ercontented,
My banished mates from home,

But be no rashness vented
Ere time for joy shall come.
No crime can outspeed Justice,
Who, resting, seems delayed—
Full faith accord the angel
Who points the patient blade.

The traitor still may nestle
In balmy bed of state,
But mark the Warder, watching
His guardsman at his gate.
He wears the crown, a monarch—
Of knaves and stony hearts;
But though they're blessed by Senates,
None can escape the darts!

Though shored by spear and crozier,
All know the arrant cheat,
And shun the square of pavement
Uncertain at his feet!
Yea, spare the wretch, each brooding
And secret-leaguers' chief,
And make no pistol-target
Of stars upon the thief.

The knell of God strikes seldom
But in the aptest hour;
And when the life is sweetest,
The worm will feel His power!

THE DESPATCH OF THE DOOM.

("Pendant que dans l'auberge.")

{Bk. IV. xiii., Jersey, November, 1852.}
While in the jolly tavern, the bandits gayly drink,
Upon the haunted highway, sharp hoof-beats loudly clink?
Yea; past scant-buried victims, hard-spurring sturdy steed,
A mute and grisly rider is trampling grass and weed,
And by the black-sealed warrant which in his grasp shines clear,
I known it is *the Future*—God's Justicer is here!

THE SEAMAN'S SONG.

("Adieu, patrie.")

{Bk. V. ix., Aug. 1, 1852.}
  Farewell the strand,
  The sails expand
    Above!
  Farewell the land
    We love!
Farewell, old home where apples swing!
Farewell, gay song-birds on the wing!

Farewell, riff-raff
Of Customs' clerks who laugh
  And shout:
"Farewell!" We'll quaff
  One bout
To thee, young lass, with kisses sweet!
Farewell, my dear—the ship flies fleet!

The fog shuts out the last fond peep,
As 'neath the prow the cast drops weep.
Farewell, old home, young lass, the bird!
The whistling wind alone is heard:
  Farewell! Farewell!

THE RETREAT FROM MOSCOW.

("Il neigeait.")

{Bk. V. xiii., Nov. 25-30, 1852.}
It snowed. A defeat was our conquest red!
For once the eagle was hanging its head.
Sad days! the Emperor turned slowly his back
On smoking Moscow, blent orange and black.
The winter burst, avalanche-like, to reign
Over the endless blanched sheet of the plain.
Nor chief nor banner in order could keep,

The wolves of warfare were 'wildered like sheep.
The wings from centre could hardly be known
Through snow o'er horses and carts o'erthrown,
Where froze the wounded. In the bivouacs forlorn
Strange sights and gruesome met the breaking morn:
Mute were the bugles, while the men bestrode
Steeds turned to marble, unheeding the goad.
The shells and bullets came down with the snow
As though the heavens hated these poor troops below.
Surprised at trembling, though it was with cold,
Who ne'er had trembled out of fear, the veterans bold
Marched stern; to grizzled moustache hoarfrost clung
'Neath banners that in leaden masses hung.

It snowed, went snowing still. And chill the breeze
Whistled upon the glassy endless seas,
Where naked feet on, on for ever went,
With naught to eat, and not a sheltering tent.
They were not living troops as seen in war,
But merely phantoms of a dream, afar
In darkness wandering, amid the vapor dim,—
A mystery; of shadows a procession grim,
Nearing a blackening sky, unto its rim.
Frightful, since boundless, solitude behold
Where only Nemesis wove, mute and cold,
A net all snowy with its soft meshes dense,
A shroud of magnitude for host immense;
Till every one felt as if left alone
In a wide wilderness where no light shone,
To die, with pity none, and none to see

That from this mournful realm none should get free.
Their foes the frozen North and Czar—That, worst.
Cannon were broken up in haste accurst
To burn the frames and make the pale fire high,
Where those lay down who never woke or woke to die.
Sad and commingled, groups that blindly fled
Were swallowed smoothly by the desert dread.

'Neath folds of blankness, monuments were raised
O'er regiments. And History, amazed,
Could not record the ruin of this retreat,
Unlike a downfall known before or the defeat
Of Hannibal—reversed and wrapped in gloom!
Of Attila, when nations met their doom!
Perished an army—fled French glory then,
Though there the Emperor! he stood and gazed
At the wild havoc, like a monarch dazed
In woodland hoar, who felt the shrieking saw—
He, living oak, beheld his branches fall, with awe.
Chiefs, soldiers, comrades died. But still warm love
Kept those that rose all dastard fear above,
As on his tent they saw his shadow pass—
Backwards and forwards, for they credited, alas!
His fortune's star! it could not, could not be
That he had not his work to do—a destiny?
To hurl him headlong from his high estate,
Would be high treason in his bondman, Fate.
But all the while he felt himself alone,
Stunned with disasters few have ever known.
Sudden, a fear came o'er his troubled soul,

What more was written on the Future's scroll?
Was this an expiation? It must be, yea!
He turned to God for one enlightening ray.
"Is this the vengeance, Lord of Hosts?" he sighed,
But the first murmur on his parched lips died.
"Is this the vengeance? Must my glory set?"
A pause: his name was called; of flame a jet
Sprang in the darkness;—a Voice answered; "No!
Not yet."

  Outside still fell the smothering snow.
Was it a voice indeed? or but a dream?
It was the vulture's, but how like the *sea-bird's scream.*

TORU DUTT.

THE OCEAN'S SONG.

("Nous nous promenions à Rozel-Tower.")

{Bk. VI. iv., October, 1852.}
We walked amongst the ruins famed in story
  Of Rozel-Tower,
And saw the boundless waters stretch in glory
  And heave in power.

O ocean vast! we heard thy song with wonder,

 Whilst waves marked time.
"Appeal, O Truth!" thou sang'st with tone of thunder,
 "And shine sublime!

"The world's enslaved and hunted down by beagles,—
 To despots sold,
Souls of deep thinkers, soar like mighty eagles,
 The Right uphold.

"Be born; arise; o'er earth and wild waves bounding
 Peoples and suns!
Let darkness vanish;—tocsins be resounding,
 And flash, ye guns!

"And you,—who love no pomps of fog, or glamour,
 Who fear no shocks,
Brave foam and lightning, hurricane and clamor,
 Exiles—the rocks!"

TORU DUTT

THE TRUMPETS OF THE MIND.

("Sonnez, clairons de la pensée!")

{Bk. VII. i., March 19, 1853.}

Poems

Sound, sound for ever, Clarions of Thought!

When Joshua 'gainst the high-walled city fought,
He marched around it with his banner high,
His troops in serried order following nigh,
But not a sword was drawn, no shaft outsprang,
Only the trumpets the shrill onset rang.
At the first blast, smiled scornfully the king,
And at the second sneered, half wondering:
"Hop'st thou with noise my stronghold to break down?"
At the third round, the ark of old renown
Swept forward, still the trumpets sounding loud,
And then the troops with ensigns waving proud.
Stepped out upon the old walls children dark
With horns to mock the notes and hoot the ark.
At the fourth turn, braving the Israelites,
Women appeared upon the crenelated heights—
Those battlements embrowned with age and rust—
And hurled upon the Hebrews stones and dust,
And spun and sang when weary of the game.
At the fifth circuit came the blind and lame,
And with wild uproar clamorous and high
Railed at the clarion ringing to the sky.
At the sixth time, upon a tower's tall crest,
So high that there the eagle built his nest,
So hard that on it lightning lit in vain,
Appeared in merriment the king again:
"These Hebrew Jews musicians are, meseems!"
He scoffed, loud laughing, "but they live on dreams."
The princes laughed submissive to the king,

Laughed all the courtiers in their glittering ring,
And thence the laughter spread through all the town.

At the seventh blast—the city walls fell down.

TORU DUTT.

AFTER THE COUP D'ÉTAT.

("Devant les trahisons.")

{Bk. VII, xvi., Jersey, Dec. 2, 1852.}
Before foul treachery and heads hung down,
I'll fold my arms, indignant but serene.
Oh! faith in fallen things—be thou my crown,
My force, my joy, my prop on which I lean:

Yes, whilst *he's* there, or struggle some or fall,
O France, dear France, for whom I weep in vain.
Tomb of my sires, nest of my loves—my all,
I ne'er shall see thee with these eyes again.

I shall not see thy sad, sad sounding shore,
France, save my duty, I shall all forget;
Amongst the true and tried, I'll tug my oar,
And rest proscribed to brand the fawning set.

O bitter exile, hard, without a term,
Thee I accept, nor seek nor care to know
Who have down-truckled 'mid the men deemed firm,
And who have fled that should have fought the foe.

If true a thousand stand, with them I stand;
A hundred? 'tis enough: we'll Sylla brave;
Ten? put my name down foremost in the band;
One?—well, alone—until I find my grave.

TORU DUTT.

PATRIA.{1}

("Là-haut, qui sourit.")

{Bk. VII. vii., September, 1853.}
Who smiles there? Is it
A stray spirit,
Or woman fair?
Sombre yet soft the brow!
Bow, nations, bow;
O soul in air,
Speak—what art thou?

In grief the fair face seems—
What means those sudden gleams?
Our antique pride from dreams
Starts up, and beams
Its conquering glance,—
To make our sad hearts dance,
And wake in woods hushed long
The wild bird's song.
Angel of Day!
Our Hope, Love, Stay,
Thy countenance
Lights land and sea
Eternally,
Thy name is France
Or Verity.

Fair angel in thy glass
When vile things move or pass,
Clouds in the skies amass;
Terrible, alas!
Thy stern commands are then:
"Form your battalions, men,
The flag display!"
And all obey.
Angel of might
Sent kings to smite,
The words in dark skies glance,
"Mené, Mené," hiss
Bolts that never miss!
Thy name is France,

Or Nemesis.

As halcyons in May,
O nations, in his ray
Float and bask for aye,
Nor know decay!
One arm upraised to heaven
Seals the past forgiven;
One holds a sword
To quell hell's horde,
Angel of God!
Thy wings stretch broad
As heaven's expanse!
To shield and free
Humanity!
Thy name is France,
Or Liberty!

{Footnote 1: Written to music by Beethoven.}

THE UNIVERSAL REPUBLIC.

("Temps futurs.")

{Part "Lux," Jersey, Dec. 16-20, 1853.}
O vision of the coming time!

When man has 'scaped the trackless slime
And reached the desert spring;
When sands are crossed, the sward invites
The worn to rest 'mid rare delights
And gratefully to sing.

E'en now the eye that's levelled high,
Though dimly, can the hope espy
So solid soon, one day;
For every chain must then be broke,
And hatred none will dare evoke,
And June shall scatter May.

E'en now amid our misery
The germ of Union many see,
And through the hedge of thorn,
Like to a bee that dawn awakes,
On, Progress strides o'er shattered stakes,
With solemn, scathing scorn.

Behold the blackness shrink, and flee!
Behold the world rise up so free
Of coroneted things!
Whilst o'er the distant youthful States,
Like Amazonian bosom-plates,
Spread Freedom's shielding wings.

Ye, liberated lands, we hail!
Your sails are whole despite the gale!
Your masts are firm, and will not fail—

The triumph follows pain!
Hear forges roar! the hammer clanks—
It beats the time to nations' thanks—
At last, a *peaceful* strain!

'Tis rust, not gore, that gnaws the guns,
And shattered shells are but the runs
Where warring insects cope;
And all the headsman's racks and blades
And pincers, tools of tyrants' aids,
Are buried with the rope.

Upon the sky-line glows i' the dark
The Sun that now is but a spark;
But soon will be unfurled—
The glorious banner of us all,
The flag that rises ne'er to fall,
Republic of the World!

LES CONTEMPLATIONS.—1830-56.

THE VALE TO YOU, TO ME THE HEIGHTS.

A FABLE.

{Bk. III. vi., October, 1846.}
A lion camped beside a spring, where came the Bird
Of Jove to drink:
When, haply, sought two kings, without their courtier herd,
The moistened brink,
Beneath the palm—*they* always tempt pugnacious hands—
Both travel-sore;
But quickly, on the recognition, out flew brands
Straight to each core;
As dying breaths commingle, o'er them rose the call
Of Eagle shrill:
"Yon crownèd couple, who supposed the world too small,
Now one grave fill!
Chiefs blinded by your rage! each bleachèd sapless bone
Becomes a pipe
Through which siroccos whistle, trodden 'mong the stone
By quail and snipe.
Folly's liege-men, what boots such murd'rous raid,
And mortal feud?
I, Eagle, dwell as friend with Leo—none afraid—
In solitude:

At the same pool we bathe and quaff in placid mood.
Kings, he and I;
For I to him leave prairie, desert sands and wood,
And he to me the sky."

H.L.W.

CHILDHOOD.

("L'enfant chantait.")

{Bk. I. xxiii., Paris, January, 1835.}
The small child sang; the mother, outstretched on the low bed,
With anguish moaned,—fair Form pain should possess not long;
For, ever nigher, Death hovered around her head:
I hearkened there this moan, and heard even there that song.

The child was but five years, and, close to the lattice, aye
Made a sweet noise with games and with his laughter bright;
And the wan mother, aside this being the livelong day
Carolling joyously, coughed hoarsely all the night.

The mother went to sleep 'mong them that sleep alway;
And the blithe little lad began anew to sing...
Sorrow is like a fruit: God doth not therewith weigh
Earthward the branch strong yet but for the blossoming.

NELSON R. TYERMAN.

SATIRE ON THE EARTH.

("Une terre au flanc maigre.")

{Bk. III. xi., October, 1840.}
A clod with rugged, meagre, rust-stained, weather-worried face,
Where care-filled creatures tug and delve to keep a worthless race;
And glean, begrudgedly, by all their unremitting toil,
Sour, scanty bread and fevered water from the ungrateful soil;
Made harder by their gloom than flints that gash their harried hands,
And harder in the things they call their hearts than wolfish bands,
Perpetuating faults, inventing crimes for paltry ends,
And yet, perversest beings! hating Death, their best of friends!
Pride in the powerful no more, no less than in the poor;
Hatred in both their bosoms; love in one, or, wondrous! two!
Fog in the valleys; on the mountains snowfields, ever new,
That only melt to send down waters for the liquid hell,
In which, their strongest sons and fairest daughters vilely fell!
No marvel, Justice, Modesty dwell far apart and high,
Where they can feebly hear, and, rarer, answer victims' cry.
At both extremes, unflinching frost, the centre scorching hot;
Land storms that strip the orchards nude, leave beaten grain to rot;
Oceans that rise with sudden force to wash the bloody land,
Where War, amid sob-drowning cheers, claps weapons in each hand.
And this to those who, luckily, abide afar—
This is, ha! ha! *a star*!

HOW BUTTERFLIES ARE BORN.

("Comme le matin rit sur les roses.")

{Bk. I. xii.}
The dawn is smiling on the dew that covers
The tearful roses—lo, the little lovers—
That kiss the buds and all the flutterings
In jasmine bloom, and privet, of white wings
That go and come, and fly, and peep, and hide
With muffled music, murmured far and wide!
Ah, Springtime, when we think of all the lays
That dreamy lovers send to dreamy Mays,
Of the proud hearts within a billet bound,
Of all the soft silk paper that men wound,
The messages of love that mortals write,
Filled with intoxication of delight,
Written in April, and before the Maytime
Shredded and flown, playthings for the winds' playtime.
We dream that all white butterflies above,
Who seek through clouds or waters souls to love,
And leave their lady mistress to despair,
To flirt with flowers, as tender and more fair,
Are but torn love-letters, that through the skies
Flutter, and float, and change to Butterflies.

A. LANG.

HAVE YOU NOTHING TO SAY FOR YOURSELF?

("Si vous n'avez rien à me dire.")

{Bk. II. iv., May, 18—.}
Speak, if you love me, gentle maiden!
Or haunt no more my lone retreat.
If not for me thy heart be laden,
Why trouble mine with smiles so sweet?

Ah! tell me why so mute, fair maiden,
Whene'er as thus so oft we meet?
If not for me thy heart be, Aideen,
Why trouble mine with smiles so sweet?

Why, when my hand unconscious pressing,
Still keep untold the maiden dream?
In fancy thou art thus caressing
The while we wander by the stream.

If thou art pained when I am near thee,
Why in my path so often stray?
For in my heart I love yet fear thee,
And fain would fly, yet fondly stay.

C.H. KENNY.

INSCRIPTION FOR A CRUCIFIX.{1}

("Vous qui pleurez, venez à ce Dieu.")

{Bk. III. iv., March, 1842.}
Ye weepers, the Mourner o'er mourners behold!
Ye wounded, come hither—the Healer enfold!
Ye gloomy ones, brighten 'neath smiles quelling care—
Or pass—for *this* Comfort is found ev'rywhere.

{Footnote 1: Music by Gounod.}

DEATH, IN LIFE.

("Ceux-ci partent.")

{Bk. III. v., February, 1843.}
  We pass—these sleep
Beneath the shade where deep-leaved boughs
Bend o'er the furrows the Great Reaper ploughs,
And gentle summer winds in many sweep
  Whirl in eddying waves
  The dead leaves o'er the graves.

  And the living sigh:

Forgotten ones, so soon your memories die.
Ye never more may list the wild bird's song,
Or mingle in the crowded city-throng.
 Ye must ever dwell in gloom,
 'Mid the silence of the tomb.

And the dead reply:
God giveth us His life. Ye die,
Your barren lives are tilled with tears,
For glory, ye are clad with fears.
 Oh, living ones! oh, earthly shades!
 We live; your beauty clouds and fades.

THE DYING CHILD TO ITS MOTHER.

("Oh! vous aurez trop dit.")

{Bk. III. xiv., April, 1843.}
Ah, you said too often to your angel
There are other angels in the sky—
There, where nothing changes, nothing suffers,
Sweet it were to enter in on high.

To that dome on marvellous pilasters,
To that tent roofed o'er with colored bars,
That blue garden full of stars like lilies,

And of lilies beautiful as stars.

And you said it was a place most joyous,
All our poor imaginings above,
With the wingèd cherubim for playmates,
And the good God evermore to love.

Sweet it were to dwell there in all seasons,
Like a taper burning day and night,
Near to the child Jesus and the Virgin,
In that home so beautiful and bright.

But you should have told him, hapless mother,
Told your child so frail and gentle too,
That you were all his in life's beginning,
But that also he belonged to you.

For the mother watches o'er the infant,
He must rise up in her latter days,
She will need the man that was her baby
To stand by her when her strength decays.

Ah, you did not tell enough your darling
That God made us in this lower life,
Woman for the man, and man for woman,
In our pains, our pleasures and our strife.

So that one sad day, O loss, O sorrow!
The sweet creature left you all alone;
'Twas your own hand hung the cage door open,

Mother, and your pretty bird is flown.

BP. ALEXANDER.

EPITAPH.

("Il vivait, il jouait.")

{Bk. III. xv., May, 1843.}
He lived and ever played, the tender smiling thing.
What need, O Earth, to have plucked this flower from blossoming?
Hadst thou not then the birds with rainbow-colors bright,
The stars and the great woods, the wan wave, the blue sky?
What need to have rapt this child from her thou hadst placed him by—
Beneath those other flowers to have hid this flower from sight?

Because of this one child thou hast no more of might,
O star-girt Earth, his death yields thee not higher delight!
But, ah! the mother's heart with woe for ever wild,
This heart whose sovran bliss brought forth so bitter birth—
This world as vast as thou, even *thou*, O sorrowless Earth,
Is desolate and void because of this one child!

NELSON K. TYERMAN.

ST. JOHN.

("Un jour, le morne esprit.")

{Bk. VI. vii., Jersey, September, 1855.}
One day, the sombre soul, the Prophet most sublime
  At Patmos who aye dreamed,
And tremblingly perused, without the vast of Time,
  Words that with hell-fire gleamed,

Said to his eagle: "Bird, spread wings for loftiest flight—
  Needs must I see His Face!"
The eagle soared. At length, far beyond day and night,
  Lo! the all-sacred Place!

And John beheld the Way whereof no angel knows
  The name, nor there hath trod;
And, lo! the Place fulfilled with shadow that aye glows
  Because of very God.

NELSON R. TYERMAN.

THE POET'S SIMPLE FAITH.

You say, "Where goest thou?" I cannot tell,
And still go on. If but the way be straight,
It cannot go amiss! before me lies
Dawn and the Day; the Night behind me; that
Suffices me; I break the bounds; I *see*,
And nothing more; *believe*, and nothing less.
My future is not one of my concerns.

PROF. E. DOWDEN.
I AM CONTENT.

("J'habite l'ombre.")

{1855.}
True; I dwell lone,
  Upon sea-beaten cape,
Mere raft of stone;
  Whence all escape
Save one who shrinks not from the gloom,
And will not take the coward's leap i' the tomb.

My bedroom rocks
  With breezes; quakes in storms,
When dangling locks
  Of seaweed mock the forms
Of straggling clouds that trail o'erhead
Like tresses from disrupted coffin-lead.

Upon the sky
 Crape palls are often nailed
With stars. Mine eye
 Has scared the gull that sailed
To blacker depths with shrillest scream,
Still fainter, till like voices in a dream.

My days become
 More plaintive, wan, and pale,
While o'er the foam
 I see, borne by the gale,
Infinity! in kindness sent—
To find me ever saying: "I'm content!"

LA LÉGENDE DES SIÈCLES.

CAIN.

("Lorsque avec ses enfants Cain se fût enfui.")

{Bk. II}
Then, with his children, clothed in skins of brutes,
Dishevelled, livid, rushing through the storm,
Cain fled before Jehovah. As night fell
The dark man reached a mount in a great plain,
And his tired wife and his sons, out of breath,
Said: "Let us lie down on the earth and sleep."
Cain, sleeping not, dreamed at the mountain foot.
Raising his head, in that funereal heaven
He saw an eye, a great eye, in the night
Open, and staring at him in the gloom.
"I am too near," he said, and tremblingly woke up
His sleeping sons again, and his tired wife,
And fled through space and darkness. Thirty days
He went, and thirty nights, nor looked behind;
Pale, silent, watchful, shaking at each sound;
No rest, no sleep, till he attained the strand
Where the sea washes that which since was Asshur.
"Here pause," he said, "for this place is secure;
Here may we rest, for this is the world's end."
And he sat down; when, lo! in the sad sky,

The selfsame Eye on the horizon's verge,
And the wretch shook as in an ague fit.
"Hide me!" he cried; and all his watchful sons,
Their finger on their lip, stared at their sire.
Cain said to Jabal (father of them that dwell
In tents): "Spread here the curtain of thy tent,"
And they spread wide the floating canvas roof,
And made it fast and fixed it down with lead.
"You see naught now," said Zillah then, fair child
The daughter of his eldest, sweet as day.
But Cain replied, "That Eye—I see it still."
And Jubal cried (the father of all those
That handle harp and organ): "I will build
A sanctuary;" and he made a wall of bronze,
And set his sire behind it. But Cain moaned,
"That Eye is glaring at me ever." Henoch cried:
"Then must we make a circle vast of towers,
So terrible that nothing dare draw near;
Build we a city with a citadel;
Build we a city high and close it fast."
Then Tubal Cain (instructor of all them
That work in brass and iron) built a tower—
Enormous, superhuman. While he wrought,
His fiery brothers from the plain around
Hunted the sons of Enoch and of Seth;
They plucked the eyes out of whoever passed,
And hurled at even arrows to the stars.
They set strong granite for the canvas wall,
And every block was clamped with iron chains.
It seemed a city made for hell. Its towers,

With their huge masses made night in the land.
The walls were thick as mountains. On the door
They graved: "Let not God enter here." This done,
And having finished to cement and build
In a stone tower, they set him in the midst.
To him, still dark and haggard, "Oh, my sire,
Is the Eye gone?" quoth Zillah tremblingly.
But Cain replied: "Nay, it is even there."
Then added: "I will live beneath the earth,
As a lone man within his sepulchre.
I will see nothing; will be seen of none."
They digged a trench, and Cain said: "'Tis enow,"
As he went down alone into the vault;
But when he sat, so ghost-like, in his chair,
And they had closed the dungeon o'er his head,
The Eye was in the tomb and fixed on Cain.

Dublin University Magazine

BOAZ ASLEEP.

("Booz s'était couché.")

{Bk. II. vi.}
At work within his barn since very early,
Fairly tired out with toiling all the day,
Upon the small bed where he always lay

Boaz was sleeping by his sacks of barley.

Barley and wheat-fields he possessed, and well,
Though rich, loved justice; wherefore all the flood
That turned his mill-wheels was unstained with mud
And in his smithy blazed no fire of hell.

His beard was silver, as in April all
A stream may be; he did not grudge a stook.
When the poor gleaner passed, with kindly look,
Quoth he, "Of purpose let some handfuls fall."

He walked his way of life straight on and plain,
With justice clothed, like linen white and clean,
And ever rustling towards the poor, I ween,
Like public fountains ran his sacks of grain.

Good master, faithful friend, in his estate
Frugal yet generous, beyond the youth
He won regard of woman, for in sooth
The young man may be fair—the old man's great.

Life's primal source, unchangeable and bright,
The old man entereth, the day eterne;
And in the young man's eye a flame may burn,
But in the old man's eye one seeth light.

As Jacob slept, or Judith, so full deep
Slept Boaz 'neath the leaves. Now it betided,
Heaven's gate being partly open, that there glided

A fair dream forth, and hovered o'er his sleep.

And in his dream to heaven, the blue and broad,
Right from his loins an oak tree grew amain.
His race ran up it far, like a long chain;
Below it sung a king, above it died a God.

Whereupon Boaz murmured in his heart,
"The number of my years is past fourscore:
How may this be? I have not any more,
Or son, or wife; yea, she who had her part.

"In this my couch, O Lord! is now in Thine;
And she, half living, I half dead within,
Our beings still commingle and are twin,
It cannot be that I should found a line!

"Youth hath triumphal mornings; its days bound
From night, as from a victory. But such
A trembling as the birch-tree's to the touch
Of winter is an eld, and evening closes round.

"I bow myself to death, as lone to meet
The water bow their fronts athirst." He said.
The cedar feeleth not the rose's head,
Nor he the woman's presence at his feet!

For while he slept, the Moabitess Ruth
Lay at his feet, expectant of his waking.
He knowing not what sweet guile she was making;

She knowing not what God would have in sooth.

Asphodel scents did Gilgal's breezes bring—
Through nuptial shadows, questionless, full fast
The angels sped, for momently there passed
A something blue which seemed to be a wing.

Silent was all in Jezreel and Ur—
The stars were glittering in the heaven's dusk meadows.
Far west among those flowers of the shadows.
The thin clear crescent lustrous over her,

Made Ruth raise question, looking through the bars
Of heaven, with eyes half-oped, what God, what comer
Unto the harvest of the eternal summer,
Had flung his golden hook down on the field of stars.

BP. ALEXANDER.

SONG OF THE GERMAN LANZKNECHT

("Sonnex, clarions!")

{Bk. VI. vii.}
Flourish the trumpet! and rattle the drum!
The *Reiters* are mounted! the Reiters will come!

When our bullets cease singing
And long swords cease ringing
 On backplates of fearsomest foes in full flight,
We'll dig up their dollars
To string for girls' collars—
 They'll jingle around them before it is night!
  When flourish the trumpets, etc.

We're the Emperor's winners
Of right royal dinners,
 Where cities are served up and flanked by estates,
While we wallow in claret,
Knowing not how to spare it,
 Though beer is less likely to muddle our pates—
  While flourish the trumpets, etc.

Gods of battle! red-handed!
Wise it was to have banded
 Such arms as are these for embracing of gain!
Hearken to each war-vulture
Crying, "Down with all culture
 Of land or religion!" *Hoch*! to our refrain
  Of flourish the trumpets, etc.

Give us "bones of the devil"
To exchange in our revel
 The ingot, the gem, and yellow doubloon;
Coronets are but playthings—
We reck not who say things

When the Reiters have ridden to death! none too soon!—
To flourish of trumpet and rattle of drum,
The Reiters will finish as firm as they come!

H.L.W.

KING CANUTE.

("Un jour, Kanut mourut.")

{Bk. X. i.}
King Canute died.{1} Encoffined he was laid.
Of Aarhuus came the Bishop prayers to say,
And sang a hymn upon his tomb, and held
That Canute was a saint—Canute the Great,
That from his memory breathed celestial perfume,
And that they saw him, they the priests, in glory,
Seated at God's right hand, a prophet crowned.

I.

    Evening came,
And hushed the organ in the holy place,
And the priests, issuing from the temple doors,
Left the dead king in peace. Then he arose,
Opened his gloomy eyes, and grasped his sword,
And went forth loftily. The massy walls
Yielded before the phantom, like a mist.

There is a sea where Aarhuus, Altona,
And Elsinore's vast domes and shadowy towers
Glass in deep waters. Over this he went
Dark, and still Darkness listened for his foot
Inaudible, itself being but a dream.
Straight to Mount Savo went he, gnawed by time,

And thus, "O mountain buffeted of storms,
Give me of thy huge mantle of deep snow
To frame a winding-sheet." The mountain knew him,
Nor dared refuse, and with his sword Canute
Cut from his flank white snow, enough to make
The garment he desired, and then he cried,
"Old mountain! death is dumb, but tell me thou
The way to God." More deep each dread ravine
And hideous hollow yawned, and sadly thus
Answered that hoar associate of the clouds:
"Spectre, I know not, I am always here."
Canute departed, and with head erect,
All white and ghastly in his robe of snow,
Went forth into great silence and great night
By Iceland and Norway. After him
Gloom swallowed up the universe. He stood
A sovran kingdomless, a lonely ghost
Confronted with Immensity. He saw
The awful Infinite, at whose portal pale
Lightning sinks dying; Darkness, skeleton
Whose joints are nights, and utter Formlessness
Moving confusedly in the horrible dark
Inscrutable and blind. No star was there,
Yet something like a haggard gleam; no sound
But the dull tide of Darkness, and her dumb
And fearful shudder. "'Tis the tomb," he said,
"God is beyond!" Three steps he took, then cried:
'Twas deathly as the grave, and not a voice
Responded, nor came any breath to sway
The snowy mantle, with unsullied white

Emboldening the spectral wanderer.
Sudden he marked how, like a gloomy star,
A spot grew broad upon his livid robe;
Slowly it widened, raying darkness forth;
And Canute proved it with his spectral hands
It was a drop of blood.

R. GARNETT.

II.

But he saw nothing; space was black—no sound.
"Forward," said Canute, raising his proud head.
There fell a second stain beside the first,
Then it grew larger, and the Cimbrian chief
Stared at the thick vague darkness, and saw naught.
Still as a bloodhound follows on his track,
Sad he went on. 'There fell a third red stain
On the white winding-sheet. He had never fled;
Howbeit Canute forward went no more,
But turned on that side where the sword arm hangs.
A drop of blood, as if athwart a dream,
Fell on the shroud, and reddened his right hand.
Then, as in reading one turns back a page,
A second time he changed his course, and turned
To the dim left. There fell a drop of blood.
Canute drew back, trembling to be alone,
And wished he had not left his burial couch.
But, when a blood-drop fell again, he stopped,
Stooped his pale head, and tried to make a prayer.

Then fell a drop, and the prayer died away
In savage terror. Darkly he moved on,
A hideous spectre hesitating, white,
And ever as he went, a drop of blood
Implacably from the darkness broke away
And stained that awful whiteness. He beheld
Shaking, as doth a poplar in the wind,
Those stains grow darker and more numerous:
Another, and another, and another.
They seem to light up that funereal gloom,
And mingling in the folds of that white sheet,
Made it a cloud of blood. He went, and went,
And still from that unfathomable vault
The red blood dropped upon him drop by drop,
Always, for ever—without noise, as though
From the black feet of some night-gibbeted corpse.
Alas! Who wept those formidable tears?
The Infinite!—Toward Heaven, of the good
Attainable, through the wild sea of night,
That hath not ebb nor flow, Canute went on,
And ever walking, came to a closed door,
That from beneath showed a mysterious light.
Then he looked down upon his winding-sheet,
For that was the great place, the sacred place,
That was a portion of the light of God,
And from behind that door Hosannas rang.
The winding-sheet was red, and Canute stopped.
This is why Canute from the light of day
Draws ever back, and hath not dared appear
Before the Judge whose face is as the sun.

This is why still remaineth the dark king
Out in the night, and never having power
To bring his robe back to its first pure state,
But feeling at each step a blood-drop fall,
Wanders eternally 'neath the vast black heaven.

Dublin University Magazine

{Footnote 1: King Canute slew his old father, Sweno, to obtain the crown.}

THE BOY-KING'S PRAYER.

("Le cheval galopait toujours.")

{Bk. XV. ii. 10.}
The good steed flew o'er river and o'er plain,
Till far away,—no need of spur or rein.
The child, half rapture, half solicitude,
Looks back anon, in fear to be pursued;
Shakes lest some raging brother of his sire
Leap from those rocks that o'er the path aspire.

On the rough granite bridge, at evening's fall,
The white horse paused by Compostella's wall,
('Twas good St. James that reared those arches tall,)

Through the dim mist stood out each belfry dome,
And the boy hailed the paradise of home.

Close to the bridge, set on high stage, they meet
A Christ of stone, the Virgin at his feet.
A taper lighted that dear pardoning face,
More tender in the shade that wrapped the place,
And the child stayed his horse, and in the shine
Of the wax taper knelt down at the shrine.

"O, my good God! O, Mother Maiden sweet!"
He said, "I was the worm beneath men's feet;
My father's brethren held me in their thrall,
But Thou didst send the Paladin of Gaul,
O Lord! and show'dst what different spirits move
The good men and the evil; those who love
And those who love not. I had been as they,
But Thou, O God! hast saved both life and soul to-day.
I saw Thee in that noble knight; I saw
Pure light, true faith, and honor's sacred law,
My Father,—and I learnt that monarchs must
Compassionate the weak, and unto all be just.
O Lady Mother! O dear Jesus! thus
Bowed at the cross where Thou didst bleed for us,
I swear to hold the truth that now I learn,
Leal to the loyal, to the traitor stern,
And ever just and nobly mild to be,
Meet scholar of that Prince of Chivalry;
And here Thy shrine bear witness, Lord, for me."

The horse of Roland, hearing the boy tell
His vow, looked round and spoke: "O King, 'tis well!"
Then on the charger mounted the child-king,
And rode into the town, while all the bells 'gan ring.

Dublin University Magazine

EVIRADNUS.

THE KNIGHT ERRANT.

("Qu'est-ce que Sigismond et Ladislas ont dit.")

{Bk. XV. iii. 1.}
I.

THE ADVENTURER SETS OUT.

What was it Sigismond and Ladisläus said?

I know not if the rock, or tree o'erhead,
Had heard their speech;—but when the two spoke low,
Among the trees, a shudder seemed to go
Through all their branches, just as if that way
A beast had passed to trouble and dismay.
More dark the shadow of the rock was seen,

And then a morsel of the shade, between
The sombre trees, took shape as it would seem
Like spectre walking in the sunset's gleam.

It is not monster rising from its lair,
Nor phantom of the foliage and the air,
It is not morsel of the granite's shade
That walks in deepest hollows of the glade.
'Tis not a vampire nor a spectre pale
But living man in rugged coat of mail.
It is Alsatia's noble Chevalier,
Eviradnus the brave, that now is here.

The men who spoke he recognized the while
He rested in the thicket; words of guile
Most horrible were theirs as they passed on,
And to the ears of Eviradnus one—
One word had come which roused him. Well he knew
The land which lately he had journeyed through.

He down the valley went into the inn
Where he had left his horse and page, Gasclin.
The horse had wanted drink, and lost a shoe;
And now, "Be quick!" he said, "with what you do,
For business calls me, I must not delay."
He strides the saddle and he rides away.

II.

EVIRADNUS.

Eviradnus was growing old apace,
The weight of years had left its hoary trace,
But still of knights the most renowned was he,
Model of bravery and purity.
His blood he spared not; ready day or night
To punish crime, his dauntless sword shone bright
In his unblemished hand; holy and white
And loyal all his noble life had been,
A Christian Samson coming on the scene.
With fist alone the gate he battered down
Of Sickingen in flames, and saved the town.
'Twas he, indignant at the honor paid
To crime, who with his heel an onslaught made
Upon Duke Lupus' shameful monument,
Tore down, the statue he to fragments rent;
Then column of the Strasburg monster bore
To bridge of Wasselonne, and threw it o'er
Into the waters deep. The people round
Blazon the noble deeds that so abound
From Altorf unto Chaux-de-Fonds, and say,
When he rests musing in a dreamy way,
"Behold, 'tis Charlemagne!" Tawny to see
And hairy, and seven feet high was he,
Like John of Bourbon. Roaming hill or wood
He looked a wolf was striving to do good.
Bound up in duty, he of naught complained,
The cry for help his aid at once obtained.
Only he mourned the baseness of mankind,
And—that the beds too short he still doth find.

When people suffer under cruel kings,
With pity moved, he to them succor brings.
'Twas he defended Alix from her foes
As sword of Urraca—he ever shows
His strength is for the feeble and oppressed;
Father of orphans he, and all distressed!
Kings of the Rhine in strongholds were by him
Boldly attacked, and tyrant barons grim.
He freed the towns—confronting in his lair
Hugo the Eagle; boldly did he dare
To break the collar of Saverne, the ring
Of Colmar, and the iron torture thing
Of Schlestadt, and the chain that Haguenau bore.
Such Eviradnus was a wrong before,
Good but most terrible. In the dread scale
Which princes weighted with their horrid tale
Of craft and violence, and blood and ill,
And fire and shocking deeds, his sword was still
God's counterpoise displayed. Ever alert
More evil from the wretched to avert,
Those hapless ones who 'neath Heaven's vault at night
Raise suppliant hands. His lance loved not the plight
Of mouldering in the rack, of no avail,
His battle-axe slipped from supporting nail
Quite easily; 'twas ill for action base
To come so near that he the thing could trace.
The steel-clad champion death drops all around
As glaciers water. Hero ever found
Eviradnus is kinsman of the race
Of Amadys of Gaul, and knights of Thrace,

He smiles at age. For he who never asked
For quarter from mankind—shall he be tasked
To beg of Time for mercy? Rather he
Would girdle up his loins, like Baldwin be.
Aged he is, but of a lineage rare;
The least intrepid of the birds that dare
Is not the eagle barbed. What matters age,
The years but fire him with a holy rage.
Though late from Palestine, he is not spent,—
With age he wrestles, firm in his intent.

III.

IN THE FOREST.

If in the woodland traveller there had been
That eve, who lost himself, strange sight he'd seen.
Quite in the forest's heart a lighted space
Arose to view; in that deserted place
A lone, abandoned hall with light aglow
The long neglect of centuries did show.
The castle-towers of Corbus in decay
Were girt by weeds and growths that had their way.
Couch-grass and ivy, and wild eglantine
In subtle scaling warfare all combine.
Subject to such attacks three hundred years,
The donjon yields, and ruin now appears,
E'en as by leprosy the wild boars die,
In moat the crumbled battlements now lie;
Around the snake-like bramble twists its rings;

Freebooter sparrows come on daring wings
To perch upon the swivel-gun, nor heed
Its murmuring growl when pecking in their greed
The mulberries ripe. With insolence the thorn
Thrives on the desolation so forlorn.
But winter brings revenges; then the Keep
Wakes all vindictive from its seeming sleep,
Hurls down the heavy rain, night after night,
Thanking the season's all-resistless might;
And, when the gutters choke, its gargoyles four
From granite mouths in anger spit and pour
Upon the hated ivy hour by hour.

As to the sword rust is, so lichens are
To towering citadel with which they war.
Alas! for Corbus—dreary, desolate,
And yet its woes the winters mitigate.
It rears itself among convulsive throes
That shake its ruins when the tempest blows.
Winter, the savage warrior, pleases well,
With its storm clouds, the mighty citadel,—
Restoring it to life. The lightning flash
Strikes like a thief and flies; the winds that crash
Sound like a clarion, for the Tempest bluff
Is Battle's sister. And when wild and rough,
The north wind blows, the tower exultant cries
"Behold me!" When hail-hurling gales arise
Of blustering Equinox, to fan the strife,
It stands erect, with martial ardor rife,
A joyous soldier! When like yelping hound

Pursued by wolves, November comes to bound
In joy from rock to rock, like answering cheer
To howling January now so near—
"Come on!" the Donjon cries to blasts o'erhead—
It has seen Attila, and knows not dread.
Oh, dismal nights of contest in the rain
And mist, that furious would the battle gain,
'The tower braves all, though angry skies pour fast
The flowing torrents, river-like and vast.
From their eight pinnacles the gorgons bay,
And scattered monsters, in their stony way,
Are growling heard; the rampart lions gnaw
The misty air and slush with granite maw,
The sleet upon the griffins spits, and all
The Saurian monsters, answering to the squall,
Flap wings; while through the broken ceiling fall
Torrents of rain upon the forms beneath,
Dragons and snak'd Medusas gnashing teeth
In the dismantled rooms. Like armored knight
The granite Castle fights with all its might,
Resisting through the winter. All in vain,
The heaven's bluster, January's rain,
And those dread elemental powers we call
The Infinite—the whirlwinds that appall—
Thunder and waterspouts; and winds that shake
As 'twere a tree its ripened fruit to take.
The winds grow wearied, warring with the tower,
The noisy North is out of breath, nor power
Has any blast old Corbus to defeat,
It still has strength their onslaughts worst to meet.

Thus, spite of briers and thistles, the old tower
Remains triumphant through the darkest hour;
Superb as pontiff, in the forest shown,
Its rows of battlements make triple crown;
At eve, its silhouette is finely traced
Immense and black—showing the Keep is placed
On rocky throne, sublime and high; east, west,
And north and south, at corners four, there rest
Four mounts; Aptar, where flourishes the pine,
And Toxis, where the elms grow green and fine;
Crobius and Bleyda, giants in their might,
Against the stormy winds to stand and fight,
And these above its diadem uphold
Night's living canopy of clouds unrolled.

The herdsman fears, and thinks its shadow creeps
To follow him; and superstition keeps
Such hold that Corbus as a terror reigns;
Folks say the Fort a target still remains
For the Black Archer—and that it contains
The cave where the Great Sleeper still sleeps sound.
The country people all the castle round
Are frightened easily, for legends grow
And mix with phantoms of the mind; we know
The hearth is cradle of such fantasies,
And in the smoke the cotter sees arise
From low-thatched but he traces cause of dread.
Thus rendering thanks that he is lowly bred,
Because from such none look for valorous deeds.
The peasant flies the Tower, although it leads

A noble knight to seek adventure there,
And, from his point of honor, dangers dare.

Thus very rarely passer-by is seen;
But—it might be with twenty years between,
Or haply less—at unfixed interval
There would a semblance be of festival.
A Seneschal and usher would appear,
And troops of servants many baskets bear.
Then were, in mystery, preparations made,
And they departed—for till night none stayed.
But 'twixt the branches gazers could descry
The blackened hall lit up most brilliantly.
None dared approach—and this the reason why.

IV.

THE CUSTOM OF LUSACE.

When died a noble Marquis of Lusace
'Twas custom for the heir who filled his place
Before assuming princely pomp and power
To sup one night in Corbus' olden tower.
From this weird meal he passed to the degree
Of Prince and Margrave; nor could ever he
Be thought brave knight, or she—if woman claim
The rank—be reckoned of unblemished fame
Till they had breathed the air of ages gone,
The funeral odors, in the nest alone
Of its dead masters. Ancient was the race;

To trace the upward stem of proud Lusace
Gives one a vertigo; descended they
From ancestor of Attila, men say;
Their race to him—through Pagans—they hark back;
Becoming Christians, race they thought to track
Through Lechus, Plato, Otho to combine
With Ursus, Stephen, in a lordly line.
Of all those masters of the country round
That were on Northern Europe's boundary found—
At first were waves and then the dykes were reared—
Corbus in double majesty appeared,
Castle on hill and town upon the plain;
And one who mounted on the tower could gain
A view beyond the pines and rocks, of spires
That pierce the shade the distant scene acquires;
A walled town is it, but 'tis not ally
Of the old citadel's proud majesty;
Unto itself belonging this remained.
Often a castle was thus self-sustained
And equalled towns; witness in Lombardy
Crama, and Plato too in Tuscany,
And in Apulia Barletta;—each one
Was powerful as a town, and dreaded none.
Corbus ranked thus; its precincts seemed to hold
The reflex of its mighty kings of old;
Their great events had witness in these walls,
Their marriages were here and funerals,
And mostly here it was that they were born;
And here crowned Barons ruled with pride and scorn;
Cradle of Scythian majesty this place.

Now each new master of this ancient race
A duty owed to ancestors which he
Was bound to carry on. The law's decree
It was that he should pass alone the night
Which made him king, as in their solemn sight.
Just at the forest's edge a clerk was met
With wine in sacred cup and purpose set,
A wine mysterious, which the heir must drink
To cause deep slumber till next day's soft brink.
Then to the castle tower he wends his way,
And finds a supper laid with rich display.
He sups and sleeps: then to his slumbering eyes
The shades of kings from Bela all arise.
None dare the tower to enter on this night,
But when the morning dawns, crowds are in sight
The dreamer to deliver,—whom half dazed,
And with the visions of the night amazed,
They to the old church take, where rests the dust
Of Borivorus; then the bishop must,
With fervent blessings on his eyes and mouth,
Put in his hands the stony hatchets both,
With which—even like death impartially—
Struck Attila, with one arm dexterously
The south, and with the other arm the north.

This day the town the threatening flag set forth
Of Marquis Swantibore, the monster he
Who in the wood tied up his wife, to be
Devoured by wolves, together with the bull
Of which with jealousy his heart was full.

Even when woman took the place of heir
The tower of Corbus claimed the supper there;
'Twas law—the woman trembled, but must dare.

V.

THE MARCHIONESS MAHAUD.

Niece of the Marquis—John the Striker named—
Mahaud to-day the marquisate has claimed.
A noble dame—the crown is hers by right:
As woman she has graces that delight.
A queen devoid of beauty is not queen,
She needs the royalty of beauty's mien;
God in His harmony has equal ends
For cedar that resists, and reed that bends,
And good it is a woman sometimes rules,
Holds in her hand the power, and manners schools,
And laws and mind;—succeeding master proud,
With gentle voice and smile she leads the crowd,
The sombre human troop. But sweet Mahaud
On evil days had fallen; gentle, good,
Alas! she held the sceptre like a flower;
Timid yet gay, imprudent for the hour,
And careless too. With Europe all in throes,
Though twenty years she now already knows,
She has refused to marry, although oft
Entreated. It is time an arm less soft
Than hers—a manly arm—supported her;

Like to the rainbow she, one might aver,
Shining on high between the cloud and rain,
Or like the ewe that gambols on the plain
Between the bear and tiger; innocent,
She has two neighbors of most foul intent:
For foes the Beauty has, in life's pure spring,
The German Emp'ror and the Polish King.

VI.

THE TWO NEIGHBORS.

The difference this betwixt the evil pair,
Faithless to God—for laws without a care—
One was the claw, the other one the will
Controlling. Yet to mass they both went still,
And on the rosary told their beads each day.
But none the less the world believed that they
Unto the powers of hell their souls had sold.
Even in whispers men each other told
The details of the pact which they had signed
With that dark power, the foe of human kind;
In whispers, for the crowd had mortal dread
Of them so high, and woes that they had spread.
One might be vengeance and the other hate,
Yet lived they side by side, in powerful state
And close alliance. All the people near
From red horizon dwelt in abject fear,
Mastered by them; their figures darkly grand
Had ruddy reflex from the wasted land,

And fires, and towns they sacked. Besides the one,
Like David, poet was, the other shone
As fine musician—rumor spread their fame,
Declaring them divine, until each name
In Italy's fine sonnets met with praise.
The ancient hierarch in those old days
Had custom strange, a now forgotten thing,
It was a European plan that King
Of France was marquis, and th' imperial head
Of Germany was duke; there was no need
To class the other kings, but barons they,
Obedient vassals unto Rome, their stay.
The King of Poland was but simple knight,
Yet now, for once, had strange unwonted right,
And, as exception to the common state,
This one Sarmatian King was held as great
As German Emperor; and each knew how
His evil part to play, nor mercy show.
The German had one aim, it was to take
All land he could, and it his own to make.
The Pole already having Baltic shore,
Seized Celtic ports, still needing more and more.
On all the Northern Sea his crafts roused fear:
Iceland beheld his demon navy near.
Antwerp the German burnt; and Prussias twain
Bowed to the yoke. The Polish King was fain
To help the Russian Spotocus—his aid
Was like the help that in their common trade
A sturdy butcher gives a weaker one.
The King it is who seizes, and this done,

The Emp'ror pillages, usurping right
In war Teutonic, settled but by might.
The King in Jutland cynic footing gains,
The weak coerced, the while with cunning pains
The strong are duped. But 'tis a law they make
That their accord themselves should never break.
From Arctic seas to cities Transalpine,
Their hideous talons, curved for sure rapine,
Scrape o'er and o'er the mournful continent,
Their plans succeed, and each is well content.
Thus under Satan's all paternal care
They brothers are, this royal bandit pair.
Oh, noxious conquerors! with transient rule
Chimera heads—ambition can but fool.
Their misty minds but harbor rottenness
Loathsome and fetid, and all barrenness—
Their deeds to ashes turn, and, hydra-bred,
The mystic skeleton is theirs to dread.
The daring German and the cunning Pole
Noted to-day a woman had control
Of lands, and watched Mahaud like evil spies;
And from the Emp'ror's cruel mouth—with dyes
Of wrath empurpled—came these words of late:
"The empire wearies of the wallet weight
Hung at its back—this High and Low Lusace,
Whose hateful load grows heavier apace,
That now a woman holds its ruler's place."
Threatening, and blood suggesting, every word;
The watchful Pole was silent—but he heard.

Two monstrous dangers; but the heedless one
Babbles and smiles, and bids all care begone—
Likes lively speech—while all the poor she makes
To love her, and the taxes off she takes.
A life of dance and pleasure she has known—
A woman always; in her jewelled crown
It is the pearl she loves—not cutting gems,
For these can wound, and mark men's diadems.
She pays the hire of Homer's copyists,
And in the Courts of Love presiding, lists.

Quite recently unto her Court have come
Two men—unknown their names or native home,
Their rank or race; but one plays well the lute,
The other is a troubadour; both suit
The taste of Mahaud, when on summer eve,
'Neath opened windows, they obtain her leave
To sing upon the terrace, and relate
The charming tales that do with music mate.
In August the Moravians have their fête,
But it is radiant June in which Lusace
Must consecrate her noble Margrave race.
Thus in the weird and old ancestral tower
For Mahaud now has come the fateful hour,
The lonely supper which her state decrees.
What matters this to flowers, and birds, and trees,
And clouds and fountains? That the people may
Still bear their yoke—have kings to rule alway?
The water flows, the wind in passing by
In murmuring tones takes up the questioning cry.

VII.

THE BANQUET HALL.

The old stupendous hall has but one door,
And in the dusk it seems that more and more
The walls recede in space unlimited.
At the far end there is a table spread
That in the dreary void with splendor shines;
For ceiling we behold but rafter lines.
The table is arranged for one sole guest,
A solitary chair doth near it rest,
Throne-like, 'neath canopy that droopeth down
From the black beams; upon the walls are shown
The painted histories of the olden might,
The King of the Wends Thassilo's stern fight
On land with Nimrod, and on ocean wide
With Neptune. Rivers too personified
Appear—the Rhine as by the Meuse betrayed,
And fading groups of Odin in the shade,
And the wolf Fenrir and the Asgard snake.
One might the place for dragons' stable take.
The only lights that in the shed appear
Spring from the table's giant chandelier
With seven iron branches—brought from hell
By Attila Archangel, people tell,
When he had conquered Mammon—and they say
That seven souls were the first flames that day.
This banquet hall looks an abyss outlined

With shadowy vagueness, though indeed we find
In the far depth upon the table spread
A sudden, strong, and glaring light is shed,
Striking upon the goldsmith's burnished works,
And on the pheasants killed by traitor hawks.
Loaded the table is with viands cold,
Ewers and flagons, all enough of old
To make a love feast. All the napery
Was Friesland's famous make; and fair to see
The dishes, silver-gilt and bordered round
With flowers; for fruit, here strawberries were found
And citrons, apples too, and nectarines.
The wooden bowls were carved in cunning lines
By peasants of the Murg, whose skilful hands
With patient toil reclaim the barren lands
And make their gardens flourish on a rock,
Or mountain where we see the hunters flock.
Gold fountain-cup, with handles Florentine,
Shows Acteons horned, though armed and booted fine,
Who fight with sword in hand against the hounds.
Roses and gladioles make up bright mounds
Of flowers, with juniper and aniseed;
While sage, all newly cut for this great need,
Covers the Persian carpet that is spread
Beneath the table, and so helps to shed
Around a perfume of the balmy spring.
Beyond is desolation withering.
One hears within the hollow dreary space
Across the grove, made fresh by summer's grace,
The wind that ever is with mystic might

A spirit ripple of the Infinite.
The glass restored to frames to creak is made
By blustering wind that comes from neighboring glade.
Strange in this dream-like place, so drear and lone,
The guest expected should be living one!
The seven lights from seven arms make glow
Almost with life the staring eyes that show
On the dim frescoes—and along the walls
Is here and there a stool, or the light falls
O'er some long chest, with likeness to a tomb.
Yet was displayed amid the mournful gloom
Some copper vessels, and some crockery ware.
The door—as if it must, yet scarcely dare—
Had opened widely to the night's fresh air.

No voice is heard, for man has fled the place;
But Terror crouches in the corners' space,
And waits the coming guest. This banquet hall
Of Titans is so high, that he who shall
With wandering eye look up from beam to beam
Of the confused wild roof will haply seem
To wonder that the stars he sees not there.
Giants the spiders are, that weave with care
Their hideous webs, which float the joists amid,
Joists whose dark ends in griffins' jaws are hid.
The light is lurid, and the air like death,
And dark and foul. Even Night holds its breath
Awhile. One might suppose the door had fear
To move its double leaves—their noise to hear.

VIII.

WHAT MORE WAS TO BE SEEN.

But the great hall of generations dead
Has something more sepulchral and more dread
Than lurid glare from seven-branched chandelier
Or table lone with stately daïs near—
Two rows of arches o'er a colonnade
With knights on horseback all in mail arrayed,
Each one disposed with pillar at his back
And to another vis-à-vis. Nor lack
The fittings all complete; in each right hand
A lance is seen; the armored horses stand
With chamfrons laced, and harness buckled sure;
The cuissarts' studs are by their clamps secure;
The dirks stand out upon the saddle-bow;
Even unto the horses' feet do flow
Caparisons,—the leather all well clasped,
The gorget and the spurs with bronze tongues hasped,
The shining long sword from the saddle hung,
The battle-axe across the back was flung.
Under the arm a trusty dagger rests,
Each spiked knee-piece its murderous power attests.
Feet press the stirrups—hands on bridle shown
Proclaim all ready, with the visors down,
And yet they stir not, nor is audible
A sound to make the sight less terrible.

Each monstrous horse a frontal horn doth bear,

If e'er the Prince of Darkness herdsman were,
These cattle black were his by surest right,
Like things but seen in horrid dreams of night.
The steeds are swathed in trappings manifold,
The armed knights are grave, and stern, and cold,
Terrific too; the clench'd fists seem to hold
Some frightful missive, which the phantom hands
Would show, if opened out at hell's commands.
The dusk exaggerates their giant size,
The shade is awed—the pillars coldly rise.
Oh, Night! why are these awful warriors here?

Horses and horsemen that make gazers fear
Are only empty armor. But erect
And haughty mien they all affect
And threatening air—though shades of iron still.
Are they strange larvae—these their statues ill?
No. They are dreams of horror clothed in brass,
Which from profoundest depths of evil pass
With futile aim to dare the Infinite!
Souls tremble at the silent spectre sight,
As if in this mysterious cavalcade
They saw the weird and mystic halt was made
Of them who at the coming dawn of day
Would fade, and from their vision pass away.
A stranger looking in, these masks to see,
Might deem from Death some mandate there might be
At times to burst the tombs—the dead to wear
A human shape, and mustering ranks appear
Of phantoms, each confronting other shade.

Grave-clothes are not more grim and sombre made
Than are these helms; the deaf and sealed-up graves
Are not more icy than these arms; the staves
Of hideous biers have not their joints more strong
Than are the joinings of these legs; the long
Scaled gauntlet fingers look like worms that shine,
And battle robes to shroud-like folds incline.
The heads are skull-like, and the stony feet
Seem for the charnel house but only meet.
The pikes have death's-heads carved, and seem to be
Too heavy; but the shapes defiantly
Sit proudly in the saddle—and perforce
The rider looks united to the horse!
The network of their mail doth clearly cross.
The Marquis' mortar beams near Ducal wreath,
And on the helm and gleaming shield beneath
Alternate triple pearls with leaves displayed
Of parsley, and the royal robes are made
So large that with the knightly harness they
Seem to o'ermaster palfreys every way.
To Rome the oldest armor might be traced,
And men and horses' armor interlaced
Blent horribly; the man and steed we feel
Made but one hydra with its scales of steel.
Yet is there history here. Each coat of mail
Is representant of some stirring tale.
Each delta-shaped escutcheon shines to show
A vision of the chief by it we know.
Here are the blood-stained Dukes' and Marquis' line,

Barbaric lords, who amid war's rapine
Bore gilded saints upon their banners still
Painted on fishes' skin with cunning skill.
Here Geth, who to the Slaves cried "Onward go,"
And Mundiaque and Ottocar—Plato
And Ladisläus Kunne; and Welf who bore
These words upon his shield his foes before;
"Nothing there is I fear." Otho blear-eyed,
Zultan and Nazamustus, and beside
The later Spignus, e'en to Spartibor
Of triple vision, and yet more and more
As if a pause at every age were made,
And Antaeus' fearful dynasty portrayed.

What do they here so rigid and erect?
What wait they for—and what do they expect?
Blindness fills up the helm 'neath iron brows;
Like sapless tree no soul the hero knows.
Darkness is now where eyes with flame were fraught,
And thrice-bored visor serves for mask of naught.
Of empty void is spectral giant made,
And each of these all-powerful knights displayed
Is only rind of pride and murderous sin;
Themselves are held the icy grave within.
Rust eats the casques enamoured once so much
Of death and daring—which knew kiss-like touch
Of banner—mistress so august and dear—
But not an arm can stir its hinges here;
Behold how mute are they whose threats were heard
Like savage roar—whose gnashing teeth and word

Poems

Deadened the clarion's tones; the helmets dread
Have not a sound, and all the armor spread,
The hauberks, that strong breathing seemed to sway,
Are stranded now in helplessness alway
To see the shadows, still prolonged, that seem
To take at night the image of a dream.

These two great files reach from the door afar
To where the table and the daïs are,
Leaving between their fronts a narrow lane.
On the left side the Marquises maintain
Their place, but the right side the Dukes retain,
And till the roof, embattled by Spignus,
But worn by time that even that subdues,
Shall fall upon their heads, these forms will stand
The grades confronting—one on either hand.
While in advance beyond, with haughty head—
As if commander of this squadron dread—
All waiting signal of the Judgment Day,
In stone was seen in olden sculptors' way
Charlemagne the King, who on the earth had found
Only twelve knights to grace his Table Round.

The crests were an assembly of strange things,
Of horrors such as nightmare only brings.
Asps, and spread eagles without beak or feet,
Sirens and mermaids here and dragons meet,
And antlered stags and fabled unicorn,
And fearful things of monstrous fancy born.
Upon the rigid form of morion's sheen

Winged lions and the Cerberus are seen,
And serpents winged and finned; things made to fright
The timid foe, alone by sense of sight.
Some leaning forward and the others back,
They looked a growing forest that did lack
No form of terror; but these things of dread
That once on barons' helms the battle led
Beneath the giant banners, now are still,

As if they gaped and found the time but ill,
Wearied the ages passed so slowly by,
And that the gory dead no more did lie
Beneath their feet—pined for the battle-cry,
The trumpet's clash, the carnage and the strife,
Yawning to taste again their dreadful life.
Like tears upon the palfreys' muzzles were
The hard reflections of the metal there;
From out these spectres, ages past exhumed,
And as their shadows on the roof-beams loomed,
Cast by the trembling light, each figure wan
Seemed growing, and a monstrous shape to don,
So that the double range of horrors made
The darkened zenith clouds of blackest shade,
That shaped themselves to profiles terrible.

All motionless the coursers horrible,
That formed a legion lured by Death to war,
These men and horses masked, how dread they are!
Absorbed in shadows of the eternal shore,
Among the living all their tasks are o'er.

Silent, they seem all mystery to brave,
These sphinxes whom no beacon light can save
Upon the threshold of the gulf so near,
As if they faced the great enigma here;
Ready with hoofs, between the pillars blue
To strike out sparks, and combats to renew,
Choosing for battle-field the shades below,
Which they provoked by deeds we cannot know,
In that dark realm thought dares not to expound
False masks from heaven lowered to depths profound.

IX.

A NOISE ON THE FLOOR.

This is the scene on which now enters in
Eviradnus; and follows page Gasclin.

The outer walls were almost all decayed,
The door, for ancient Marquises once made—
Raised many steps above the courtyard near—
Commanded view of the horizon clear.
The forest looked a great gulf all around,
And on the rock of Corbus there were found
Secret and blood-stained precipices tall.
Duke Plato built the tower and banquet hall
Over great pits,—so was it Rumor said.
The flooring sounds 'neath Eviradnus' tread
Above abysses many.
    "Page," said he,

"Come here, your eyes than mine can better see,
For sight is woman-like and shuns the old;
Ah! he can see enough, when years are told,
Who backwards looks. But, boy, turn towards the glade
And tell me what you see."
    The boy obeyed,
And leaned across the threshold, while the bright,
Full moon shed o'er the glade its white, pure light.

"I see a horse and woman on it now,"
Said Gasclin, "and companions also show."
"Who are they?" asked the seeker of sublime
Adventures. "Sir, I now can hear like chime
The sound of voices, and men's voices too,
Laughter and talk; two men there are in view,
Across the road the shadows clear I mark
Of horses three."
    "Enough. Now, Gasclin, hark!"
Exclaimed the knight, "you must at once return
By other path than that which you discern,
So that you be not seen. At break of day
Bring back our horses fresh, and every way
Caparisoned; now leave me, boy, I say."
The page looked at his master like a son,
And said, "Oh! if I might stay on,
For they are two."

    "Go—I suffice alone!"

X.

EVIRADNUS MOTIONLESS.

And lone the hero is within the hall,
And nears the table where the glasses all
Show in profusion; all the vessels there,
Goblets and glasses gilt, or painted fair,
Are ranged for different wines with practised care.
He thirsts; the flagons tempt; but there must stay
One drop in emptied glass, and 'twould betray
The fact that some one living had been here.
Straight to the horses goes he, pauses near
That which is next the table shining bright,
Seizes the rider—plucks the phantom knight
To pieces—all in vain its panoply
And pallid shining to his practised eye;
Then he conveys the severed iron remains
To corner of the hall where darkness reigns;
Against the wall he lays the armor low
In dust and gloom like hero vanquished now—
But keeping pond'rous lance and shield so old,
Mounts to the empty saddle, and behold!
A statue Eviradnus has become,
Like to the others in their frigid home.
With visor down scarce breathing seemed maintained
Throughout the hall a death-like silence reigned.

XI.

A LITTLE MUSIC.

Listen! like hum froth unseen nests we hear
A mirthful buzz of voices coming near,
Of footsteps—laughter—from the trembling trees.
And now the thick-set forest all receives
A flood of moonlight—and there gently floats
The sound of a guitar of Inspruck; notes
Which blend with chimes—vibrating to the hand—
Of tiny bell—where sounds a grain of sand.
A man's voice mixes with the melody,
And vaguely melts to song in harmony.

"If you like we'll dream a dream.
  Let us mount on palfreys two;
Birds are singing,—let it seem
  You lure me—and I take you.

"Let us start—'tis eve, you see,
  I'm thy master and thy prey.
My bright steed shall pleasure be;
  Yours, it shall be love, I say.

"Journeying leisurely we go,
  We will make our steeds touch heads,
Kiss for fodder,—and we so
  Satisfy our horses' needs.

"Come! the two delusive things
  Stamp impatiently it seems,
Yours has heavenward soaring wings,
  Mine is of the land of dreams.

"What's our baggage? only vows,
  Happiness, and all our care,
And the flower that sweetly shows
  Nestling lightly in your hair.

"Come, the oaks all dark appear,
  Twilight now will soon depart,
Railing sparrows laugh to hear
  Chains thou puttest round my heart.

"Not my fault 'twill surely be
  If the hills should vocal prove,
And the trees when us they see,
  All should murmur—let us love!

"Oh, be gentle!—I am dazed,
  See the dew is on the grass,
Wakened butterflies amazed
  Follow thee as on we pass.

"Envious night-birds open wide
  Their round eyes to gaze awhile,
Nymphs that lean their urns beside
  From their grottoes softly smile,

"And exclaim, by fancy stirred,
  'Hero and Leander they;
We in listening for a word
  Let our water fall away.'

"Let us journey Austrian way,
  With the daybreak on our brow;
I be great, and you I say
  Rich, because we love shall know.

"Let us over countries rove,
  On our charming steeds content,
In the azure light of love,
  And its sweet bewilderment.

"For the charges at our inn,
  You with maiden smiles shall pay;
I the landlord's heart will win
  In a scholar's pleasant way.

"You, great lady—and I, Count—
Come, my heart has opened quite,
We this tale will still recount,
  To the stars that shine at night."

The melody went on some moments more
Among the trees the calm moon glistened o'er,
Then trembled and was hushed; the voice's thrill
Stopped like alighting birds, and all was still.

XII.

GREAT JOSS AND LITTLE ZENO.

Quite suddenly there showed across the door,
Three heads which all a festive aspect wore.
Two men were there; and, dressed in cloth of gold,
A woman. Of the men one might have told
Some thirty years, the other younger seemed,
Was tall and fair, and from his shoulder gleamed
A gay guitar with ivy leaves enlaced.
The other man was dark, but pallid-faced
And small. At the first glance they seemed to be
But made of perfume and frivolity.
Handsome they were, but through their comely mien
A grinning demon might be clearly seen.
April has flowers where lurk the slugs between.

"Big Joss and little Zeno, pray come here;
Look now—how dreadful! can I help but fear!"
Madame Mahaud was speaker. Moonlight there
Caressingly enhanced her beauty rare,
Making it shine and tremble, as if she
So soft and gentle were of things that be
Of air created, and are brought and ta'en
By heavenly flashes. Now, she spoke again
"Certes, 'tis heavy purchase of a throne,
To pass the night here utterly alone.
Had you not slyly come to guard me now,
I should have died of fright outright I know."

The moonbeams through the open door did fall,
And shine upon the figure next the wall.

Said Zeno, "If I played the Marquis part,
I'd send this rubbish to the auction mart;
Out of the heap should come the finest wine,
Pleasure and gala-fêtes, were it all mine."
And then with scornful hand he touched the thing,
And made the metal like a soul's cry ring.
He laughed—the gauntlet trembled at his stroke.
"Let rest my ancestors"—'twas Mahaud spoke;
Then murmuring added she, "For you are much
Too small their noble armor here to touch."

And Zeno paled, but Joss with laugh exclaimed,
"Why, all these good black men so grandly named
Are only nests for mice. By Jove, although
They lifelike look and terrible, we know
What is within; just listen, and you'll hear
The vermins' gnawing teeth, yet 'twould appear
These figures once were proudly named Otho,
And Ottocar, and Bela, and Plato.
Alas! the end's not pleasant—puts one out;
To have been kings and dukes—made mighty rout—
Colossal heroes filling tombs with slain,
And, Madame, this to only now remain;
A peaceful nibbling rat to calmly pierce
A prince's noble armor proud and fierce."

"Sing, if you will—but do not speak so loud;

Besides, such things as these," said fair Mahaud,
"In your condition are not understood."
"Well said," made answer Zeno, "'tis a place
Of wonders—I see serpents, and can trace
Vampires, and monsters swarming, that arise
In mist, through chinks, to meet the gazer's eyes."

Then Mahaud shuddered, and she said: "The wine
The Abbé made me drink as task of mine,
Will soon enwrap me in the soundest sleep—
Swear not to leave me—that you here will keep."
"I swear," cried Joss, and Zeno, "I also;
But now at once to supper let us go."

XIII.

THEY SUP.

With laugh and song they to the table went.
Said Mahaud gayly: "It is my intent
To make Joss chamberlain. Zeno shall be
A constable supreme of high degree."
All three were joyous, and were fair to see.
Joss ate—and Zeno drank; on stools the pair,
With Mahaud musing in the regal chair.
The sound of separate leaf we do not note—
And so their babble seemed to idly float,
And leave no thought behind. Now and again
Joss his guitar made trill with plaintive strain
Or Tyrolean air; and lively tales they told

Mingled with mirth all free, and frank, and bold.
Said Mahaud: "Do you know how fortunate
You are?" "Yes, we are young at any rate—
Lovers half crazy—this is truth at least."
"And more, for you know Latin like a priest,
And Joss sings well."
   "Ah, yes, our master true,
Yields us these gifts beyond the measure due."
"Your master!—who is he?" Mahaud exclaimed.
"Satan, we say—but Sin you'd think him named,"
Said Zeno, veiling words in raillery.
"Do not laugh thus," she said with dignity;
"Peace, Zeno. Joss, you speak, my chamberlain."
"Madame, Viridis, Countess of Milan,
Was deemed superb; Diana on the mount
Dazzled the shepherd boy; ever we count
The Isabel of Saxony so fair,
And Cleopatra's beauty all so rare—
Aspasia's, too, that must with theirs compare—
That praise of them no fitting language hath.
Divine was Rhodope—and Venus' wrath
Was such at Erylesis' perfect throat,
She dragged her to the forge where Vulcan smote
Her beauty on his anvil. Well, as much
As star transcends a sequin, and just such
As temple is to rubbish-heap, I say,
You do eclipse their beauty every way.
Those airy sprites that from the azure smile,
Peris and elfs the while they men beguile,
Have brows less youthful pure than yours; besides

Dishevelled they whose shaded beauty hides
In clouds."
  "Flatt'rer," said Mahaud, "you but sing
Too well."
  Then Joss more homage sought to bring;
"If I were angel under heav'n," said he,
"Or girl or demon, I would seek to be
By you instructed in all art and grace,
And as in school but take a scholar's place.
Highness, you are a fairy bright, whose hand
For sceptre vile gave up your proper wand."
Fair Mahaud mused—then said, "Be silent now;
You seem to watch me; little 'tis I know,
Only that from Bohemia Joss doth come,
And that in Poland Zeno hath his home.
But you amuse me; I am rich, you poor—
What boon shall I confer and make secure?
What gift? ask of me, poets, what you will
And I will grant it—promise to fulfil."
"A kiss," said Joss.
  "A kiss!" and anger fraught
Amazed at minstrel having such a thought—
While flush of indignation warmed her cheek.
"You do forget to whom it is you speak,"
She cried.
  "Had I not known your high degree,
Should I have asked this royal boon," said he,
"Obtained or given, a kiss must ever be.
No gift like king's—no kiss like that of queen!"
Queen! And on Mahaud's face a smile was seen.

XIV.

AFTER SUPPER.

But now the potion proved its subtle power,
And Mahaud's heavy eyelids 'gan to lower.
Zeno, with finger on his lip, looked on—
Her head next drooped, and consciousness was gone.
Smiling she slept, serene and very fair,
He took her hand, which fell all unaware.

"She sleeps," said Zeno, "now let chance or fate
Decide for us which has the marquisate,
And which the girl."

   Upon their faces now
A hungry tiger's look began to show.
"My brother, let us speak like men of sense,"
Said Joss; "while Mahaud dreams in innocence,
We grasp all here—and hold the foolish thing—
Our Friend below to us success will bring.
He keeps his word; 'tis thanks to him I say,
No awkward chance has marred our plans to-day.
All has succeeded—now no human power
Can take from us this woman and her dower.
Let us conclude. To wrangle and to fight
For just a yes or no, or to prove right
The Arian doctrines, all the time the Pope
Laughs in his sleeve at you—or with the hope
Some blue-eyed damsel with a tender skin

And milkwhite dainty hands by force to win—
This might be well in days when men bore loss
And fought for Latin or Byzantine Cross;
When Jack and Rudolf did like fools contend,
And for a simple wench their valor spend—
When Pepin held a synod at Leptine,
And times than now were much less wise and fine.
We do no longer heap up quarrels thus,
But better know how projects to discuss.
Have you the needful dice?"

   "Yes, here they wait
For us."

   "Who wins shall have the Marquisate;
Loser, the girl."

   "Agreed."

   "A noise I hear?"
"Only the wind that sounds like some one near—
Are you afraid?" said Zeno.

   "Naught I fear
Save fasting—and that solid earth should gape.
Let's throw and fate decide—ere time escape."
Then rolled the dice.

   "'Tis four."

'Twas Joss to throw.
"Six!—and I neatly win, you see; and lo!
At bottom of this box I've found Lusace,
And henceforth my orchestra will have place;
To it they'll dance. Taxes I'll raise, and they
In dread of rope and forfeit well will pay;
Brass trumpet-calls shall be my flutes that lead,
Where gibbets rise the imposts grow and spread."

Said Zeno, "I've the girl and so is best,"
"She's beautiful," said Joss.

   "Yes, 'tis confess'd."
"What shall you do with her?" asked Joss.

   "I know.
Make her a corpse," said Zeno; "marked you how
The jade insulted me just now! Too small
She called me—such the words her lips let fall.
I say, that moment ere the dice I threw
Had yawning Hell cried out, 'My son, for you
The chance is open still: take in a heap
The fair Lusace's seven towns, and reap
The corn, and wine, and oil of counties ten,
With all their people diligent, and then
Bohemia with its silver mines, and now
The lofty land whence mighty rivers flow
And not a brook returns; add to these counts
The Tyrol with its lovely azure mounts
And France with her historic fleurs-de-lis;

Come now, decide, what 'tis your choice must be?'
I should have answered, 'Vengeance! give to me
Rather than France, Bohemia, or the fair
Blue Tyrol, I my choice, O Hell! declare
For government of darkness and of death,
Of grave and worms.' Brother, this woman hath
As marchioness with absurdity set forth
To rule o'er frontier bulwarks of the north.
In any case to us a danger she,
And having stupidly insulted me
'Tis needful that she die. To blurt all out—
I know that you desire her; without doubt
The flame that rages in my heart warms yours;
To carry out these subtle plans of ours,
We have become as gypsies near this doll,
You as her page—I dotard to control—
Pretended gallants changed to lovers now.
So, brother, this being fact for us to know
Sooner or later, 'gainst our best intent
About her we should quarrel. Evident
Is it our compact would be broken through.
There is one only thing for us to do,
And that is, kill her."

    "Logic very clear,"
Said musing Joss, "but what of blood shed here?"
Then Zeno stooped and lifted from the ground
An edge of carpet—groped until he found
A ring, which, pulled, an opening did disclose,
With deep abyss beneath; from it there rose

The odor rank of crime. Joss walked to see
While Zeno pointed to it silently.
But eyes met eyes, and Joss, well pleased, was fain
By nod of head to make approval plain.

XV.

THE OUBLIETTES.

If sulphurous light had shone from this vile well
One might have said it was a mouth of hell,
So large the trap that by some sudden blow
A man might backward fall and sink below.
Who looked could see a harrow's threatening teeth,
But lost in night was everything beneath.
Partitions blood-stained have a reddened smear,
And Terror unrelieved is master here.
One feels the place has secret histories
Replete with dreadful murderous mysteries,
And that this sepulchre, forgot to-day,
Is home of trailing ghosts that grope their way
Along the walls where spectre reptiles crawl.
"Our fathers fashioned for us after all
Some useful things," said Joss; then Zeno spoke:
"I know what Corbus hides beneath its cloak,
I and the osprey know the castle old,
And what in bygone times the justice bold."

"And are you sure that Mahaud will not wake?"
"Her eyes are closed as now my fist I make;

She is in mystic and unearthly sleep;
The potion still its power o'er her must keep."
"But she will surely wake at break of day?"
"In darkness."

"What will all the courtiers say
When in the place of her they find two men?"
"To them we will declare ourselves—and then
They at our feet will fall."

"Where leads this hole?"
"To where the crow makes feast and torrents roll
To desolation. Let us end it now."

These young and handsome men had seemed to grow
Deformed and hideous—so doth foul black heart
Disfigure man, till beauty all depart.
So to the hell within the human face
Transparent is. They nearer move apace;
And Mahaud soundly sleeps as in a bed.
"To work."

Joss seizes her and holds her head
Supporting her beneath her arms, in his;
And then he dared to plant a monstrous kiss
Upon her rosy lips,—while Zeno bent
Before the massive chair, and with intent
Her robe disordered as he raised her feet;
Her dainty ankles thus their gaze to meet.
And while the mystic sleep was all profound,

The pit gaped wide like grave in burial ground.

XVI.

WHAT THEY ATTEMPT BECOMES DIFFICULT.

Bearing the sleeping Mahaud they moved now
Silent and bent with heavy step and slow.
Zeno faced darkness—Joss turned towards the light—
So that the hall to Joss was quite in sight.
Sudden he stopped—and Zeno, "What now!" called,
But Joss replied not, though he seemed appalled,
And made a sign to Zeno, who with speed
Looked back. Then seemed they changed to stone indeed.
For both perceived that in the vaulted hall
One of the grand old knights ranged by the wall
Descended from his horse. Like phantom he
Moved with a horrible tranquillity.
Masked by his helm towards them he came; his tread
Made the floor tremble—and one might have said
A spirit of th' abyss was here; between
Them and the pit he came—a barrier seen;
Then said, with sword in hand and visor down,
In measured tones that had sepulchral grown
As tolling bell, "Stop, Sigismond, and you,
King Ladisläus;" at those words, though few,
They dropped the Marchioness, and in such a way
That at their feet like rigid corpse she lay.

The deep voice speaking from the visor's grate

Proceeded—while the two in abject state
Cowered low. Joss paled, by gloom and dread o'ercast,
And Zeno trembled like a yielding mast.
"You two who listen now must recollect
The compact all your fellow-men suspect.
'Tis this: 'I, Satan, god of darkened sphere,
The king of gloom and winds that bring things drear,
Alliance make with my two brothers dear,
The Emperor Sigismond and Polish King
Named Ladisläus. I to surely bring
Aid and protection to them both alway,
And never to absent myself or say
I'm weary. And yet more—I, being lord
Of sea and land, to Sigismond award
The earth; to Ladisläus all the sea.
With this condition that they yield to me
When I the forfeit claim—the King his head,
But shall the Emperor give his soul instead.'"

Said Joss, "Is't he?—Spectre with flashing eyes,
And art thou Satan come to us surprise?"
"Much less am I and yet much more.
Oh, kings of crimes and plots! your day is o'er,
But I your lives will only take to-day;
Beneath the talons black your souls let stay
To wrestle still."

  The pair looked stupefied
And crushed. Exchanging looks 'twas Zeno cried,
Speaking to Joss, "Now who—who can it be?"

Joss stammered, "Yes, no refuge can I see;
The doom is on us. But oh, spectre! say
Who are you?"

"I'm the judge."

"Then mercy, pray."
The voice replied: "God guides His chosen hand
To be th' Avenger in your path to stand.
Your hour has sounded, nothing now indeed
Can change for you the destiny decreed,
Irrevocable quite. Yes, I looked on.
Ah! little did you think that any one
To this unwholesome gloom could knowledge bring
That Joss a kaiser was, and Zeno king.
You spoke just now—but why?—too late to plead.
The forfeit's due and hope should all be dead.
Incurables! For you I am the grave.
Oh, miserable men! that naught can save.
Yes, Sigismond a kaiser is, and you
A king, O Ladisläus!—it is true.
You thought of God but as a wheel to roll
Your chariot on; you who have king's control
O'er Poland and its many towns so strong.
You, Milan's Duke, to whom at once belong
The gold and iron crowns. You, Emperor made
By Rome, a son of Hercules 'tis said;
And you of Spartibor. And your two crowns
Are shining lights; and yet your shadow frowns
From every mountain land to trembling sea.

You are at giddy heights twin powers to be
A glory and a force for all that's great—
But 'neath the purple canopy of state,
Th' expanding and triumphant arch you prize,
'Neath royal power that sacred veils disguise,
Beneath your crowns of pearls and jewelled stars,
Beneath your exploits terrible and wars,
You, Sigismond, have but a monster been,
And, Ladisläus, you are scoundrel seen.
Oh, degradation of the sceptre's might
And swords—when Justice has a hand like night,
Foul and polluted; and before this thing,
This hydra, do the Temple's hinges swing—
The throne becomes the haunt of all things base
Oh, age of infamy and foul disgrace!
Oh, starry heavens looking on the shame,
No brow but reddens with resentful flame—
And yet the silent people do not stir!
Oh, million arms! what things do you deter—
Poor sheep, whom vermin-majesties devour,
Have you not nails with strong desiring power
To rend these royalties, that you so cower?
But two are taken,—such as will amaze
E'en hell itself, when it on them shall gaze.
Ah, Sigismond and Ladisläus, you
Were once triumphant, splendid to the view,
Stifling with your prosperity—but now
The hour of retribution lays you low.
Ah, do the vulture and the crocodile
Shed tears! At such a sight I fain must smile.

It seems to me 'tis very good sometimes
That princes, conquerors stained with bandits' crimes,
Sparkling with splendor, wearing crowns of gold,
Should know the deadly sweat endured of old,
That of Jehoshaphat; should sob and fear,
And after crime th' unclean be brought to bear.
'Tis well—God rules—and thus it is that I
These masters of the world can make to lie
In ashes at my feet. And this was he
Who reigned—and this a Caesar known to be!
In truth, my old heart aches with very shame
To see such cravens with such noble name.
But let us finish—what has just passed here
Demands thick shrouding, and the time is near.
Th' accursed dice that rolled at Calvary
You rolled a woman's murder to decree
It was a dark disastrous game to play;
But not for me a moral to essay.
This moment to the misty grave is due,
And far too vile and little human you
To see your evil ways. Your fingers lack
The human power your shocking deeds to track.
What use in darkness mirror to uphold?
What use your doings to be now retold?
Drink of the darkness—greedy of the ill
To which from habit you're attracted still,
Not recognizing in the draught you take
The stench that your atrocities must make.
I only tell you that this burdened age
Tires of your Highnesses, that soil its page,

And of your villanies—and this is why
You now must swell the stream that passes by
Of refuse filth. Oh, horrid scene to show
Of these young men and that young girl just now!
Oh! can you really be of human kind
Breathing pure air of heaven? Do we find
That you are men? Oh, no! for when you laid
Foul lips upon the mouth of sleeping maid,
You seemed but ghouls that had come furtively
From out the tombs; only a horrid lie
Your human shape; of some strange frightful beast
You have the soul. To darkness I at least
Remit you now. Oh, murderer Sigismond
And Ladisläus pirate, both beyond
Release—two demons that have broken ban!
Therefore 'tis time their empire over man
And converse with the living, should be o'er;
Tyrants, behold your tomb your eyes before;
Vampires and dogs, your sepulchre is here.
Enter."

   He pointed to the gulf so near.
All terrified upon their knees they fell.
"Oh! take us not in your dread realm to dwell,"
Said Sigismond. "But, phantom! do us tell
What thou wouldst have from us—we will obey.
Oh, mercy!—'tis for mercy now we pray."
"Behold us at your feet, oh, spectre dread!"
And no old crone in feebler voice could plead
Than Ladisläus did.

But not a word
Said now the figure motionless, with sword
In hand. This sovereign soul seemed to commune
With self beneath his metal sheath; yet soon
And suddenly, with tranquil voice said he,
"Princes, your craven spirit wearies me.
No phantom—only man am I. Arise!
I like not to be dreaded otherwise
Than with the fear to which I'm used; know me,
For it is Eviradnus that you see!"

XVII.

THE CLUB.

As from the mist a noble pine we tell
Grown old upon the heights of Appenzel,
When morning freshness breathes round all the wood,
So Eviradnus now before them stood,
Opening his visor, which at once revealed
The snowy beard it had so well concealed.
Thin Sigismond was still as dog at gaze,
But Ladisläus leaped, and howl did raise,
And laughed and gnashed his teeth, till, like a cloud
That sudden bursts, his rage was all avowed.
"'Tis but an old man after all!" he cried.

Then the great knight, who looked at both, replied,
"Oh, kings! an old man of my time can cope

With two much younger ones of yours, I hope.
To mortal combat I defy you both
Singly; or, if you will, I'm nothing loth
With two together to contend; choose here
From out the heap what weapon shall appear
Most fit. As you no cuirass wear, I see,
I will take off my own, for all must be
In order perfect—e'en your punishment."

Then Eviradnus, true to his intent,
Stripped to his Utrecht jerkin; but the while
He calmly had disarmed—with dexterous guile
Had Ladisläus seized a knife that lay
Upon the damask cloth, and slipped away
His shoes; then barefoot, swiftly, silently
He crept behind the knight, with arm held high.
But Eviradnus was of all aware,
And turned upon the murderous weapon there,
And twisted it away; then in a trice
His strong colossal hand grasped like a vice
The neck of Ladisläus, who the blade
Now dropped; over his eyes a misty shade
Showed that the royal dwarf was near to death.

"Traitor!" said Eviradnus in his wrath,
"I rather should have hewn your limbs away,
And left you crawling on your stumps, I say,—
But now die fast."

   Ghastly, with starting eyes,

The King without a cry or struggle dies.
One dead—but lo! the other stands bold-faced,
Defiant; for the knight, when he unlaced
His cuirass, had his trusty sword laid down,
And Sigismond now grasps it as his own.
The monster-youth laughed at the silv'ry beard,
And, sword in hand, a murderer glad appeared.
Crossing his arms, he cried, "'Tis my turn now!"
And the black mounted knights in solemn row
Were judges of the strife. Before them lay
The sleeping Mahaud—and not far away
The fatal pit, near which the champion knight
With evil Emperor must contend for right,
Though weaponless he was. And yawned the pit
Expectant which should be engulfed in it.

"Now we shall see for whom this ready grave,"
Said Sigismond, "you dog, whom naught can save!"
Aware was Eviradnus that if he
Turned for a blade unto the armory,
He would be instant pierced—what can he do?
The moment is for him supreme. But, lo!
He glances now at Ladisläus dead,
And with a smile triumphant and yet dread,
And air of lion caged to whom is shown
Some loophole of escape, he bends him down.

"Ha! ha! no other club than this I need!"
He cried, as seizing in his hands with speed
The dead King's heels, the body lifted high,

Then to the frightened Emperor he came nigh,
And made him shake with horror and with fear,
The weapon all so ghastly did appear.
The head became the stone to this strange sling,
Of which the body was the potent string;
And while 'twas brandished in a deadly way,
The dislocated arms made monstrous play
With hideous gestures, as now upside down
The bludgeon corpse a giant force had grown.
"'Tis well!" said Eviradnus, and he cried,
"Arrange between yourselves, you two allied;
If hell-fire were extinguished, surely it
By such a contest might be all relit;
From kindling spark struck out from dead King's brow,
Batt'ring to death a living Emperor now."

And Sigismond, thus met and horrified,
Recoiled to near the unseen opening wide;
The human club was raised, and struck again * * *
And Eviradnus did alone remain
All empty-handed—but he heard the sound
Of spectres two falling to depths profound;
Then, stooping o'er the pit, he gazed below,
And, as half-dreaming now, he murmured low,
"Tiger and jackal meet their portion here,
'Tis well together they should disappear!"

XVIII.

DAYBREAK.

Then lifts he Mahaud to the ducal chair,
And shuts the trap with noiseless, gentle care;
And puts in order everything around,
So that, on waking, naught should her astound.

"No drop of blood the thing has cost," mused he,
"And that is best indeed."

    But suddenly
Some distant bells clang out. The mountains gray
Have scarlet tips, proclaiming dawning day;
The hamlets are astir, and crowds come out—
Bearing fresh branches of the broom—about
To seek their Lady, who herself awakes
Rosy as morn, just when the morning breaks;
Half-dreaming still, she ponders, can it be
Some mystic change has passed, for her to see
One old man in the place of two quite young!
Her wondering eyes search carefully and long.
It may be she regrets the change: meanwhile,
The valiant knight salutes her with a smile,
And then approaching her with friendly mien,
Says, "Madam, has your sleep all pleasant been?"

MRS. NEWTON CROSLAND.

Poems

THE SOUDAN, THE SPHINXES, THE CUP, THE LAMP.

("Zim-Zizimi, Soudan d'Égypte.")

{Bk. XVI. i.}
Zim Zizimi—(of the Soudan of burnt Egypt,
The Commander of Believers, a Bashaw
Whose very robes were from Asia's greatest stript,
More powerful than any lion with resistless paw)
A master weighed on by his immense splendor—
Once had a dream when he was at his evening feast,
When the broad table smoked like a perfumed censer,
And its grateful odors the appetite increased.
The banquet was outspread in a hall, high as vast,
With pillars painted, and with ceiling bright with gold,
Upreared by Zim's ancestors in the days long past,
And added to till now worth a sum untold.
Howe'er rich no rarity was absent, it seemed,
Fruit blushed upon the side-boards, groaning 'neath rich meats,
With all the dainties palate ever dreamed
In lavishness to waste—for dwellers in the streets
Of cities, whether Troy, or Tyre, or Ispahan,
Consume, in point of cost, food at a single meal
Much less than what is spread before this crowned man—-
Who rules his couchant nation with a rod of steel,
And whose servitors' chiefest arts it was to squeeze
The world's full teats into his royal helpless mouth.

Each hard-sought dainty that never failed to please,
All delicacies, wines, from east, west, north or south,
Are plenty here—for Sultan Zizimi drinks wine
In its variety, trying to find what never sates.
Laughs at the holy writings and the text divine,
O'er which the humble dervish prays and venerates.
There is a common saying which holds often good:
That cruel is he who is sparing in his cups.
That they are such as are most thirsty of man's blood—
Yet he will see a slave beheaded whilst he sups.
But be this as it all may, glory gilds his reign,
He has overrun Africa, the old and black;
Asia as well—holding them both beneath a rain
Of bloody drops from scaffold, pyre, the stake, or rack,
To leave his empire's confines, one must run a race
Far past the river Baxtile southward; in the north,
To the rude, rocky, barren land of Thrace,
Yet near enough to shudder when great Zim is wroth.
Conquering in every field, he finds delight
In battle-storms; his music is the shout of camps.
On seeing him the eagle speeds away in fright,
Whilst hid 'mong rocks, the grisly wolf its victim champs.
Mysore's as well as Agra's rajah is his kin;
The great sheiks of the arid sands confess him lord;
Omar, who vaunting cried: "Through me doth Allah win!"
Was of his blood—a dreaded line of fire and sword.
The waters of Nagain, sands of Sahara warm,
The Atlas and the Caucasus, snow-capped and lone,
Mecca, Marcatta, these were massed in part to form
A portion of the giant shadow of Zim's throne.

Before his might, to theirs, as hardest rock to dust,
There have recoiled a horde of savage, warlike chiefs,
Who have been into Afric's fiery furnace thrust—
Its scorching heat to his rage greatest of reliefs.
There is no being but fears Zim; to him bows down
Even the sainted Llama in the holy place;
And the wild Kasburder chieftain at his dark power
Turns pale, and seeks a foeman of some lesser race.
Cities and states are bought and sold by Soudan Zim,
Whose simple word their thousand people hold as law.
He ruins them at will, for what are men to him,
More than to stabled cattle is the sheaf of straw?

The Soudan is not pleased, for he is e'er alone,
For who may in his royal sports or joys be leagued.
He must never speak to any one in equal tones,
But be by his own dazzling weightiness fatigued.
He has exhausted all the pastimes of the earth;
In vain skilled men have fought with sword, the spear, or lance,
The quips and cranks most laughed at have to him no mirth;
He gives a regal yawn as fairest women dance;
Music has outpoured all its notes, the soft and loud,
But dully on his wearied ear its accents roll,
As dully as the praises of the servile crowd
Who falsely sing the purity of his black soul.
He has had before his daïs from the prison brought
Two thieves, whose terror makes their chains to loudly ring,

Then gaping most unkingly, he dismissed his slaves,
And tranquilly, half rising, looked around to seek
In the weighty stillness—such as broods round graves—
Something within his royal scope to which to speak.

The throne, on which at length his eyes came back to rest,
Is upheld by rose-crowned Sphinxes, which lyres hold,
All cut in whitest marble, with uncovered breast,
While their eyes contain that enigma never told.
Each figure has its title carved upon its head:
Health, and *Voluptuousness, Greatness, Joy,* and *Play,*
With *Victory, Beauty, Happiness,* may be read,
Adorning brands they wear unblushing in the day.

The Soudan cried: "O, Sphinxes, with the torch-like eye,
I am the Conqueror—my name is high-arrayed
In characters like flame upon the vaulted sky,
Far from oblivion's reach or an effacing shade.
Upon a sheaf of thunderbolts I rest my arm,
And gods might wish my exploits with them were their own.
I live—I am not open to the points of harm,
And e'en my throne will be with age an altar-stone.
When the time comes for me to cast off earthly robe,
And enter—being Day—into the realms of light,
The gods will say, we call Zizimi from his globe
That we may have our brother nearer to our sight!
Glory is but my menial, Pride my own chained slave,
Humbly standing when Zizimi is in his seat.
I scorn base man, and have sent thousands to the grave.

They are but as a rushen carpet to my feet.
Instead of human beings, eunuchs, blacks, or mutes,
Be yours, oh, Sphinxes, with the glad names on your fronts!
The task, with voice attuned to emulate the flute's,
To charm the king, whose chase is man, and wars his hunts.

"Some portion of your splendor back on me reflect,
Sing out in praiseful chains of melodious links!
Oh, throne, which I with bloody spoils have so bedecked,
Speak to your lord! Speak you, the first rose-crested Sphinx!"

Soon on the summons, once again was stillness broke,
For the ten figures, in a voice which all else drowned,
Parting their stony lips, alternatively spoke—
Spoke clearly, with a deeply penetrative sound.

THE FIRST SPHINX.

So lofty as to brush the heavens' dome,
Upon the highest terrace of her tomb
Is Queen Nitrocis, thinking all alone,
Upon her line, long tenants of the throne,
Terrors, scourges of the Greeks and Hebrews,
Harsh and bloodthirsty, narrow in their views.
Against the pure scroll of the sky, a blot,
Stands out her sepulchre, a fatal spot
That seems a baneful breath around to spread.
The birds which chance to near it, drop down dead.
The queen is now attended on by shades,

Which have replaced, in horrid guise, her maids.
No life is here—the law says such as bore
A corpse alone may enter through yon door.
Before, behind, around the queen, her sight
Encounters but the same blank void of night.
Above, the pilasters are like to bars,
And, through their gaps, the dead look at the stars,
While, till the dawn, around Nitrocis' bones,
Spectres hold council, crouching on the stones.

THE SECOND SPHINX.

Howe'er great is pharaoh, the magi, king,
Encompassed by an idolizing ring,
None is so high as Tiglath Pileser.
Who, like the God before whom pales the star,
Has temples, with a prophet for a priest,
Who serves up daily sacrilegious feast.
His anger there are none who dare provoke,
His very mildness is looked on as a yoke;
And under his, more feared than other rules,
He holds his people bound, like tamèd bulls.
Asia is banded with his paths of war;
He is more of a scourge than Attila.
He triumphs glorious—but, day by day,
The earth falls at his feet, piecemeal away;
And the bricks for his tomb's wall, one by one,
Are being shaped—are baking in the sun.

THE THIRD SPHINX.

Equal to archangel, for one short while,
Was Nimroud, builder of tall Babel's pile.
His sceptre reached across the space between
The sites where Sol to rise and set is seen.
Baal made him terrible to all alike,
The greatest cow'ring when he rose to strike.
Unbelief had shown in ev'ry eye,
Had any dared to say: "Nimroud will die!"
He lived and ruled, but is—at this time, where?
Winds blow free o'er his realm—a desert bare!

THE FOURTH SPHINX.

There is a statue of King Chrem of old,
Of unknown date and maker, but of gold.
How many grandest rulers in his day
Chrem pluckèd down, there are now none can say.
Whether he ruled with gentle hand or rough,
None know. He once was—no longer is—enough,
Crowned Time, whose seat is on a ruined mass,
Holds, and aye turns, a strange sand in his glass,
A sand scraped from the mould, brushed from the shroud
Of all passed things, mean, great, lowly, or proud.
Thus meting with the ashes of the dead
How hours of the living have quickly fled.
The sand runs, monarchs! the clepsydra weeps.
Wherefore? They see through future's gloomy deeps,
Through the church wall, into the catacomb,
And mark the change when thrones do graves become.

THE FIFTH SPHINX.

To swerve the earth seemed from its wonted path
When marched the Four of Asia in their wrath,
And when they were bound slaves to Cyrus' car,
The rivers shrank back from their banks afar.
"Who can this be," was Nineveh's appeal;
"Who dares to drag the gods at his car-wheel?"
The ground is still there that these wheel-rims tore—
The people and the armies are no more.

THE SIXTH SPHINX.

Never again Cambyses earth will tread.
He slept, and rotted, for his ghost had fled.
So long as sovereigns live, the subjects kneel,
Crouching like spaniels at their royal heel;
But when their might flies, they are shunned by all,
Save worms, which—human-like—still to them crawl
On Troy or Memphis, on Pyrrhus the Great,
Or on Psammeticus, alike falls fate.
Those who in rightful purple are arrayed,
The prideful vanquisher, like vanquished, fade.
Death grins as he the fallen man bestrides—
And less of faults than of his glories hides.

THE SEVENTH SPHINX.

The time is come for Belus' tomb to fall,

Long has been ruined its high granite wall;
And its cupola, sister of the cloud,
Has now to lowest mire its tall head bowed.
The herdsman comes to it to choose the stones
To build a hut, and overturns the bones,
From which he has just scared a jackal pack,
Waiting to gnaw them when he turns his back.
Upon this scene the night is doubly night,
And the lone passer vainly strains his sight,
Musing: Was Belus not buried near this spot?
The royal resting-place is now forgot.

THE EIGHTH SPHINX.

The inmates of the Pyramids assume
The hue of Rhamesis, black with the gloom.
A Jailer who ne'er needs bolts, bars, or hasps,
Is Death. With unawed hand a god he grasps,
He thrusts, to stiffen, in a narrow case,
Or cell, where struggling air-blasts constant moan;
Walling them round with huge, damp, slimy stone;
And (leaving mem'ry of bloodshed as drink,
And thoughts of crime as food) he stops each chink.

THE NINTH SPHINX.

Who would see Cleopatra on her bed?
Come in. The place is filled with fog like lead,
Which clammily has settled on the frame
Of her who was a burning, dazzling flame

To all mankind—who durst not lift their gaze,
And meet the brightness of her beauty's rays.
Her teeth were pearls, her breath a rare perfume.
Men died with love on entering her room.
Poised 'twixt the world and her—acme of joys!
Antony took her of the double choice.
The ice-cold heart that passion seldom warms,
Would find heat torrid in that queen's soft arms.
She won without a single woman's wile,
Illumining the earth with peerless smile.
Come in!—but muffle closely up your face,
No grateful scents have ta'en sweet odors' place.

THE TENTH SPHINX.

What did the greatest king that e'er earth bore,
Sennacherib? No matter—he's no more!
What were the words Sardanapalus said?
Who cares to hear—that ruler long is dead.

The Soudan, turning pale, stared at the TEN aghast.
"Before to-morrow's night," he said, "in dust to rest,
These walls with croaking images shall be downcast;
I will not have fiends speak when angels are addressed."
But while Zim at the Sphinxes clenched his hand and shook,
The cup in which it seems the rich wine sweetly breathes,
The cup with jewels sparkling, met his lowered look,
Dwelling on the rim which the rippling wine enwreathes.
"Ha! You!" Zim cried, "have often cleared my heated head

Of heavy thoughts which your great lord have come to seek
And torture with their pain and weight like molten lead.
Let us two—power, I—you, wine—together speak."

THE CUP.

"Phur," spoke the Cup, "O king, dwelt as Day's god,
Ruled Alexandria with sword and rod.
He from his people drew force after force,
Leaving in ev'ry clime an army's corse.
But what gained he by having, like the sea,
Flooded with human waves to enslave the free?
Where lies the good in having been the chief
In conquering, to cause a nation's grief?
Darius, Assar-addon, Hamilcar;
Who have led men in legions out to war,
Or have o'er Time's shade cast rays from their seat,
Or throngs in worship made their name repeat,
These were, but all the cup of life have drank;
Rising 'midst clamor, they in stillness sank.
Death's dart beat down the sword—the kings high reared,
Were brought full low—judges, like culprits, feared.
The body—when the soul had ceased its sway—
Was placed where earth upon it heavy lay,
While seek the mouldering bones rare oils anoint
Claw of tree's root and tooth of rocky point.
Weeds thrive on them who made the world a mart
Of human flesh, plants force their joints apart.
No deed of eminence the greatest saves,
And of mausoleums make panthers caves."

The Cup, Zim, in his fury, dashed upon the floor,
Crying aloud for lights. Slaves, at his angry call,
In to him hastily, a candelabra bore,
And set it, branching o'er the table, in the hall,
From whose wide bounds it hunted instantly the gloom.
"Ah, light!" exclaimed the Soudan, "welcome light, all hail!
Dull witnesses were yonder Sphinxes of this room;
The Cup was always drunk, in wit did ever fail;
But you fling gleams forth brightly, dazzling as a torch;
Vainly to quell your power all Night's attempts are spent;
The murky, black-eyed clouds you eat away and scorch,
Making where'er you spring to life an Orient.
To charm your lord give voice, thou spark of paradise!
Speak forth against the Sphinxes' enigmatic word,
And 'gainst the Wine-Cup, with its sharp and biting spice!"

THE LAMP.

Oh, Crusher of Countless Cities, such as earth knew
Scarce once before him, Ninus (who his brother slew),
Was borne within the walls which, in Assyrian rite,
Were built to hide dead majesty from outer sight.
If eye of man the gift uncommon could assume,
And pierce the mass, thick, black as hearse's plume,
To where lays on a horrifying bed
What was King Ninus, now hedged round with dread,
'Twould see by what is shadow of the light,
A line of feath'ry dust, bones marble-white.
A shudder overtakes the pois'nous snakes

When they glide near that powder, laid in flakes.
Death comes at times to him—*Life* comes no more!
And sets a jug and loaf upon the floor.
He then with bony foot the corpse o'erturns,
And says: "It is I, Ninus! 'Tis Death who spurns!
I bring thee, hungry king, some bread and meat."
"I have no hands," Ninus replies. "Yet, eat!"
Zim pierced to the very quick by these repeated stabs,
Sprang to his feet, while from him pealed a fearful shout,
And, furious, flung down upon the marble slabs
The richly carved and golden Lamp, whose light went out—
Then glided in a form strange-shaped,
In likeness of a woman, moulded in dense smoke,
Veiled in thick, ebon fog, in utter darkness draped,
A glimpse of which, in short, one's inmost fears awoke.
Zim was alone with her, this Goddess of the Night.
The massy walls of stone like vapor part and fade,
Zim, shuddering, tried to call guard or satellite,
But as the figure grasped him firmly, "Come!" she said.

BP. ALEXANDER
A QUEEN FIVE SUMMERS OLD.

("Elle est toute petite.")

{Bk. XXVI.}
She is so little—in her hands a rose:
A stern duenna watches where she goes,
What sees Old Spain's Infanta—the clear shine
Of waters shadowed by the birch and pine.

What lies before? A swan with silver wing,
The wave that murmurs to the branch's swing,
Or the deep garden flowering below?
Fair as an angel frozen into snow,
The royal child looks on, and hardly seems to know.

As in a depth of glory far away,
Down in the green park, a lofty palace lay,
There, drank the deer from many a crystal pond,
And the starred peacock gemmed the shade beyond.
Around that child all nature shone more bright;
Her innocence was as an added light.
Rubies and diamonds strewed the grass she trode,
And jets of sapphire from the dolphins flowed.

Still at the water's side she holds her place,
Her bodice bright is set with Genoa lace;
O'er her rich robe, through every satin fold,
Wanders an arabesque in threads of gold.
From its green urn the rose unfolding grand,
Weighs down the exquisite smallness of her hand.
And when the child bends to the red leafs tip,
Her laughing nostril, and her carmine lip,
The royal flower purpureal, kissing there,
Hides more than half that young face bright and fair,
So that the eye deceived can scarcely speak
Where shows the rose, or where the rose-red cheek.
Her eyes look bluer from their dark brown frame:
Sweet eyes, sweet form, and Mary's sweeter name.
All joy, enchantment, perfume, waits she there,

Heaven in her glance, her very name a prayer.

Yet 'neath the sky, and before life and fate,
Poor child, she feels herself so vaguely great.
With stately grace she gives her presence high
To dawn, to spring, to shadows flitting by,
To the dark sunset glories of the heaven,
And all the wild magnificence of even;
On nature waits, eternal and serene,
With all the graveness of a little queen.
She never sees a man but on his knee,
She Duchess of Brabant one day will be,
Or rule Sardinia, or the Flemish crowd
She is the Infanta, five years old, and proud.

Thus is it with kings' children, for they wear
A shadowy circlet on their forehead fair;
Their tottering steps are towards a kingly chair.
Calmly she waits, and breathes her gathered flower
Till one shall cull for her imperial power.
Already her eye saith, "It is my right;"
Even love flows from her, mingled with affright.
If some one seeing her so fragile stand,
Were it to save her, should put forth his hand,
Ere he had made a step, or breathed a vow,
The scaffold's shadow were upon his brow.
While the child laughs, beyond the bastion thick
Of that vast palace, Roman Catholic,
Whose every turret like a mitre shows,
Behind the lattice something dreadful goes.

Men shake to see a shadow from beneath
Passing from pane to pane, like vapory wreath,
Pale, black, and still it glides from room to room;
In the same spot, like ghost upon a tomb;
Or glues its dark brown to the casement wan,
Dim shade that lengthens as the night draws on.
Its step funereal lingers like the swing
Of passing bell—'tis death, or else the king.
'Tis he, the man by whom men live and die;
But could one look beyond that phantom eye,
As by the wall he leans a little space,
And see what shadows fill his soul's dark place,
Not the fair child, the waters clear, the flowers
Golden with sunset—not the birds, the bowers—
No; 'neath that eye, those fatal brows that keep
The fathomless brain, like ocean, dark and deep,
There, as in moving mirage, should one find
A fleet of ships that go before the wind:
On the foamed wave, and 'neath the starlight pale,
The strain and rattle of a fleet in sail,
And through the fog an isle on her white rock
Hearkening from far the thunder's coming shock.

Still by the water's edge doth silent stand
The Infanta with the rose-flower in her hand,
Caresses it with eyes as blue as heaven;
Sudden a breeze, such breeze as panting even
From her full heart flings out to field and brake,
Ruffles the waters, bids the rushes shake,
And makes through all their green recesses swell

The massive myrtle and the asphodel.
To the fair child it comes, and tears away
On its strong wing the rose-flower from the spray.
On the wild waters casts it bruised and torn,
And the Infanta only holds a thorn.
Frightened, perplexed, she follows with her eyes
Into the basin where her ruin lies,
Looks up to heaven, and questions of the breeze
That had not feared her highness to displease;
But all the pond is changed; anon so clear,
Now back it swells, as though with rage and fear;
A mimic sea its small waves rise and fall,
And the poor rose is broken by them all.
Its hundred leaves tossed wildly round and round
Beneath a thousand waves are whelmed and drowned;
It was a foundering fleet you might have said;
And the duenna with her face of shade,—
"Madam," for she had marked her ruffled mind,
"All things belong to princes—but God's wind."

BP. ALEXANDER

SEA-ADVENTURERS' SONG.

("En partant du Golfe d'Otrante.")

{Bk. XXVIII.}
We told thirty when we started
From port so taut and fine,
But soon our crew were parted,
Till now we number nine.

Tom Robbins, English, tall and straight,
Left us at Aetna light;
He left us to investigate
What made the mountain bright;
"I mean to ask Old Nick himself,
(And here his eye he rolls)
If I can't bring Newcastle pelf
By selling him some coals!"

In Calabree, a lass and cup
Drove scowling Spada wild:
She only held her finger up,
And there he drank and smiled;
And over in Gaëta Bay,
Ascanio—ashore
A fool!—must wed a widow gay
Who'd buried three or four.

At Naples, woe! poor Ned they hanged—

Hemp neckcloth he disdained—
And prettily we all were banged—
And two more blades remained

To serve the Duke, and row in chains—
Thank saints! 'twas not my cast!
We drank deliverance from pains—
We who'd the ducats fast.

At Malta Dick became a monk—
(What vineyards have those priests!)
And Gobbo to quack-salver sunk,
To leech vile murrained beasts;
And lazy André, blown off shore,
Was picked up by the Turk,
And in some harem, you be sure,
Is forced at last to work.

Next, three of us whom nothing daunts,
Marched off with Prince Eugene,
To take Genoa! oh, it vaunts
Girls fit—each one—for queen!
Had they but promised us the pick,
Perchance we had joined, all;
But battering bastions built of brick—
Bah, give me wooden wall!

By Leghorn, twenty caravels
Came 'cross our lonely sail—
Spinoza's Sea-Invincibles!

But, whew! our shots like hail
Made shortish work of galley long
And chubby sailing craft—
Our making ready first to close
Sent them a-spinning aft.

Off Marseilles, ne'er by sun forsook
We friends fell-to as foes!
For Lucca Diavolo mistook
Angelo's wife for Rose,

And hang me! soon the angel slid
The devil in the sea,
And would of lass likewise be rid—
And so we fought it free!

At Palmas eight or so gave slip,
Pescara to pursue,
And more, perchance, had left the ship,
But Algiers loomed in view;
And here we cruised to intercept
Some lucky-laden rogues,
Whose gold-galleons but slowly crept,
So that we trounced the dogs!

And after making war out there,
We made love at "the Gib."
We ten—no more! we took it fair,
And kissed the gov'nor's "rib,"
And made the King of Spain our take,

Believe or not, who cares?
I tell ye that he begged till black
I' the face to have his shares.

We're rovers of the restless main,
But we've some conscience, mark!
And we know what it is to reign,
And finally did heark—
Aye, masters of the narrow Neck,
We hearkened to our heart,
And gave him freedom on our deck,
His town, and gold—in part.

My lucky mates for that were made
Grandees of Old Castile,
And maids of honor went to wed,
Somewhere in sweet Seville;

Not they for me were fair enough,
And so his Majesty
Declared his daughter—'tis no scoff!
My beauteous bride should be.

"A royal daughter!" think of that!
But I would never one.
I have a lass (I said it pat)
Who's not been bred like nun—
But, merry maid with eagle eye,
It's proud she smiles and bright,
And sings upon the cliff, to spy

My ship a-heave in sight!

My Faenzetta has my heart!
In Fiesoné she
The fairest! Nothing shall us part,
Saving, in sooth, the Sea!
And that not long! its rolling wave
And such breeze holding now
Will send me along to her I love—
And so I made my bow.

We told thirty when we started
From port so taut and fine,
But thus our crew were parted,
And now we number nine.

THE SWISS MERCENARIES.

("Lorsque le regiment des hallebardiers.")

{Bk. XXXI.}
When the regiment of Halberdiers
 Is proudly marching by,
The eagle of the mountain screams
 From out his stormy sky;
Who speaketh to the precipice,

And to the chasm sheer;
Who hovers o'er the thrones of kings,
And bids the caitiffs fear.
King of the peak and glacier,
King of the cold, white scalps—
He lifts his head, at that close tread,
The eagle of the Alps.

O shame! those men that march below—
O ignominy dire!
Are the sons of my free mountains
Sold for imperial hire.
Ah! the vilest in the dungeon!
Ah! the slave upon the seas—
Is great, is pure, is glorious,
Is grand compared with these,
Who, born amid my holy rocks,
In solemn places high,
Where the tall pines bend like rushes
When the storm goes sweeping by;

Yet give the strength of foot they learned
By perilous path and flood,
And from their blue-eyed mothers won,
The old, mysterious blood;
The daring that the good south wind
Into their nostrils blew,
And the proud swelling of the heart
With each pure breath they drew;
The graces of the mountain glens,

With flowers in summer gay;
And all the glories of the hills
To earn a lackey's pay.

Their country free and joyous—
　She of the rugged sides—
She of the rough peaks arrogant
　Whereon the tempest rides:
Mother of the unconquered thought
　And of the savage form,
Who brings out of her sturdy heart
　The hero and the storm:
Who giveth freedom unto man,
　And life unto the beast;
Who hears her silver torrents ring
　Like joy-bells at a feast;

Who hath her caves for palaces,
　And where her châlets stand—
The proud, old archer of Altorf,
　With his good bow in his hand.
Is she to suckle jailers?
　Shall shame and glory rest,
Amid her lakes and glaciers,
　Like twins upon her breast?
Shall the two-headed eagle,
　Marked with her double blow,
Drink of her milk through all those hearts
　Whose blood he bids to flow?

Say, was it pomp ye needed,
 And all the proud array
Of courtly joust and high parade
 Upon a gala day?
Look up; have not my valleys
 Their torrents white with foam—
Their lines of silver bullion
 On the blue hillocks of home?
Doth not sweet May embroider
 My rocks with pearls and flowers?
Her fingers trace a richer lace
 Than yours in all my bowers.

Are not my old peaks gilded
 When the sun arises proud,
And each one shakes a white mist plume
 Out of the thunder-cloud?
O, neighbor of the golden sky—
 Sons of the mountain sod—
Why wear a base king's colors
 For the livery of God?
O shame! despair! to see my Alps
 Their giant shadows fling
Into the very waiting-room
 Of tyrant and of king!

O thou deep heaven, unsullied yet,
 Into thy gulfs sublime—
Up azure tracts of flaming light—
 Let my free pinion climb;

Till from my sight, in that clear light,
  Earth and her crimes be gone—
The men who act the evil deeds—
  The caitiffs who look on.
Far, far into that space immense,
  Beyond the vast white veil,
Where distant stars come out and shine,
  And the great sun grows pale.

BP. ALEXANDER

THE CUP ON THE BATTLE-FIELD.

("Mon pére, ce héros au sourire.")

{Bk. XLIX. iv.}
My sire, the hero with the smile so soft,
And a tall trooper, his companion oft,
Whom he loved greatly for his courage high
And strength and stature, as the night drew nigh
Rode out together. The battle was done;
The dead strewed the field; long sunk was the sun.
It seemed in the darkness a sound they heard,—
Was it feeble moaning or uttered word?
'Twas a Spaniard left from the force in flight,
Who had crawled to the roadside after fight;

Shattered and livid, less live than dead,
Rattled his throat as hoarsely he said:
"Water, water to drink, for pity's sake!
Oh, a drop of water this thirst to slake!"
My father, moved at his speech heart-wrung,
Handed the orderly, downward leapt,
The flask of rum at the holster kept.
"Let him have some!" cried my father, as ran
The trooper o'er to the wounded man,—
A sort of Moor, swart, bloody and grim;
But just as the trooper was nearing him,
He lifted a pistol, with eye of flame,
And covered my father with murd'rous aim.
The hurtling slug grazed the very head,
And the helmet fell, pierced, streaked with red,
And the steed reared up; but in steady tone:
"Give him the whole!" said my father, "and on!"

TORU DUTT

HOW GOOD ARE THE POOR.

("Il est nuit. La cabane est pauvre.")

{Bk. LII. iii.}

'Tis night—within the close stout cabin door,
The room is wrapped in shade save where there fall
Some twilight rays that creep along the floor,
And show the fisher's nets upon the wall.

In the dim corner, from the oaken chest,
A few white dishes glimmer; through the shade
Stands a tall bed with dusky curtains dressed,
And a rough mattress at its side is laid.

Five children on the long low mattress lie—
A nest of little souls, it heaves with dreams;
In the high chimney the last embers die,
And redden the dark room with crimson gleams.

The mother kneels and thinks, and pale with fear,
She prays alone, hearing the billows shout:
While to wild winds, to rocks, to midnight drear,
The ominous old ocean sobs without.

Poor wives of fishers! Ah! 'tis sad to say,
Our sons, our husbands, all that we love best,
Our hearts, our souls, are on those waves away,

Those ravening wolves that know not ruth, nor rest.

Think how they sport with these beloved forms;
And how the clarion-blowing wind unties
Above their heads the tresses of the storms:
Perchance even now the child, the husband, dies.

For we can never tell where they may be
Who, to make head against the tide and gale,
Between them and the starless, soulless sea
Have but one bit of plank, with one poor sail.

Terrible fear! We seek the pebbly shore,
Cry to the rising billows, "Bring them home."
Alas! what answer gives their troubled roar,
To the dark thought that haunts us as we roam.

Janet is sad: her husband is alone,
Wrapped in the black shroud of this bitter night:

His children are so little, there is none
To give him aid. "Were they but old, they might."
Ah, mother! when they too are on the main,
How wilt thou weep: "Would they were young again!"

She takes his lantern—'tis his hour at last
She will go forth, and see if the day breaks,
And if his signal-fire be at the mast;
Ah, no—not yet—no breath of morning wakes.

No line of light o'er the dark water lies;
It rains, it rains, how black is rain at morn:
The day comes trembling, and the young dawn cries—
Cries like a baby fearing to be born.

Sudden her humane eyes that peer and watch
Through the deep shade, a mouldering dwelling find,
No light within—the thin door shakes—the thatch
O'er the green walls is twisted of the wind,

Yellow, and dirty, as a swollen rill,
"Ah, me," she saith, "here does that widow dwell;
Few days ago my good man left her ill:
I will go in and see if all be well."

She strikes the door, she listens, none replies,
And Janet shudders. "Husbandless, alone,
And with two children—they have scant supplies.
Good neighbor! She sleeps heavy as a stone."

She calls again, she knocks, 'tis silence still;
No sound—no answer—suddenly the door,
As if the senseless creature felt some thrill
Of pity, turned—and open lay before.

She entered, and her lantern lighted all
The house so still, but for the rude waves' din.
Through the thin roof the plashing rain-drops fall,
But something terrible is couched within.

"So, for the kisses that delight the flesh,
For mother's worship, and for children's bloom,
For song, for smile, for love so fair and fresh,
For laugh, for dance, there is one goal—the tomb."

And why does Janet pass so fast away?
What hath she done within that house of dread?
What foldeth she beneath her mantle gray?
And hurries home, and hides it in her bed:
With half-averted face, and nervous tread,
What hath she stolen from the awful dead?

The dawn was whitening over the sea's verge
As she sat pensive, touching broken chords
Of half-remorseful thought, while the hoarse surge
Howled a sad concert to her broken words.

"Ah, my poor husband! we had five before,
Already so much care, so much to find,
For he must work for all. I give him more.
What was that noise? His step! Ah, no! the wind.

"That I should be afraid of him I love!
I have done ill. If he should beat me now,
I would not blame him. Did not the door move?
Not yet, poor man." She sits with careful brow
Wrapped in her inward grief; nor hears the roar
Of winds and waves that dash against his prow,
Nor the black cormorant shrieking on the shore.

Sudden the door flies open wide, and lets
Noisily in the dawn-light scarcely clear,
And the good fisher, dragging his damp nets,
Stands on the threshold, with a joyous cheer.

"'Tis thou!" she cries, and, eager as a lover,
Leaps up and holds her husband to her breast;
Her greeting kisses all his vesture cover;
"'Tis I, good wife!" and his broad face expressed

How gay his heart that Janet's love made light.
"What weather was it?" "Hard." "Your fishing?" "Bad.
The sea was like a nest of thieves to-night;
But I embrace thee, and my heart is glad."

"There was a devil in the wind that blew;
I tore my net, caught nothing, broke my line,
And once I thought the bark was broken too;
What did you all the night long, Janet mine?"

She, trembling in the darkness, answered, "I!
Oh, naught—I sew'd, I watch'd, I was afraid,
The waves were loud as thunders from the sky;
But it is over." Shyly then she said—

"Our neighbor died last night; it must have been
When you were gone. She left two little ones,
So small, so frail—William and Madeline;
The one just lisps, the other scarcely runs."

The man looked grave, and in the corner cast
His old fur bonnet, wet with rain and sea,
Muttered awhile, and scratched his head,—at last
"We have five children, this makes seven," said he.

"Already in bad weather we must sleep
Sometimes without our supper. Now! Ah, well—
'Tis not my fault. These accidents are deep;
It was the good God's will. I cannot tell.

"Why did He take the mother from those scraps,
No bigger than my fist. 'Tis hard to read;
A learned man might understand, perhaps—
So little, they can neither work nor need.

"Go fetch them, wife; they will be frightened sore,
If with the dead alone they waken thus.
That was the mother knocking at our door,
And we must take the children home to us.

"Brother and sister shall they be to ours,
And they will learn to climb my knee at even;
When He shall see these strangers in our bowers,
More fish, more food, will give the God of Heaven.

"I will work harder; I will drink no wine—
Go fetch them. Wherefore dost thou linger, dear?
Not thus were wont to move those feet of thine."
She drew the curtain, saying, "They are here!"

BP. ALEXANDER

Poems

LA VOIX DE GUERNESEY.

MENTANA. {1}

(VICTOR HUGO TO GARIBALDI.)

("Ces jeunes gens, combien étaient-ils.")

{LA VOIX DE GUERNESEY, December, 1868.}
I.

Young soldiers of the noble Latin blood,
How many are ye—Boys? Four thousand odd.
How many are there dead? Six hundred: count!
Their limbs lie strewn about the fatal mount,
Blackened and torn, eyes gummed with blood, hearts rolled
Out from their ribs, to give the wolves of the wold
A red feast; nothing of them left but these
Pierced relics, underneath the olive trees,
Show where the gin was sprung—the scoundrel-trap
Which brought those hero-lads their foul mishap.
See how they fell in swathes—like barley-ears!
Their crime? to claim Rome and her glories theirs;
To fight for Right and Honor;—foolish names!
Come—Mothers of the soil! Italian dames!
Turn the dead over!—try your battle luck!
(Bearded or smooth, to her that gave him suck

The man is always child)—Stay, here's a brow
Split by the Zouaves' bullets! This one, now,
With the bright curly hair soaked so in blood,
Was yours, ma donna!—sweet and fair and good.

The spirit sat upon his fearless face
Before they murdered it, in all the grace
Of manhood's dawn. Sisters, here's yours! his lips,
Over whose bloom the bloody death-foam slips,
Lisped house-songs after you, and said your name
In loving prattle once. That hand, the same
Which lies so cold over the eyelids shut,
Was once a small pink baby-fist, and wet
With milk beads from thy yearning breasts.

Take thou
Thine eldest,—thou, thy youngest born. Oh, flow
Of tears never to cease! Oh, Hope quite gone,
Dead like the dead!—Yet could they live alone—
Without their Tiber and their Rome? and be
Young and Italian—and not also free?
They longed to see the ancient eagle try
His lordly pinions in a modern sky.
They bore—each on himself—the insults laid
On the dear foster-land: of naught afraid,
Save of not finding foes enough to dare
For Italy. Ah; gallant, free, and rare
Young martyrs of a sacred cause,—Adieu!
No more of life—no more of love—for you!
No sweet long-straying in the star-lit glades

At Ave-Mary, with the Italian maids;
No welcome home!

II.

This Garibaldi now, the Italian boys
Go mad to hear him—take to dying—take
To passion for "the pure and high";—God's sake!
It's monstrous, horrible! One sees quite clear
Society—our charge—must shake with fear,
And shriek for help, and call on us to act
When there's a hero, taken in the fact.
If Light shines in the dark, there's guilt in that!
What's viler than a lantern to a bat?

III.

Your Garibaldi missed the mark! You see
The end of life's to cheat, and not to be
Cheated: The knave is nobler than the fool!
Get all you can and keep it! Life's a pool,
The best luck wins; if Virtue starves in rags,
I laugh at Virtue; here's my money-bags!
Here's righteous metal! We have kings, I say,
To keep cash going, and the game at play;
There's why a king wants money—he'd be missed
Without a fertilizing civil list.
Do but try
The question with a steady moral eye!
The colonel strives to be a brigadier,

The marshal, constable. Call the game fair,
And pay your winners! Show the trump, I say!
A renegade's a rascal—till the day
They make him Pasha: is he rascal then?
What with these sequins? Bah! you speak to Men,
And Men want money—power—luck—life's joy—
Those take who can: we could, and fobbed Savoy;
For those who live content with honest state,
They're public pests; knock we 'em on the pate!
They set a vile example! Quick—arrest
That Fool, who ruled and failed to line his nest.
Just hit a bell, you'll see the clapper shake—
Meddle with Priests, you'll find the barrack wake—
Ah! Princes know the People's a tight boot,
March 'em sometimes to be shot and to shoot,
Then they'll wear easier. So let them preach
The righteousness of howitzers; and teach
At the fag end of prayer: "Now, slit their throats!
My holy Zouaves! my good yellow-coats!"
We like to see the Holy Father send
Powder and steel and lead without an end,
To feed Death fat; and broken battles mend.
So they!

IV.

But thou, our Hero, baffled, foiled,
The Glorious Chief who vainly bled and toiled.
The trust of all the Peoples—Freedom's Knight!
The Paladin unstained—the Sword of Right!

What wilt thou do, whose land finds thee but jails!
The banished claim the banished! deign to cheer
The refuge of the homeless—enter here,
And light upon our households dark will fall
Even as thou enterest. Oh, Brother, all,
Each one of us—hurt with thy sorrows' proof,
Will make a country for thee of his roof.
Come, sit with those who live as exiles learn:
Come! Thou whom kings could conquer but not yet turn.
We'll talk of "Palermo"{2}—"the Thousand" true,
Will tell the tears of blood of France to you;
Then by his own great Sea we'll read, together,
Old Homer in the quiet summer weather,
And after, thou shalt go to thy desire
While that faint star of Justice grows to fire.{3}

V.

Oh, Italy! hail your Deliverer,
Oh, Nations! almost he gave Rome to her!
Strong-arm and prophet-heart had all but come
To win the city, and to make it "Rome."
Calm, of the antique grandeur, ripe to be
Named with the noblest of her history.
He would have Romanized your Rome—controlled
Her glory, lordships, Gods, in a new mould.
Her spirits' fervor would have melted in
The hundred cities with her; made a twin
Vesuvius and the Capitol; and blended
Strong Juvenal's with the soul, tender and splendid,

Of Dante—smelted old with new alloy—
Stormed at the Titans' road full of bold joy
Whereby men storm Olympus. Italy,
Weep!—This man could have made one Rome of thee!

VI.

But the crime's wrought! Who wrought it?
Honest Man—
Priest Pius? No! Each does but what he can.
Yonder's the criminal! The warlike wight
Who hides behind the ranks of France to fight,
Greek Sinon's blood crossed thick with Judas-Jew's,
The Traitor who with smile which true men woos,
Lip mouthing pledges—hand grasping the knife—
Waylaid French Liberty, and took her life.
Kings, he is of you! fit companion! one
Whom day by day the lightning looks upon
Keen; while the sentenced man triples his guard
And trembles; for his hour approaches hard.
Ye ask me "when?" I say *soon*! Hear ye not
Yon muttering in the skies above the spot?
Mark ye no coming shadow, Kings? the shroud
Of a great storm driving the thunder-cloud?
Hark! like the thief-catcher who pulls the pin,
God's thunder asks to *speak to one within*!

VII.

And meanwhile this death-odor—this corpse-scent

Which makes the priestly incense redolent
Of rotting men, and the Te Deums stink—
Reeks through the forests—past the river's brink,
O'er wood and plain and mountain, till it fouls
Fair Paris in her pleasures; then it prowls,
A deadly stench, to Crete, to Mexico,
To Poland—wheresoe'er kings' armies go:
And Earth one Upas-tree of bitter sadness,
Opening vast blossoms of a bloody madness.
Throats cut by thousands—slain men by the ton!
Earth quite corpse-cumbered, though the half not done!
They lie, stretched out, where the blood-puddles soak,
Their black lips gaping with the last cry spoke.
"Stretched;" nay! *sown broadcast*; yes, the word is "sown."
The fallows Liberty—the harsh wind blown
Over the furrows, Fate: and these stark dead
Are grain sublime, from Death's cold fingers shed
To make the Abyss conceive: the Future bear
More noble Heroes! Swell, oh, Corpses dear!
Rot quick to the green blade of Freedom! Death!
Do thy kind will with them! They without breath,
Stripped, scattered, ragged, festering, slashed and blue,
Dangle towards God the arms French shot tore through
And wait in meekness, Death! for Him and You!

VIII.

Oh, France! oh, People! sleeping unabashed!
Liest thou like a hound when it was lashed?
Thou liest! thine own blood fouling both thy hands,

And on thy limbs the rust of iron bands,
And round thy wrists the cut where cords went deep.
Say did they numb thy soul, that thou didst sleep?
Alas! sad France is grown a cave for sleeping,
Which a worse night than Midnight holds in keeping,
Thou sleepest sottish—lost to life and fame—
While the stars stare on thee, and pale for shame.
Stir! rouse thee! Sit! if thou know'st not to rise;
Sit up, thou tortured sluggard! ope thine eyes!
Stretch thy brawn, Giant! Sleep is foul and vile!
Art fagged, art deaf, art dumb? art blind this while?
They lie who say so! Thou dost know and feel
The things they do to thee and thine. The heel
That scratched thy neck in passing—whose? Canst say?
Yes, yes, 'twas *his*, and this is his *fête-day*.
Oh, thou that wert of humankind—couched so—
A beast of burden on this dunghill! oh!
Bray to them, Mule! Oh, Bullock! bellow then!
Since they have made thee blind, grope in thy den!
Do something, Outcast One, that wast so grand!
Who knows if thou putt'st forth thy poor maimed hand,
There may be venging weapon within reach!
Feel with both hands—with both huge arms go stretch
Along the black wall of thy cellar. Nay,
There *may* be some odd thing hidden away?
Who knows—there *may*! Those great hands might so come
In course of ghastly fumble through the gloom,
Upon a sword—a *sword*! The hands once clasp
Its hilt, must wield it with a Victor's grasp.

EDWIN ARNOLD, C.S.I.

{Footnote 1: The Battle of Mentana, so named from a village by Rome, was fought between the allied French and Papal Armies and the Volunteer Forces of Garibaldi, Nov. 3, 1867.}

{Footnote 2: Palermo was taken immediately after the Garibaldian volunteers, 1000 strong, landed at Marsala to inaugurate the rising which made Italy free.}

{Footnote 3: Both poet and his idol lived to see the French Republic for the fourth time proclaimed. When Hugo rose in the Senate, on the first occasion after his return to Paris after the expulsion of the Napoleons, and his white head was seen above that of Rouher, ex-Prime Minister of the Empire, all the house shuddered, and in a nearly unanimous voice shouted: "The judgment of God! expiation!"}

Poems

LES CHANSONS DES RUES ET DES BOIS.

LOVE OF THE WOODLAND.

―――――――――

("*Orphée au bois du Caystre.*")

{Bk. I. ii.}
Orpheus, through the hellward wood
Hurried, ere the eve-star glowed,
For the fauns' lugubrious hoots
Followed, hollow, from crookèd roots;
Aeschylus, where Aetna smoked,
Gods of Sicily evoked
With the flute, till sulphur taint
Dulled and lulled the echoes faint;
Pliny, soon his style mislaid,
Dogged Miletus' merry maid,
As she showed eburnean limbs
All-multiplied by brooklet brims;
Plautus, see! like Plutus, hold
Bosomfuls of orchard-gold,
Learns he why that mystic core
Was sweet Venus' meed of yore?
Dante dreamt (while spirits pass
As in wizard's jetty glass)
Each black-bossed Briarian trunk

Waved live arms like furies drunk;
Winsome Will, 'neath Windsor Oak,
Eyed each elf that cracked a joke
At poor panting grease-hart fast—
Obese, roguish Jack harassed;
At Versailles, Molière did court
Cues from Pan (in heron port,
Half in ooze, half treeward raised),
"Words so witty, that Boileau's 'mazed!"

Foliage! fondly you attract!
Dian's faith I keep intact,
And declare that thy dryads dance
Still, and will, in thy green expanse!

SHOOTING STARS.

{FOR MY LITTLE CHILD ONLY.}

("Tas de feux tombants.")

{Bk. III. vii.}
See the scintillating shower!
Like a burst from golden mine—
Incandescent coals that pour
From the incense-bowl divine,

And around us dewdrops, shaken,
Mirror each a twinkling ray
'Twixt the flowers that awaken
In this glory great as day.
Mists and fogs all vanish fleetly;
And the birds begin to sing,
Whilst the rain is murm'ring sweetly
As if angels echoing.
And, methinks, to show she's grateful
For this seed from heaven come,
Earth is holding up a plateful
Of the birds and buds a-bloom!

L'ANNÉE TERRIBLE.

TO LITTLE JEANNE.

("Vous eûtes donc hier un an.")

{September, 1870.}
You've lived a year, then, yesterday, sweet child,
Prattling thus happily! So fledglings wild,
New-hatched in warmer nest 'neath sheltering bough,
Chirp merrily to feel their feathers grow.

Your mouth's a rose, Jeanne! In these volumes grand
Whose pictures please you—while I trembling stand
To see their big leaves tattered by your hand—
Are noble lines; but nothing half your worth,
When all your tiny frame rustles with mirth
To welcome me. No work of author wise
Can match the thought half springing to your eyes,
And your dim reveries, unfettered, strange,
Regarding man with all the boundless range
Of angel innocence. Methinks, 'tis clear
That God's not far, Jeanne, when I see you here.

Ah! twelve months old: 'tis quite an age, and brings
Grave moments, though your soul to rapture clings,
You're at that hour of life most like to heaven,
When present joy no cares, no sorrows leaven
When man no shadow feels: if fond caress
Round parent twines, children the world possess.
Your waking hopes, your dreams of mirth and love
From Charles to Alice, father to mother, rove;
No wider range of view your heart can take
Than what her nursing and his bright smiles make;
They two alone on this your opening hour
Can gleams of tenderness and gladness pour:
They two—none else, Jeanne! Yet 'tis just, and I,
Poor grandsire, dare but to stand humbly by.
You come—I go: though gloom alone my right,
Blest be the destiny which gives you light.

Your fair-haired brother George and you beside

Me play—in watching you is all my pride;
And all I ask—by countless sorrows tried—
The grave; o'er which in shadowy form may show
Your cradles gilded by the morning's glow.

Pure new-born wonderer! your infant life
Strange welcome found, Jeanne, in this time of strife.
Like wild-bee humming through the woods your play,
And baby smiles have dared a world at bay:
Your tiny accents lisp their gentle charms
To mighty Paris clashing mighty arms.
Ah! when I see you, child, and when I hear
You sing, or try, with low voice whispering near,
And touch of fingers soft, my grief to cheer,
I dream this darkness, where the tempests groan,
Trembles, and passes with half-uttered moan.
For though these hundred towers of Paris bend,
Though close as foundering ship her glory's end,
Though rocks the universe, which we defend;
Still to great cannon on our ramparts piled,
God sends His blessing by a little child.

MARWOOD TUCKER.

TO A SICK CHILD DURING THE SIEGE OF PARIS.

("Si vous continuez toute pâle.")

{November, 1870.}
If you continue thus so wan and white;
If I, one day, behold
You pass from out our dull air to the light,
You, infant—I, so old:
If I the thread of our two lives must see
Thus blent to human view,
I who would fain know death was near to me,
And far away for you;
If your small hands remain such fragile things;
If, in your cradle stirred,
You have the mien of waiting there for wings,
Like to some new-fledged bird;
Not rooted to our earth you seem to be.
If still, beneath the skies,
You turn, O Jeanne, on our mystery
Soft, discontented eyes!
If I behold you, gay and strong no more;
If you mope sadly thus;
If you behind you have not shut the door,
Through which you came to us;
If you no more like some fair dame I see
Laugh, walk, be well and gay;
If like a little soul you seem to me

That fain would fly away—
I'll deem that to this world, where oft are blent
The pall and swaddling-band,
You came but to depart—an angel sent
To bear me from the land.

LUCY H. HOOPER.

THE CARRIER PIGEON.

("Oh! qu'est-ce que c'est donc que l'Inconnu.")

{January, 1871.}
Who then—oh, who, is like our God so great,
Who makes the seed expand beneath the mountain's weight;
Who for a swallow's nest leaves one old castle wall,
Who lets for famished beetles savory apples fall,
Who bids a pigmy win where Titans fail, in yoke,
And, in what we deem fruitless roar and smoke,
Makes Etna, Chimborazo, still His praises sing,
And saves a city by a word lapped 'neath a pigeon's wing!

TOYS AND TRAGEDY.

("Enfants, on vous dira plus tard.")

{January, 1871.}
In later years, they'll tell you grandpapa
Adored his little darlings; for them did
His utmost just to pleasure them and mar
No moments with a frown or growl amid
Their rosy rompings; that he loved them so
(Though men have called him bitter, cold, and stern,)
That in the famous winter when the snow
Covered poor Paris, he went, old and worn,
To buy them dolls, despite the falling shells,
At which laughed Punch, and they, and shook his bells.

MOURNING.

("Charle! ô mon fils!")

{March, 1871.}
Charles, Charles, my son! hast thou, then, quitted me?
  Must all fade, naught endure?
Hast vanished in that radiance, clear for thee,
  But still for us obscure?

My sunset lingers, boy, thy morn declines!
  Sweet mutual love we've known;
For man, alas! plans, dreams, and smiling twines
  With others' souls his own.

He cries, "This has no end!" pursues his way:
  He soon is downward bound:
He lives, he suffers; in his grasp one day
  Mere dust and ashes found.

I've wandered twenty years, in distant lands,
  With sore heart forced to stay:
Why fell the blow Fate only understands!
  God took my home away.

To-day one daughter and one son remain
  Of all my goodly show:
Wellnigh in solitude my dark hours wane;
  God takes my children now.

Linger, ye two still left me! though decays
  Our nest, our hearts remain;
In gloom of death your mother silent prays,
  I in this life of pain.

Martyr of Sion! holding Thee in sight,
  I'll drain this cup of gall,
And scale with step resolved that dangerous height,
  Which rather seems a fall.

Truth is sufficient guide; no more man needs
Than end so nobly shown.
Mourning, but brave, I march; where duty leads,
I seek the vast unknown.

MARWOOD TUCKER.

THE LESSON OF THE PATRIOT DEAD.

("O caresse sublime.")

{April, 1871.}
Upon the grave's cold mouth there ever have caresses clung
For those who died ideally good and grand and pure and young;
Under the scorn of all who clamor: "There is nothing just!"
And bow to dread inquisitor and worship lords of dust;
Let sophists give the lie, hearts droop, and courtiers play the worm,
Our martyrs of Democracy the Truth sublime affirm!
And when all seems inert upon this seething, troublous round,
And when the rashest knows not best to flee ar stand his ground,
When not a single war-cry from the sombre mass will rush,
When o'er the universe is spread by Doubting utter hush,

Then he who searches well within the walls that close immure
Our teachers, leaders, heroes slain because they lived too pure,
May glue his ear upon the ground where few else came to grieve,
And ask the austere shadows: "Ho! and must one still believe?
Read yet the orders: 'Forward, march!' and 'charge!'" Then from the lime,
Which burnt the bones but left the soul (Oh! tyrants' useless crime!)
Will rise reply: "Yes!" "yes!" and "yes!" the thousand, thousandth time!

H.L.W.

THE BOY ON THE BARRICADE.

("Sur une barricade.")

{June, 1871.}
Like Casabianca on the devastated deck,
In years yet younger, but the selfsame core.
Beside the battered barricado's restless wreck,
A lad stood splashed with gouts of guilty gore,
But gemmed with purest blood of patriot more.

Upon his fragile form the troopers' bloody grip

Was deeply dug, while sharply challenged they:
"Were you one of this currish crew?"—pride pursed his lip,
As firm as bandog's, brought the bull to bay—
While answered he: "I fought with others. Yea!"

"Prepare then to be shot! Go join that death-doomed row."
As paced he pertly past, a volley rang—
And as he fell in line, mock mercies once more flow
Of man's lead-lightning's sudden scathing pang,
But to his home-turned thoughts the balls but sang.

"Here's half-a-franc I saved to buy my mother's bread!"—
The captain started—who mourns not a dear,
The dearest! mother!—"Where is she, wolf-cub?" he said
Still gruffly. "There, d'ye see? not far from here."
"Haste! make it hers! then back to swell *their* bier."

He sprang aloof as springald from detested school,
Or ocean-rover from protected port.
"The little rascal has the laugh on us! no fool
To breast our bullets!"—but the scoff was short,
For soon! the rogue is racing from his court;

And with still fearless front he faces them and calls:
"READY! but level low—*she's* kissed these eyes!"
From cooling hands of *men* each rifle falls,
 And their gray officer, in grave surprise,
Life grants the lad whilst his last comrade dies.

Brave youth! I know not well what urged thy act,

Whether thou'lt pass in palace, or die rackt;
But *then*, shone on the guns, a sublime soul.—
A Bayard-boy's, bound by his pure parole!
Honor redeemed though paid by parlous price,
Though lost be sunlit sports, wild boyhood's spice,
The Gates, the cheers of mates for bright device!

Greeks would, whilom, have choicely clasped and circled thee,
Set thee the first to shield some new Thermopylae;
Thy deed had touched and tuned their true Tyrtaeus tongue,
And staged by Aeschylus, grouped thee grand gods among.

And thy lost name (now known no more) been gilt and graved
On cloud-kissed column, by the sweet south ocean laved.
From us no crown! no honors from the civic sheaf—
Purely this poet's tear-bejewelled, aye-green leaf!

H.L.W.

TO HIS ORPHAN GRANDCHILDREN.

("O Charles, je te sens près de moi.")

{July, 1871.}
I feel thy presence, Charles. Sweet martyr! down
  In earth, where men decay,
I search, and see from cracks which rend thy tomb,
  Burst out pale morning's ray.

Close linked are bier and cradle: here the dead,
  To charm us, live again:
Kneeling, I mourn, when on my threshold sounds
  Two little children's strain.

George, Jeanne, sing on! George, Jeanne, unconscious play!
  Your father's form recall,
Now darkened by his sombre shade, now gilt
  By beams that wandering fall.

Oh, knowledge! what thy use? did we not know
  Death holds no more the dead;
But Heaven, where, hand in hand, angel and star
  Smile at the grave we dread?

A Heaven, which childhood represents on earth.
  Orphans, may God be nigh!
That God, who can your bright steps turn aside

From darkness, where I sigh.

All joy be yours, though sorrow bows me down!
 To each his fitting wage:
Children, I've passed life's span, and men are plagued
 By shadows at that stage.

Hath any done—nay, only half performed—
 The good he might for others?
Hath any conquered hatred, or had strength
 To treat his foes like brothers?

E'en he, who's tried his best, hath evil wrought:
 Pain springs from happiness:
My heart has triumphed in defeat, my pulse
 Ne'er quickened at success.

I seemed the greater when I felt the blow:
 The prick gives sense of gain;
Since to make others bleed my courage fails,
 I'd rather bear the pain.

To grow is sad, since evils grow no less;
 Great height is mark for all:
The more I have of branches, more of clustering boughs,
 The ghastlier shadows fall.

Thence comes my sadness, though I grant your charms:
 Ye are the outbursting
Of the soul in bloom, steeped in the draughts

Of nature's boundless spring.

George is the sapling, set in mournful soil;
  Jeanne's folding petals shroud
A mind which trembles at our uproar, yet
  Half longs to speak aloud.

Give, then, my children—lowly, blushing plants,
  Whom sorrow waits to seize—
Free course to instincts, whispering 'mid the flowers,
  Like hum of murmuring bees.

Some day you'll find that chaos comes, alas!
  That angry lightning's hurled,
When any cheer the People, Atlas huge,
  Grim bearer of the world!

You'll see that, since our fate is ruled by chance,
  Each man, unknowing, great,
Should frame life so, that at some future hour
  Fact and his dreamings meet.

I, too, when death is past, one day shall grasp
  That end I know not now;
And over you will bend me down, all filled
  With dawn's mysterious glow.

I'll learn what means this exile, what this shroud
  Enveloping your prime;
And why the truth and sweetness of one man

Seem to all others crime.

I'll hear—though midst these dismal boughs you sang—
  How came it, that for me,
Who every pity feel for every woe,
  So vast a gloom could be.

I'll know why night relentless holds me, why
  So great a pile of doom:
Why endless frost enfolds me, and methinks
  My nightly bed's a tomb:

Why all these battles, all these tears, regrets,
  And sorrows were my share;
And why God's will of me a cypress made,
  When roses bright ye were.

MARWOOD TUCKER.

TO THE CANNON "VICTOR HUGO."
———————

{Bought with the proceeds of Readings of "Les Châtiments" during
the Siege of Paris.}

{1872.}

Thou deadly crater, moulded by my muse,
Cast thou thy bronze into my bowed and wounded heart,
And let my soul its vengeance to thy bronze impart!

L'ART D'ÊTRE GRANDPÊRE.

THE CHILDREN OF THE POOR.

("Prenez garde à ce petit être.")

{LAUS PUER: POEM V.}
Take heed of this small child of earth;
He is great: in him is God most high.
Children before their fleshly birth
Are lights in the blue sky.

In our brief bitter world of wrong
They come; God gives us them awhile.
His speech is in their stammering tongue,
And His forgiveness in their smile.

Their sweet light rests upon our eyes:
Alas! their right to joy is plain.
If they are hungry, Paradise
Weeps, and if cold, Heaven thrills with pain.

The want that saps their sinless flower
Speaks judgment on Sin's ministers.
Man holds an angel in his power.
Ah! deep in Heaven what thunder stirs.

When God seeks out these tender things,
Whom in the shadow where we keep,
He sends them clothed about with wings,
And finds them ragged babes that weep!

Dublin University Magazine.

THE EPIC OF THE LION.

("Un lion avait pris un enfant.")

{XIII.}

A Lion in his jaws caught up a child—
Not harming it—and to the woodland, wild
With secret streams and lairs, bore off his prey—
The beast, as one might cull a bud in May.
It was a rosy boy, a king's own pride,
A ten-year lad, with bright eyes shining wide,
And save this son his majesty beside
Had but one girl, two years of age, and so
The monarch suffered, being old, much woe;
His heir the monster's prey, while the whole land
In dread both of the beast and king did stand;
Sore terrified were all.

    By came a knight

That road, who halted, asking, "What's the fright?"
They told him, and he spurred straight for the site!
The beast was seen to smile ere joined they fight,
The man and monster, in most desperate duel,
Like warring giants, angry, huge, and cruel.
Stout though the knight, the lion stronger was,
And tore that brave breast under its cuirass,
Scrunching that hero, till he sprawled, alas!
Beneath his shield, all blood and mud and mess:
Whereat the lion feasted: then it went
Back to its rocky couch and slept content.
Sudden, loud cries and clamors! striking out
Qualm to the heart of the quiet, horn and shout
Causing the solemn wood to reel with rout.
Terrific was this noise that rolled before;
It seemed a squadron; nay, 'twas something more—
A whole battalion, sent by that sad king
With force of arms his little prince to bring,
Together with the lion's bleeding hide.

Which here was right or wrong? Who can decide?
Have beasts or men most claim to live? God wots!
He is the unit, we the cipher-dots.
Ranged in the order a great hunt should have,
They soon between the trunks espy the cave.
"Yes, that is it! the very mouth of the den!"
The trees all round it muttered, warning men;
Still they kept step and neared it. Look you now,
Company's pleasant, and there were a thou—
Good Lord! all in a moment, there's its face!

Frightful! they saw the lion! Not one pace
Further stirred any man; but bolt and dart
Made target of the beast. He, on his part,
As calm as Pelion in the rain or hail,
Bristled majestic from the teeth to tail,
And shook full fifty missiles from his hide,
But no heed took he; steadfastly he eyed,
And roared a roar, hoarse, vibrant, vengeful, dread,
A rolling, raging peal of wrath, which spread,
Making the half-awakened thunder cry,
"Who thunders there?" from its black bed of sky.
This ended all! Sheer horror cleared the coast;
As fogs are driven by the wind, that valorous host
Melted, dispersed to all the quarters four,
Clean panic-stricken by that monstrous roar.
Then quoth the lion, "Woods and mountains, see,
A thousand men, enslaved, fear one beast free!"
He followed towards the hill, climbed high above,
Lifted his voice, and, as the sowers sow
The seed down wind, thus did that lion throw
His message far enough the town to reach:
"King! your behavior really passes speech!
Thus far no harm I've wrought to him your son;
But now I give you notice—when night's done,
I will make entry at your city-gate,
Bringing the prince alive; and those who wait
To see him in my jaws—your lackey-crew—
Shall see me eat him in your palace, too!"
Next morning, this is what was viewed in town:
Dawn coming—people going—some adown

Praying, some crying; pallid cheeks, swift feet,
And a huge lion stalking through the street.
It seemed scarce short of rash impiety
To cross its path as the fierce beast went by.
So to the palace and its gilded dome
With stately steps unchallenged did he roam;
He enters it—within those walls he leapt!
No man!

  For certes, though he raged and wept,
His majesty, like all, close shelter kept,
Solicitous to live, holding his breath
Specially precious to the realm. Now death
Is not thus viewed by honest beasts of prey;
And when the lion found *him* fled away,
Ashamed to be so grand, man being so base,
He muttered to himself, "A wretched king!
'Tis well; I'll eat his boy!" Then, wandering,
Lordly he traversed courts and corridors,
Paced beneath vaults of gold on shining floors,
Glanced at the throne deserted, stalked from hall
To hall—green, yellow, crimson—empty all!
Rich couches void, soft seats unoccupied!
And as he walked he looked from side to side
To find some pleasant nook for his repast,
Since appetite was come to munch at last
The princely morsel!—Ah! what sight astounds
That grisly lounger?

  In the palace grounds

An alcove on a garden gives, and there
A tiny thing—forgot in the general fear,
Lulled in the flower-sweet dreams of infancy,
Bathed with soft sunlight falling brokenly
Through leaf and lattice—was at that moment waking;
A little lovely maid, most dear and taking,
The prince's sister—all alone, undressed—
She sat up singing: children sing so best.
Charming this beauteous baby-maid; and so
The beast caught sight of her and stopped—

    And then
Entered—the floor creaked as he stalked straight in.
Above the playthings by the little bed
The lion put his shaggy, massive head,
Dreadful with savage might and lordly scorn,
More dreadful with that princely prey so borne;
Which she, quick spying, "Brother, brother!" cried,
"Oh, my own brother!" and, unterrified,
She gazed upon that monster of the wood,
Whose yellow balls not Typhon had withstood,
And—well! who knows what thoughts these small heads hold?
She rose up in her cot—full height, and bold,
And shook her pink fist angrily at him.
Whereon—close to the little bed's white rim,
All dainty silk and laces—this huge brute
Set down her brother gently at her foot,
Just as a mother might, and said to her,
"Don't be put out, now! There he is, dear, there!"

Poems

EDWIN ARNOLD, C.S.I.

Poems

LES QUATRE VENTS DE L'ESPRIT.

ON HEARING THE PRINCESS ROYAL{1} SING.

("Dans ta haute demeure.")

{Bk. III. ix., 1881.}
In thine abode so high
Where yet one scarce can breathe,
Dear child, most tenderly
A soft song thou dost wreathe.

Thou singest, little girl—
Thy sire, the King is he:
Around thee glories whirl,
But all things sigh in thee.

Thy thought may seek not wings
Of speech; dear love's forbidden;
Thy smiles, those heavenly things,
Being faintly born, are chidden.

Thou feel'st, poor little Bride,
A hand unknown and chill
Clasp thine from out the wide
Deep shade so deathly still.

Thy sad heart, wingless, weak,
Is sunk in this black shade
So deep, thy small hands seek,
Vainly, the pulse God made.

Thou art yet but highness, thou
That shaft be majesty:
Though still on thy fair brow
Some faint dawn-flush may be,

Child, unto armies dear,
Even now we mark heaven's light
Dimmed with the fume and fear
And glory of battle-might.

Thy godfather is he,
Earth's Pope,—he hails thee, child!
Passing, armed men you see
Like unarmed women, mild.

As saint all worship thee;
Thyself even hast the strong
Thrill of divinity
Mingled with thy small song.

Each grand old warrior
Guards thee, submissive, proud;
Mute thunders at thy door
Sleep, that shall wake most loud.

Around thee foams the wild
Bright sea, the lot of kings.
Happier wert thou, my child,
I' the woods a bird that sings!

NELSON R. TYERMAN.

{Footnote 1: Marie, daughter of King Louis Philippe, afterwards Princess
of Würtemburg.}

MY HAPPIEST DREAM.

("J'aime à me figure.")

{Bk. III. vii. and viii.}
I love to look, as evening fails,
On vestals streaming in their veils,
Within the fane past altar rails,
　Green palms in hand.
My darkest moods will always clear
When I can fancy children near,
With rosy lips a-laughing—dear,
　Light-dancing band!

Enchanting vision, too, displayed,
That of a sweet and radiant maid,
Who knows not why she is afraid,—
 Love's yet unseen!
Another—rarest 'mong the rare—
To see the gaze of chosen fair
Return prolonged and wistful stare
 Of eager een.

But—dream o'er all to stir my soul,
And shine the brightest on the roll,
Is when a land of tyrant's toll
 By sword is rid.
I say not dagger—with the sword
When Right enchampions the horde,
All in broad day—so that the bard
May sing the victor with the starred
 Bayard and Cid!

AN OLD-TIME LAY.

("*Jamais elle ne raille.*")

{Bk. III. xiii.}
 Where your brood seven lie,
 Float in calm heavenly,

Life passing evenly,
Waterfowl, waterfowl! often I dream
  For a rest
  Like your nest,
Skirting the stream.

Shine the sun tearfully
Ere the clouds clear fully,
Still you skim cheerfully,
Swallow, oh! swallow swift! often I sigh
  For a home
  Where you roam
Nearing the sky!

Guileless of pondering;
Swallow-eyes wandering;
Seeking no fonder ring
Than the rose-garland Love gives thee apart!
  Grant me soon—
  Blessed boon!
Home in thy heart!

JERSEY.

("Jersey dort dans les flots.")

{Bk. III. xiv., Oct. 8, 1854.}

Dear Jersey! jewel jubilant and green,
'Midst surge that splits steel ships, but sings to thee!
Thou fav'rest Frenchmen, though from England seen,
Oft tearful to that mistress "North Countree";
Returned the third time safely here to be,
I bless my bold Gibraltar of the Free.

Yon lighthouse stands forth like a fervent friend,
One who our tempest buffets back with zest,
And with twin-steeple, eke our helmsman's end,
Forms arms that beckon us upon thy breast;
Rose-posied pillow, crystallized with spray,
Where pools pellucid mirror sunny ray.

A frigate fretting yonder smoothest sky,
Like pauseless petrel poising o'er a wreck,
Strikes bright athwart the dearly dazzled eye,
Until it lessens to scarce certain speck,
'Neath Venus, sparkling on the agate-sprinkled beach,
For fisher's sailing-signal, just and true,
Until Aurora frights her from the view.

In summer, steamer-smoke spreads as thy veil,
And mists in winter sudden screen thy sight,
When at thy feet the galley-breakers wail
And toss their tops high o'er the lofty flight
Of horrid storm-worn steps with shark-like bite,
That only ope to swallow up in spite.

L'ENVOY.

But penitent in calm, thou givest a balm,
To many a man who's felt thy rage,
And many a sea-bird—thanks be heard!—
Thou shieldest—sea-bird—exiled bard and sage.

THEN, MOST, I SMILE.

("Il est un peu tard.")

{Bk. III. xxx., Oct. 30, 1854.}
Late it is to look so proud,
Daisy queen! come is the gloom
Of the winter-burdened cloud!—
"But, in winter, most I bloom!"

Star of even! sunk the sun!
Lost for e'er the ruddy line;
And the earth is veiled in dun,—
"Nay, in darkness, best I shine!"

O, my soul! art 'bove alarm,
Quaffing thus the cup of gall—
Canst thou face the grave with calm?—
"Yes, the Christians smile at all."

THE EXILE'S DESIRE.

("Si je pouvais voir, O patrie!")

{Bk. III. xxxvii.}
Would I could see you, native land,
Where lilacs and the almond stand
Behind fields flowering to the strand—
　But no!

Can I—oh, father, mother, crave
Another final blessing save
To rest my head upon your grave?—
　But no!

In the one pit where ye repose,
Would I could tell of France's woes,
My brethren, who fell facing foes—
　But no!

Would I had—oh, my dove of light,
After whose flight came ceaseless night,
One plume to clasp so purely white.—
　But no!

Far from ye all—oh, dead, bewailed!
The fog-bell deafens me empaled
Upon this rock—I feel enjailed—
　Though free.

Like one who watches at the gate
Lest some shall 'scape the doomèd strait.
I watch! the tyrant, howe'er late,
  Must fall!

THE REFUGEE'S HAVEN.

("Vous voilà dans la froide Angleterre.")

{Bk. III. xlvii., Jersey, Sept. 19, 1854.}
You may doubt I find comfort in England
But, there, 'tis a refuge from dangers!
Where a Cromwell dictated to Milton,
Republicans ne'er can be strangers!

Poems

VARIOUS PIECES.

TO THE NAPOLEON COLUMN.

{Oct. 9, 1830.}
When with gigantic hand he placed,
For throne, on vassal Europe based,
That column's lofty height—
Pillar, in whose dread majesty,
In double immortality,
Glory and bronze unite!
Aye, when he built it that, some day,
Discord or war their course might stay,
Or here might break their car;
And in our streets to put to shame
Pigmies that bear the hero's name
Of Greek and Roman war.
It was a glorious sight; the world
His hosts had trod, with flags unfurled,
In veteran array;
Kings fled before him, forced to yield,
He, conqueror on each battlefield,
Their cannon bore away.
Then, with his victors back he came;
All France with booty teemed, her name
Was writ on sculptured stone;
And Paris cried with joy, as when

The parent bird comes home again
To th' eaglets left alone.
Into the furnace flame, so fast,
Were heaps of war-won metal cast,
The future monument!
His thought had formed the giant mould,
And piles of brass in the fire he rolled,
From hostile cannon rent.
When to the battlefield he came,
He grasped the guns spite tongues of flame,
And bore the spoil away.
This bronze to France's Rome he brought,
And to the founder said, "Is aught
Wanting for our array?"
And when, beneath a radiant sun,
That man, his noble purpose done,
With calm and tranquil mien,
Disclosed to view this glorious fane,
And did with peaceful hand contain
The warlike eagle's sheen.
Round *thee*, when hundred thousands placed,
As some great Roman's triumph graced,
The little Romans all;
We boys hung on the procession's flanks,
Seeking some father in thy ranks,
And loud thy praise did call.
Who that surveyed thee, when that day
Thou deemed that future glory ray
Would here be ever bright;
Feared that, ere long, all France thy grave

From pettifoggers vain would crave
Beneath that column's height?

Author of "Critical Essays."

CHARITY.

("Je suis la Charité.")

{February, 1837.}
"Lo! I am Charity," she cries,
"Who waketh up before the day;
While yet asleep all nature lies,
God bids me rise and go my way."

How fair her glorious features shine,
Whereon the hand of God hath set
An angel's attributes divine,
With all a woman's sweetness met.

Above the old man's couch of woe
She bows her forehead, pure and even.
There's nothing fairer here below,
There's nothing grander up in heaven,

Than when caressingly she stands

(The cold hearts wakening 'gain their beat),
And holds within her holy hands
The little children's naked feet.

To every den of want and toil
She goes, and leaves the poorest fed;
Leaves wine and bread, and genial oil,
And hopes that blossom in her tread,

And fire, too, beautiful bright fire,
That mocks the glowing dawn begun,
Where, having set the blind old sire,
He dreams he's sitting in the sun.

Then, over all the earth she runs,
And seeks, in the cold mists of life,
Those poor forsaken little ones
Who droop and weary in the strife.

Ah, most her heart is stirred for them,
Whose foreheads, wrapped in mists obscure,
Still wear a triple diadem—
The young, the innocent, the poor.

And they are better far than we,
And she bestows a worthier meed;
For, with the loaf of charity,
She gives the kiss that children need.

She gives, and while they wondering eat

The tear-steeped bread by love supplied,
She stretches round them in the street
Her arm that passers push aside.

If, with raised head and step alert,
She sees the rich man stalking by,
She touches his embroidered skirt,
And gently shows them where they lie.

She begs for them of careless crowd,
Of earnest brows and narrow hearts,
That when it hears her cry aloud,
Turns like the ebb-tide and departs.

O miserable he who sings
Some strain impure, whose numbers fall
Along the cruel wind that brings
Death to some child beneath his wall.

O strange and sad and fatal thing,
When, in the rich man's gorgeous hall,
The huge fire on the hearth doth fling
A light on some great festival,

To see the drunkard smile in state,
In purple wrapt, with myrtle crowned,
While Jesus lieth at the gate
With only rags to wrap him round.

Dublin University Magazine

SWEET SISTER.

("Vous qui ne savez pas combien l'enfance est belle.")
Sweet sister, if you knew, like me,
The charms of guileless infancy,
No more you'd envy riper years,
Or smiles, more bitter than your tears.

But childhood passes in an hour,
As perfume from a faded flower;
The joyous voice of early glee
Flies, like the Halcyon, o'er the sea.

Enjoy your morn of early Spring;
Soon time maturer thoughts must bring;
Those hours, like flowers that interclimb,
Should not be withered ere their time.

Too soon you'll weep, as we do now,
O'er faithless friend, or broken vow,
And hopeless sorrows, which our pride
In pleasure's whirl would vainly hide.

Laugh on! unconscious of thy doom,
All innocence and opening bloom;
Laugh on! while yet thine azure eye
Mirrors the peace that reigns on high.

MRS. B. SOMERS.

THE PITY OF THE ANGELS.

("Un Ange vit un jour.")

{LA PITIÉ SUPREME VIII., 1881.}
When an angel of kindness
Saw, doomed to the dark,
Men framed in his likeness,
He sought for a spark—
Stray gem of God's glory
 That shines so serene—
And, falling like lark,
To brighten our story,
 Pure Pity was seen.

THE SOWER.

Sitting in a porchway cool,
Fades the ruddy sunlight fast,
Twilight hastens on to rule—
Working hours are wellnigh past

Shadows shoot across the lands;
But one sower lingers still,
Old, in rags, he patient stands,—

Looking on, I feel a thrill.

Black and high his silhouette
Dominates the furrows deep!
Now to sow the task is set,
Soon shall come a time to reap.

Marches he along the plain,
To and fro, and scatters wide
From his hands the precious grain;
Moody, I, to see him stride.

Darkness deepens. Gone the light.
Now his gestures to mine eyes
Are august; and strange—his height
Seems to touch the starry skies.

TORU DUTT.

OH, WHY NOT BE HAPPY?{1}

("A quoi bon entendre les oiseaux?")

{RUY BLAS, Act II.}
Oh, why not be happy this bright summer day,
'Mid perfume of roses and newly-mown hay?
Great Nature is smiling—the birds in the air

Sing love-lays together, and all is most fair.
  Then why not be happy
   This bright summer day,
   'Mid perfume of roses
   And newly-mown hay?

The streamlets they wander through meadows so fleet,
Their music enticing fond lovers to meet;
The violets are blooming and nestling their heads
In richest profusion on moss-coated beds.
  Then why not be happy
   This bright summer day,
   When Nature is fairest
   And all is so gay?

LEOPOLD WRAY.

{Footnote 1: Music composed by Elizabeth Philip.}

FREEDOM AND THE WORLD.

{Inscription under a Statue of the Virgin and Child, at Guernsey.—The
  poet sees in the emblem a modern Atlas, i.e., Freedom supporting the
  World.}

("Le peuple est petit.")
Weak is the People—but will grow beyond all other—
Within thy holy arms, thou fruitful victor-mother!
O Liberty, whose conquering flag is never furled—
Thou bearest Him in whom is centred all the World.

SERENADE.

("Quand tu chantes.")
When the voice of thy lute at the eve
  Charmeth the ear,
In the hour of enchantment believe
  What I murmur near.
That the tune can the Age of Gold
  With its magic restore.
Play on, play on, my fair one,
  Play on for evermore.

When thy laugh like the song of the dawn
  Riseth so gay
That the shadows of Night are withdrawn
  And melt away,
I remember my years of care
  And misgiving no more.
Laugh on, laugh on, my fair one,

Laugh on for evermore.

When thy sleep like the moonlight above
  Lulling the sea,
Doth enwind thee in visions of love,
  Perchance, of me!
I can watch so in dream that enthralled me,
  Never before!
Sleep on, sleep on, my fair one!
  Sleep on for evermore.

HENRY F. CHORLEY.

AN AUTUMNAL SIMILE.

("*Les feuilles qui gisaient.*")
The leaves that in the lonely walks were spread,
Starting from off the ground beneath the tread,
  Coursed o'er the garden-plain;
Thus, sometimes, 'mid the soul's deep sorrowings,
Our soul a moment mounts on wounded wings,
  Then, swiftly, falls again.

Poems

TO CRUEL OCEAN.

Where are the hapless shipmen?—disappeared,
Gone down, where witness none, save Night, hath been,
Ye deep, deep waves, of kneeling mothers feared,
What dismal tales know ye of things unseen?
Tales that ye tell your whispering selves between
　The while in clouds to the flood-tide ye pour;
And this it is that gives you, as I ween,
　Those mournful voices, mournful evermore,
When ye come in at eve to us who dwell on shore.

ESMERALDA IN PRISON.

("Phoebus, n'est-il sur la terre?")

{OPERA OF "ESMERALDA," ACT IV., 1836.}
Phoebus, is there not this side the grave,
　Power to save
Those who're loving? Magic balm
That will restore to me my former calm?
Is there nothing tearful eye
Can e'er dry, or hush the sigh?
I pray Heaven day and night,
As I lay me down in fright,

To retake my life, or give
All again for which I'd live!
Phoebus, hasten from the shining sphere
  To me here!
Hither hasten, bring me Death; then Love
May let our spirits rise, ever-linked, above!

LOVER'S SONG.

("Mon âme à ton coeur s'est donnée.")

{ANGELO, Act II., May, 1835.}
My soul unto thy heart is given,
In mystic fold do they entwine,
So bound in one that, were they riven,
Apart my soul would life resign.
Thou art my song and I the lyre;
Thou art the breeze and I the brier;
The altar I, and thou the fire;
Mine the deep love, the beauty thine!
As fleets away the rapid hour
While weeping—may
My sorrowing lay
Touch thee, sweet flower.

ERNEST OSWALD COE.

A FLEETING GLIMPSE OF A VILLAGE.

("Tout vit! et se pose avec grâce.")
How graceful the picture! the life, the repose!
The sunbeam that plays on the porchstone wide;
And the shadow that fleets o'er the stream that flows,
And the soft blue sky with the hill's green side.

Fraser's Magazine.

LORD ROCHESTER'S SONG.

("Un soldat au dur visage.")

{CROMWELL, ACT I.}
"Hold, little blue-eyed page!"
So cried the watchers surly,
Stern to his pretty rage
And golden hair so curly—
"Methinks your satin cloak
Masks something bulky under;
I take this as no joke—
Oh, thief with stolen plunder!"

"I am of high repute,
And famed among the truthful:
This silver-handled lute

Is meet for one still youthful
Who goes to keep a tryst
With her who is his dearest.
I charge you to desist;
My cause is of the clearest."

But guardsmen are so sharp,
Their eyes are as the lynx's:
"That's neither lute nor harp—
Your mark is not the minxes.
Your loving we dispute—
That string of steel so cruel
For music does not suit—
You go to fight a duel!"

THE BEGGAR'S QUATRAIN.

("Aveugle comme Homère.")

{Improvised at the Café de Paris.}
Blind, as was Homer; as Belisarius, blind,
But one weak child to guide his vision dim.
The hand which dealt him bread, in pity kind—
He'll never see; God sees it, though, for him.

H.L.C., *"London Society."*

THE QUIET RURAL CHURCH.

It was a humble church, with arches low,
The church we entered there,
Where many a weary soul since long ago
Had past with plaint or prayer.

Mournful and still it was at day's decline,
The day we entered there;
As in a loveless heart, at the lone shrine,
The fires extinguished were.

Scarcely was heard to float some gentlest sound,
Scarcely some low breathed word,
As in a forest fallen asleep, is found
Just one belated bird.

A STORM SIMILE.

("Oh, regardez le ciel!")

{June, 1828.}
See, where on high the moving masses, piled
By the wind, break in groups grotesque and wild,
 Present strange shapes to view;
Oft flares a pallid flash from out their shrouds,
As though some air-born giant 'mid the clouds
 Sudden his falchion drew.

DRAMATIC PIECES.

THE FATHER'S CURSE.

("Vous, sire, écoutez-moi.")

{LE ROI S'AMUSE, Act I.}
M. ST. VALLIER (*an aged nobleman, from whom King Francis I.*
decoyed his daughter, the famous beauty, Diana of Poitiers*).

A king should listen when his subjects speak:
'Tis true your mandate led me to the block,
Where pardon came upon me, like a dream;
I blessed you then, unconscious as I was
That a king's mercy, sharper far than death,
To save a father doomed his child to shame;
Yes, without pity for the noble race
Of Poitiers, spotless for a thousand years,
You, Francis of Valois, without one spark
Of love or pity, honor or remorse,
Did on that night (thy couch her virtue's tomb),
With cold embraces, foully bring to scorn
My helpless daughter, Dian of Poitiers.
To save her father's life a knight she sought,
Like Bayard, fearless and without reproach.

She found a heartless king, who sold the boon,
Making cold bargain for his child's dishonor.
Oh! monstrous traffic! foully hast thou done!
My blood was thine, and justly, tho' it springs
Amongst the best and noblest names of France;
But to pretend to spare these poor gray locks,
And yet to trample on a weeping woman,
Was basely done; the father was thine own,
But not the daughter!—thou hast overpassed
The right of monarchs!—yet 'tis mercy deemed.
And I perchance am called ungrateful still.
Oh, hadst thou come within my dungeon walls,
I would have sued upon my knees for death,
But mercy for my child, my name, my race,
Which, once polluted, is my race no more.
Rather than insult, death to them and me.
I come not now to ask her back from thee;
Nay, let her love thee with insensate love;
I take back naught that bears the brand of shame.
Keep her! Yet, still, amidst thy festivals,
Until some father's, brother's, husband's hand
('Twill come to pass!) shall rid us of thy yoke,
My pallid face shall ever haunt thee there,
To tell thee, Francis, it was foully done!...

TRIBOULET *(the Court Jester), sneering.* The poor man raves.

ST. VILLIER. Accursed be ye both!
Oh Sire! 'tis wrong upon the dying lion

To loose thy dog! *(Turns to Triboulet)*
   And thou, whoe'er thou art,
That with a fiendish sneer and viper's tongue
Makest my tears a pastime and a sport,
My curse upon thee!—Sire, thy brow doth bear
The gems of France!—on mine, old age doth sit;
Thine decked with jewels, mine with these gray hairs;
We both are Kings, yet bear a different crown;
And should some impious hand upon thy head
Heap wrongs and insult, with thine own strong arm
Thou canst avenge them! *God avenges mine!*

FREDK. L. SLOUS.

PATERNAL LOVE.

("Ma fille! ô seul bonheur.")

{LE ROI S'AMUSE, Act II}
My child! oh, only blessing Heaven allows me!
Others have parents, brothers, kinsmen, friends,
A wife, a husband, vassals, followers,
Ancestors, and allies, or many children.
I have but thee, thee only. Some are rich;
Thou art my treasure, thou art all my riches.
And some believe in angels; I believe

In nothing but thy soul. Others have youth,
And woman's love, and pride, and grace, and health;
Others are beautiful; thou art my beauty,
Thou art my home, my country and my kin,
My wife, my mother, sister, friend—my child!
My bliss, my wealth, my worship, and my law,
My Universe! Oh, by all other things
My soul is tortured. If I should ever lose thee—
Horrible thought! I cannot utter it.
Smile, for thy smile is like thy mother's smiling.
She, too, was fair; you have a trick like her,
Of passing oft your hand athwart your brow
As though to clear it. Innocence still loves
A brow unclouded and an azure eye.
To me thou seem'st clothed in a holy halo,
My soul beholds thy soul through thy fair body;
E'en when my eyes are shut, I see thee still;
Thou art my daylight, and sometimes I wish
That Heaven had made me blind that thou might'st be
The sun that lighted up the world for me.

FANNY KEMBLE-BUTLER.

THE DEGENERATE GALLANTS.

("Mes jeunes cavaliers.")

{HERNANI, Act I., March, 1830.}
What business brings you here, young cavaliers?
Men like the Cid, the knights of bygone years,
Rode out the battle of the weak to wage,
Protecting beauty and revering age.
Their armor sat on them, strong men as true,
Much lighter than your velvet rests on you.
Not in a lady's room by stealth they knelt;
In church, by day, they spoke the love they felt.
They kept their houses' honor bright from rust,
They told no secret, and betrayed no trust;
And if a wife they wanted, bold and gay,
With lance, or axe, or falchion, and by day,
Bravely they won and wore her. As for those
Who slip through streets when honest men repose,
With eyes turned to the ground, and in night's shade
The rights of trusting husbands to invade;
I say the Cid would force such knaves as these
To beg the city's pardon on their knees;
And with the flat of his all-conquering blade
Their rank usurped and 'scutcheon would degrade.
Thus would the men of former times, I say,
Treat the degenerate minions of to-day.

LORD F. LEVESON GOWER (1ST EARL OF ELLESMERE.)

THE OLD AND THE YOUNG BRIDEGROOM.

("L'homme auquel on vous destina.")

{HERNANI, Act I.}
Listen. The man for whom your youth is destined,
Your uncle, Ruy de Silva, is the Duke
Of Pastrana, Count of Castile and Aragon.
For lack of youth, he brings you, dearest girl,
Treasures of gold, jewels, and precious gems,
With which your brow might outshine royalty;
And for rank, pride, splendor, and opulence,
Might many a queen be envious of his duchess!
Here is one picture. I am poor; my youth
I passed i' the woods, a barefoot fugitive.
My shield, perchance, may bear some noble blazons
Spotted with blood, defaced though not dishonored.
Perchance I, too, have rights, now veiled in darkness,—
Rights, which the heavy drapery of the scaffold
Now hides beneath its black and ample folds;
Rights which, if my intent deceive me not,
My sword shall one day rescue. To be brief:—
I have received from churlish Fortune nothing

But air, light, water,—Nature's general boon.
Choose, then, between us two, for you must choose;—
Say, will you wed the duke, or follow me?

DONNA SOL. I'll follow you.

HERN. What, 'mongst my rude companions,
Whose names are registered in the hangman's book?
Whose hearts are ever eager as their swords,
Edged by a personal impulse of revenge?
Will you become the queen, dear, of my band?
Will you become a hunted outlaw's bride?
When all Spain else pursued and banished me,—
In her proud forests and air-piercing mountains,
And rocks the lordly eagle only knew,
Old Catalonia took me to her bosom.
Among her mountaineers, free, poor, and brave,
I ripened into manhood, and, to-morrow,
One blast upon my horn, among her hills,
Would draw three thousand of her sons around me.
You shudder,—think upon it. Will you tread
The shores, woods, mountains, with me, among men
Like the dark spirits of your haunted dreams,—
Suspect all eyes, all voices, every footstep,—
Sleep on the grass, drink of the torrent, hear
By night the sharp hiss of the musket-ball
Whistling too near your ear,—a fugitive
Proscribed, and doomed mayhap to follow me
In the path leading to my father's scaffold?

DONNA SOL. I'll follow you.

HERN. This duke is rich, great, prosperous,
No blot attaches to his ancient name.
He is all-powerful. He offers you
His treasures, titles, honors, with his hand.

DONNA SOL. We will depart to-morrow. Do not blame
What may appear a most unwomanly boldness.

CHARLES SHERRY.

THE SPANISH LADY'S LOVE.

DONNA SOL *to* HERNANI.

("Nous partirons demain.")

{HERNANI, ACT I.}
To mount the hills or scaffold, we go to-morrow:
Hernani, blame me not for this my boldness.
Art thou mine evil genius or mine angel?
I know not, but I am thy slave. Now hear me:
Go where thou wilt, I follow thee. Remain,
And I remain. Why do I thus? I know not.
I feel that I must see thee—see thee still—

See thee for ever. When thy footstep dies,
It is as if my heart no more would beat;
When thou art gone, I am absent from myself;
But when the footstep which I love and long for
Strikes on mine ear again—then I remember
I live, and feel my soul return to me.

G. MOIR.

THE LOVER'S SACRIFICE.

("Fuyons ensemble.")

{HERNANI, Act II.}
DONNA SOL.   Together let us fly!

HERNANI. Together? No! the hour is past for flight.
Dearest, when first thy beauty smote my sight,
I offered, for the love that bade me live,
Wretch that I was, what misery had to give:
My wood, my stream, my mountain. Bolder grown,
By thy compassion to an outlaw shown,
The outlaw's meal beneath the forest shade,
The outlaw's couch far in the greenwood glade,
I offered. Though to both that couch be free,
I keep the scaffold block reserved for me.

DONNA SOL. And yet you promised?

HERNANI *(falls on his knee.)* Angel! in this hour,
Pursued by vengeance and oppressed by power—
Even in this hour when death prepares to close
In shame and pain a destiny of woes—
Yes, I, who from the world proscribed and cast,
Have nursed one dark remembrance of the past,
E'en from my birth in sorrow's garment clad,
Have cause to smile and reason to be glad;
For you have loved the outlaw and have shed
Your whispered blessings on his forfeit head.

DONNA SOL. Let me go with you.

HERNANI.   No! I will not rend
From its fair stem the flower as I descend.
Go—I have smelt its perfume. Go—resume
All that this grasp has brushed away of bloom.
Wed the old man,—believe that ne'er we met;
I seek my shade—be happy, and forget!

LORD F. LEVESON GOWER (1ST EARL OF ELLESMERE).

THE OLD MAN'S LOVE.

("*Dérision! que cet amour boiteux.*")

{HERNANI, Act III.}
O mockery! that this halting love
That fills the heart so full of flame and transport,
Forgets the body while it fires the soul!
If but a youthful shepherd cross my path,
He singing on the way—I sadly musing,
He in his fields, I in my darksome alleys—
Then my heart murmurs: "O, ye mouldering towers!
Thou olden ducal dungeon! O how gladly
Would I exchange ye, and my fields and forests,
Mine ancient name, mine ancient rank, my ruins—
My ancestors, with whom I soon shall lie,
For *his* thatched cottage and his youthful brow!"
His hair is black—his eyes shine forth like *thine*.
Him thou might'st look upon, and say, fair youth,
Then turn to me, and think that I am old.
And yet the light and giddy souls of cavaliers
Harbor no love so fervent as their words bespeak.
Let some poor maiden love them and believe them,
Then die for them—they smile. Aye! these young birds,
With gay and glittering wing and amorous song,
Can shed their love as lightly as their plumage.
The old, whose voice and colors age has dimmed,
Flatter no more, and, though less fair, are faithful.
When *we* love, we love true. Are our steps frail?

Our eyes dried up and withered? Are our brows
Wrinkled? There are no wrinkles in the heart.
Ah! when the graybeard loves, he should be spared;
The heart is young—*that* bleeds unto the last.
I love thee as a spouse,—and in a thousand
Other fashions,—as sire,—as we love
The morn, the flowers, the overhanging heavens.
Ah me! when day by day I gaze upon thee,
Thy graceful step, thy purely-polished brow,
Thine eyes' calm fire,—I feel my heart leap up,
And an eternal sunshine bathe my soul.
And think, too! Even the world admires,
When age, expiring, for a moment totters
Upon the marble margin of a tomb,
To see a wife—a pure and dove-like angel—
Watch over him, soothe him, and endure awhile
The useless old man, only fit to die;
A sacred task, and worthy of all honor,
This latest effort of a faithful heart;
Which, in his parting hour, consoles the dying,
And, without loving, wears the look of love.
Ah! thou wilt be to me this sheltering angel,
To cheer the old man's heart—to share with him
The burden of his evil years;—a daughter
In thy respect, a sister in thy pity.

DONNA SOL. My fate may be more to precede than follow.
My lord, it is no reason for long life
That we are young! Alas! I have seen too oft

The old clamped firm to life, the young torn thence;
And the lids close as sudden o'er their eyes
As gravestones sealing up the sepulchre.

G. MOIR.

THE ROLL OF THE DE SILVA RACE.

("Celui-ci, des Silvas, c'est l'aîné.")

{HERNANI, Act III.}
   In that reverend face
Behold the father of De Silva's race,
Silvius; in Rome he filled the consul's place
Three times (your patience for such honored names).
This second was Grand Master of St. James
And Calatrava; his strong limbs sustained
Armor which ours would sink beneath. He gained
Thirty pitched battles, and took, as legends tell,
Three hundred standards from the Infidel;
And from the Moorish King Motril, in war,
Won Antiquera, Suez, and Nijar;
And then died poor. Next to him Juan stands,
His son; his plighted hand was worth the hands
Of kings. Next Gaspar, of Mendoza's line—
Few noble stems but chose to join with mine:

Sandoval sometimes fears, and sometimes woos
Our smiles; Manriquez envies; Lara sues;
And Alancastre hates. Our rank we know:
Kings are but just above us, dukes below.
Vasquez, who kept for sixty years his vow—
Greater than he I pass. This reverend brow,
This was my sire's—the greatest, though the last:
The Moors his friend had taken and made fast—
Alvar Giron. What did my father then?
He cut in stone an image of Alvar,
Cunningly carved, and dragged it to the war;
He vowed a vow to yield no inch of ground
Until that image of itself turned round;
He reached Alvar—he saved him—and his line
Was old De Silva's, and his name was mine—
Ruy Gomez.

King CARLOS. Drag me from his lurking-place
The traitor!

{DON RUY *leads the* KING *to the portrait behind which* HERNANI *is hiding.*}

   Sire, your highness does me grace.
This, the last portrait, bears my form and name,
And you would write this motto on the frame!
"This last, sprung from the noblest and the best,
Betrayed his plighted troth, and sold his guest!"

LORD F. LEVESON GOWER (1ST EARL OF ELLESMERE)

THE LOVERS' COLLOQUY.

("Mon duc, rien qu'un moment.")

{HERNANI, Act V.}
One little moment to indulge the sight
With the rich beauty of the summer's night.
The harp is hushed, and, see, the torch is dim,—
Night and ourselves together. To the brim
The cup of our felicity is filled.
Each sound is mute, each harsh sensation stilled.
Dost thou not think that, e'en while nature sleeps,
Some power its amorous vigils o'er us keeps?
No cloud in heaven; while all around repose,
Come taste with me the fragrance of the rose,
Which loads the night-air with its musky breath,
While everything is still as nature's death.
E'en as you spoke—and gentle words were those
Spoken by you,—the silver moon uprose;
How that mysterious union of her ray,
With your impassioned accents, made its way
Straight to my heart! I could have wished to die
In that pale moonlight, and while thou wert by.

HERNANI. Thy words are music, and thy strain of love
Is borrowed from the choir of heaven above.

DONNA SOL. Night is too silent, darkness too profound
Oh, for a star to shine, a voice to sound—
To raise some sudden note of music now
Suited to night.

HERN. Capricious girl! your vow
Was poured for silence, and to be released
From the thronged tumult of the marriage feast.

DONNA SOL. Yes; but one bird to carol in the field,—
A nightingale, in mossy shade concealed,—
A distant flute,—for music's stream can roll
To soothe the heart, and harmonize the soul,—
O! 'twould be bliss to listen.

{*Distant sound of a horn, the signal that* HERNANI *must go to* DON RUY, *who, having saved his life, had him bound in a vow to yield it up.*}

LORD F. LEVESON GOWER (1ST EARL OF ELLESMERE).

CROMWELL AND THE CROWN.

("Ah! je le tiens enfin.")

{CROMWELL, Act II., October, 1827.}
THURLOW *communicates the intention of Parliament to offer* CROMWELL *the crown.*

CROMWELL. And is it mine? And have my feet at length
Attained the summit of the rock i' the sand?

THURLOW. And yet, my lord, you have long reigned.

CROM.   Nay, nay!
Power I have 'joyed, in sooth, but not the name.
Thou smilest, Thurlow. Ah, thou little know'st
What hole it is Ambition digs i' th' heart
What end, most seeming empty, is the mark
For which we fret and toil and dare! How hard
With an unrounded fortune to sit down!
Then, what a lustre from most ancient times
Heaven has flung o'er the sacred head of kings!
King—Majesty—what names of power! No king,
And yet the world's high arbiter! The thing
Without the word! no handle to the blade!
Away—the empire and the name are one!
Alack! thou little dream'st how grievous 'tis,
Emerging from the crowd, and at the top
Arrived, to feel that there is *something* still

Above our heads; something, nothing! no matter—
That word is everything.

LEITCH RITCHIE.

MILTON'S APPEAL TO CROMWELL.

("Non! je n'y puis tenir.")

{CROMWELL, Act III. sc. iv.}
Stay! I no longer can contain myself,
But cry you: Look on John, who bares his mind
To Oliver—to Cromwell, Milton speaks!
Despite a kindling eye and marvel deep
A voice is lifted up without your leave;
For I was never placed at council board
To speak *my* promptings. When awed strangers come
Who've seen Fox-Mazarin wince at the stings
In my epistles—and bring admiring votes
Of learned colleges, they strain to see
My figure in the glare—the usher utters,
"Behold and hearken! that's my Lord Protector's
Cousin—that, his son-in-law—that next"—who cares!
Some perfumed puppet! "Milton?" "He in black—
Yon silent scribe who trims their eloquence!"
Still 'chronicling small-beer,'—such is my duty!

Yea, one whose thunder roared through martyr bones
Till Pope and Louis Grand quaked on their thrones,
And echoed "Vengeance for the Vaudois," where
The Sultan slumbers sick with scent of roses.
He is but the mute in this seraglio—
"Pure" Cromwell's Council!
But to be dumb and blind is overmuch!
Impatient Issachar kicks at the load!
Yet diadems are burdens painfuller,
And I would spare thee that sore imposition.
Dear brother Noll, I plead against thyself!
Thou aim'st to be a king; and, in thine heart,
What fool has said: "There is no king but thou?"
For thee the multitude waged war and won—
The end thou art of wrestlings and of prayer,
Of sleepless watch, long marches, hunger, tears
And blood prolifically spilled, homes lordless,
And homeless lords! The mass must always suffer
That one should reign! the collar's but newly clamp'd,
And nothing but the name thereon is changed—
Master? still masters! mark you not the red
Of shame unutterable in my sightless white?
Still hear me, Cromwell, speaking for your sake!
These fifteen years, we, to you whole-devoted,
Have sought for Liberty—to give it thee?
To make our interests your huckster gains?
The king a lion slain that you may flay,
And wear the robe—well, worthily—I say't,
For I will not abase my brother!
No! I would keep him in the realm serene,

My own ideal of heroes! loved o'er Israel,
And higher placed by me than all the others!
And such, for tinkling titles, hollow haloes
Like that around yon painted brow—thou! thou!
Apostle, hero, saint-dishonor thyself!
And snip and trim the flag of Naseby-field
As scarf on which the maid-of-honor's dog
Will yelp, some summer afternoon! That sword
Shrink into a sceptre! brilliant bauble! Thou,
Thrown on a lonely rock in storm of state,
Brain-turned by safety's miracle, thou risest
Upon the tott'ring stone whilst ocean ebbs,
And, reeking of no storms to come to-morrow,
Or to-morrow—deem that a certain pedestal
Whereon thou'lt be adored for e'er—e'en while
It shakes—o'ersets the rider! Tremble, thou!
For he who dazzles, makes men Samson-blind,
Will see the pillars of his palace kiss
E'en at the whelming ruin! Then, what word
Of answer from your wreck when I demand
Account of Cromwell! glory of the people
Smothered in ashes! through the dust thou'lt hear;
"What didst thou with thy virtue?" Will it respond:
"When battered helm is doffed, how soft is purple
On which to lay the head, lulled by the praise
Of thousand fluttering fans of flatterers!
Wearied of war-horse, gratefully one glides
In gilded barge, or in crowned, velvet car,
From gay Whitehall to gloomy Temple Bar—"
(Where—had you slipt, that head were bleaching now!

And that same rabble, splitting for a hedge,
Had joined their rows to cheer the active headsman;
Perchance, in mockery, they'd gird the skull
With a hop-leaf crown! Bitter the brewing, Noll!)
Are crowns the end-all of ambition? Remember
Charles Stuart! and that they who make can break!
This same Whitehall may black its front with crape,
And this broad window be the portal twice
To lead upon a scaffold! Frown! or laugh!
Laugh on as they did at Cassandra's speech!
But mark—the prophetess was right! Still laugh,
Like the credulous Ethiop in his faith in stars!
But give one thought to Stuart, two for yourself!
In his appointed hour, all was forthcoming—
Judge, axe, and deathsman veiled! and my poor eyes
Descry—as would thou saw'st!—a figure veiled,
Uplooming there—afar, like sunrise, coming!
With blade that ne'er spared Judas 'midst free brethren!
Stretch not the hand of Cromwell for the prize
Meant not for him, nor his! Thou growest old,
The people are ever young! Like her i' the chase
Who drave a dart into her lover, embowered,
Piercing the incense-clouds, the popular shaft
May slay thee in a random shot at Tyranny!
Man, friend, remain a Cromwell! in thy name,
Rule! and if thy son be worthy, he and his,
So rule the rest for ages! be it grander thus
To be a Cromwell than a Carolus.
No lapdog combed by wantons, but the watch
Upon the freedom that we won! Dismiss

Your flatterers—let no harpings, no gay songs
Prevent your calm dictation of good laws
To guard, to fortify, and keep enlinked
England and Freedom! Be thine old self alone!
And make, above all else accorded me,
My most desired claim on all posterity,
That thou in Milton's verse wert foremost of the free!

FIRST LOVE.

("Vous êtes singulier.")

{MARION DELORME, Act I., June, 1829, *played* 1831.}

MARION *(smiling.)* You're strange, and yet I love you thus.

DIDIER.   You love me?
Beware, nor with light lips utter that word.
You love me!—know you what it is to love
With love that is the life-blood in one's veins,
The vital air we breathe, a love long-smothered,
Smouldering in silence, kindling, burning, blazing,
And purifying in its growth the soul.
A love that from the heart eats every passion
But its sole self; love without hope or limit,
Deep love that will outlast all happiness;
Speak, speak; is such the love you bear me?

MARION.   Truly.

DIDIER. Ha! but you do not know how I love you!
The day that first I saw you, the dark world
Grew shining, for your eyes lighted my gloom.
Since then, all things have changed; to me you are
Some brightest, unknown creature from the skies.
This irksome life, 'gainst which my heart rebelled,
Seems almost fair and pleasant; for, alas!
Till I knew you wandering, alone, oppressed,
I wept and struggled, I had never loved.

FANNY KEMBLE-BUTLER.

THE FIRST BLACK FLAG.

("Avez-vous oui dire?")

{LES BURGRAVES, Part I., March, 1843.}
JOB. Hast thou ne'er heard men say
That, in the Black Wood, 'twixt Cologne and Spire,
Upon a rock flanked by the towering mountains,
A castle stands, renowned among all castles?
And in this fort, on piles of lava built,
A burgrave dwells, among all burgraves famed?

Hast heard of this wild man who laughs at laws—
Charged with a thousand crimes—for warlike deeds
Renowned—and placed under the Empire's ban
By the Diet of Frankfort; by the Council
Of Pisa banished from the Holy Church;
Reprobate, isolated, cursed—yet still
Unconquered 'mid his mountains and in will;
The bitter foe of the Count Palatine
And Treves' proud archbishop; who has spurned
For sixty years the ladder which the Empire
Upreared to scale his walls? Hast heard that he
Shelters the brave—the flaunting rich man strips—
Of master makes a slave? That here, above
All dukes, aye, kings, eke emperors—in the eyes
Of Germany to their fierce strife a prey,
He rears upon his tower, in stern defiance,
A signal of appeal to the crushed people,
A banner vast, of Sorrow's sable hue,
Snapped by the tempest in its whirlwind wrath,
So that kings quiver as the jades at whips?
Hast heard, he touches now his hundredth year—
And that, defying fate, in face of heaven,
On his invincible peak, no force of war
Uprooting other holds—nor powerful Cæsar—
Nor Rome—nor age, that bows the pride of man—
Nor aught on earth—hath vanquished, or subdued,
Or bent this ancient Titan of the Rhine,
The excommunicated Job?

Democratic Review.

THE SON IN OLD AGE.

("Ma Regina, cette noble figure.")

{LES BURGRAVES, Part II.}
Thy noble face, Regina, calls to mind
My poor lost little one, my latest born.
He was a gift from God—a sign of pardon—
That child vouchsafed me in my eightieth year!
I to his little cradle went, and went,
And even while 'twas sleeping, talked to it.
For when one's very old, one is a child!
Then took it up and placed it on my knees,
And with both hands stroked down its soft, light hair—
Thou wert not born then—and he would stammer
Those pretty little sounds that make one smile!
And though not twelve months old, he had a mind.
He recognized me—nay, knew me right well,
And in my face would laugh—and that child-laugh,
Oh, poor old man! 'twas sunlight to my heart.
I meant him for a soldier, ay, a conqueror,
And named him George. One day—oh, bitter thought!
The child played in the fields. When thou art mother,
Ne'er let thy children out of sight to play!
The gypsies took him from me—oh, for what?
Perhaps to kill him at a witch's rite.
I weep!—now, after twenty years—I weep
As if 'twere yesterday. I loved him so!
I used to call him "my own little king!"

I was intoxicated with my joy
When o'er my white beard ran his rosy hands,
Thrilling me all through.

Foreign Quarterly Review.

THE EMPEROR'S RETURN.

("*Un bouffon manquait à cette fête.*")

{LES BURGRAVES, Part II.}
The EMPEROR FREDERICK BARBAROSSA, *believed to be dead, appearing*
 as a beggar among the Rhenish nobility at a castle, suddenly reveals
 himself.

HATTO. This goodly masque but lacked a fool!
First gypsy; next a beggar;—good! Thy name?

BARBAROSSA. Frederick of Swabia, Emperor of Almain.

ALL. The Red Beard?

BARBAROSSA. Aye, Frederick, by my mountain birthright Prince
 O' th' Romans, chosen king, crowned emperor,
 Heaven's sword-bearer, monarch of Burgundy
 And Arles—the tomb of Karl I dared profane,
 But have repented me on bended knees
 In penance 'midst the desert twenty years;
 My drink the rain, the rocky herbs my food,
 Myself a ghost the shepherds fled before,
 And the world named me as among the dead.
 But I have heard my country call—come forth,

Lifted the shroud—broken the sepulchre.
This hour is one when dead men needs must rise.
Ye own me? Ye mind me marching through these vales
When golden spur was ringing at my heel?
Now know me what I am, your master, earls!
Brave knights you deem! You say, "The sons we are
Of puissant barons and great noblemen,
Whose honors we prolong." You *do* prolong them?
Your sires were soldiers brave, not prowlers base,
Rogues, miscreants, felons, village-ravagers!
They made great wars, they rode like heroes forth,
And, worthy, won broad lands and towers and towns,
So firmly won that thirty years of strife
Made of their followers dukes, their leaders kings!
While you! like jackal and the bird of prey,
Who lurk in copses or 'mid muddy beds—
Crouching and hushed, with dagger ready drawn,
Hide in the noisome marsh that skirts the way,
Trembling lest passing hounds snuff out your lair!
Listen at eventide on lonesome path
For traveller's footfall, or the mule-bell's chime,
Pouncing by hundreds on one helpless man,
To cut him down, then back to your retreats—
You dare to vaunt your sires? I call your sires,
Bravest of brave and greatest 'mid the great,
A line of warriors! you, a pack of thieves!

Athenaeum.